Incident Response with Threat Intelligence

Practical insights into developing an incident response capability through intelligence-based threat hunting

Roberto Martínez

BIRMINGHAM—MUMBAI

Incident Response with Threat Intelligence

Group Product Manager: Vijin Boricha

Publishing Product Manager: Vijin Boricha

Senior Editor: Arun Nadar

Content Development Editor: Romy Dias

Technical Editor: Shruthi Shetty

Copy Editor: Safis Editing

Project Coordinator: Ajesh Devavaram

Proofreader: Safis Editing

Indexer: Subalakshmi Govindan

Production Designer: Alishon Mendonca

Marketing Coordinator: Sanjana Gupta

First published: May 2022

Production reference: 1180522

Published by Packt Publishing Ltd.

Livery Place

35 Livery Street

Birmingham

B3 2PB, UK.

ISBN 978-1-80107-295-3

www.packt.com

Dedicated to those who showed me the way with their love and example and taught me never to give up.

Contributors

About the author

Roberto Martínez (`@r0bertmart1nez`) has worked as senior security researcher at Kaspersky's **Global Research and Analysis Team (GReAT)** and as Watch Commander at HSBC (GCO), investigating cyberthreats, responding to security incidents, and presenting at security events worldwide.

He has collaborated as an expert associate professor at **Tecnológico de Monterrey (ITESM)** and is a member of the **High Technology Crime Investigation Association (HTCIA)**.

Roberto has more than 18 years of experience in cybersecurity fields such as offensive security, malware analysis, digital forensics, incident response, threat intelligence, and threat hunting.

He also worked as a security consultant and instructor for governments, financial institutions, and private corporations in Latin America.

I thank God; my wonderful wife, Claudia; my beloved children, Ale, Luis, Robert; my family; friends; and the loved ones who always supported me in all those endless hours on nights and weekends when I was not with them to dedicate myself to writing this book.

Special thanks to my friend Andrés Velázquez, who I esteem and admire for his outstanding professional career and agreeing to be the presenter at the book's launch.

I also thank the whole Packt team, especially Vijin Boricha, Romy Dias, Ajesh Devavaran, Vaidehi Sawant, and Troy Mitchell, for their valuable support and patience in helping me improve and make this book a reality.

About the reviewer

Troy Mitchell is a cybersecurity professional with three decades of experience in information technology and cybersecurity, both on the defensive and offensive sides.

His expertise is mainly in incident response, digital forensics, malware analysis, threat hunting, penetration testing, and threat intelligence.

Troy retains many professional certifications, including **Certified Ethical Hacker (CEH)**, **Certified Network Defense Architect (CNDA)**, VMware VCP, and MCSE: Security.

He has worked for private sector companies as well as several government agencies.

He is currently a senior cybersecurity engineer with a global engineering company.

Troy is a highly active member of the cybersecurity community, along with playing in **Capture the Flag (CTF)** events.

I'd like to thank Packt Publishing for the opportunity to be selected as a technical reviewer to review and contribute to this book.

I would also like to thank my wife and daughter for supporting me as I worked on reviewing this book after work and on weekends, accompanied by my sidekick Skittles, the tabby cat.

Table of Contents

3

Basics of the Incident Response and Triage Procedures

4

Applying First Response Procedures

Section 2: Getting to Know the Adversaries

5

Identifying and Profiling Threat Actors

6

Understanding the Cyber Kill Chain and the MITRE ATT&CK Framework

7

Using Cyber Threat Intelligence in Incident Response

Section 3: Designing and Implementing Incident Response in Organizations

8
Building an Incident Response Capability

9
Creating Incident Response Plans and Playbooks

10
Implementing an Incident Management System

11
Integrating SOAR Capabilities into Incident Response

Section 4: Improving Threat Detection in Incident Response

12

Working with Analytics and Detection Engineering in Incident Response

13

Creating and Deploying Detection Rules

14
Hunting and Investigating Security Incidents

Index

Other Books You May Enjoy

Preface

Incident response is fundamental and necessary for organizations' cybersecurity, regardless of their size. This book provides helpful information to professionals who work in large companies with a certain level of maturity in incident response and those who work in small or medium-sized companies, where there are no areas dedicated to this field.

I wrote this book with a broad approach that converges diverse disciplines, such as threat intelligence, threat hunting, and detection engineering. The different chapters show how the orchestration of these activities using the appropriate technologies can improve the capacity to respond to security incidents that can impact organizations.

There are four sections in this book. The first section covers the basic concepts of incident response, the first response procedures, and the tools to collect the artifacts from different devices.

In the second section, we will analyze the distinct types of threat actors from a broad perspective, considering their motivations and capabilities, under the principle that the best form of defense strategy is taking advantage of the knowledge of adversaries.

The third section covers the main aspects of implementing an incident response program, including the incident response plan and actionable playbooks based on different scenarios. This section also covers the technologies that support incident management and the integration of monitoring, detection, and investigation systems.

Finally, the fourth section covers critical aspects related to a proactive detection posture in the search and detection of attack indicators that speed up a threat's response and containment times to minimize its impact and thus prevent adversaries from achieving their objective.

Who this book is for

This book is for those hungry to learn and passionate about sharing knowledge and who want to start or develop their skills in the exciting field of incident response. Whether you are a beginner or have experience in this area, you can find helpful information for the incident response practice.

What this book covers

Chapter 1, Threat Landscape and Cybersecurity Incidents, covers the context of cyber threats today and how they evolve and can become a risk to the organization's security.

Chapter 2, Concepts of Digital Forensics and Incident Response, covers incident response and digital forensics investigation fundamentals and best practices.

Chapter 3, Basics of the Incident Response and Triage Procedures, teaches you about forensics artifact identification and triage procedures.

Chapter 4, Applying First Response Procedures, teaches you how to perform first response procedures and collect digital evidence in a practical way.

Chapter 5, Identifying and Profiling Threat Actors, teaches you how to profile specific threats and identify the adversaries that may cause risk to your organization.

Chapter 6, Understanding the Cyber Kill Chain and the MITRE ATT&CK Frameworks, covers two of the most relevant frameworks to map adversaries' behaviors, tactics, and procedures.

Chapter 7, Using Cyber Threat Intelligence in Incident Response, shows you how to use threat intelligence information to identify malicious behavior in a cybersecurity incident.

Chapter 8, Building an Incident Response Capability, covers the alignment of different aspects of responding to security breaches, such as business continuity, disaster recovery, and incident response.

Chapter 9, Creating Incident Response Plans and Playbooks, shows you how to create incident response plans and playbooks for different attack scenarios.

Chapter 10, Implementing an Incident Management System, teaches you how to implement and configure an incident response management system, create investigation cases, and search artifact information on threat intelligence sources.

Chapter 11, Integrating SOAR Capabilities into Incident Response, teaches you how to integrate multiple systems to automate the processes of monitoring, alerting, creating cases, and investigating security incidents.

Chapter 12, Working with Analytics and Detection Engineering in Incident Response, covers the fundamentals of detection engineering and how you can use it to improve your monitoring or incident response detection capacity.

Chapter 13, Creating and Deploying Detection Rules, covers the fundamentals of the Yara and Sigma tools and shows you how to create rules to detect compromise and malicious behavior indicators.

Chapter 14, Hunting and Investigating Security Incidents, is where you will apply the concepts learned in the book in a practical scenario where you will hunt for threats and investigate a security breach.

To get the most out of this book

Having a basic knowledge of Linux and Windows operating systems, network protocols, and the management of virtualized environments in VMware will be very useful while using this book.

All the practical exercises in the book were designed to work on virtualization environments using VMware Workstation Player (free for personal use), so I recommend you download and use the latest version available.

The minimum hardware requirements are as follows:

- 4 cores
- 16–32 GB RAM
- 120 GB of free storage space

Software/hardware covered in the book	Operating system requirements
MAGNET RAM Capture	Windows, macOS, or Linux
FTK Imager	
Velociraptor IR	
Kape	
MITRE ATT&CK Navigator	
Threat Report ATT&CK Mapper (TRAM)	
Visual Studio Code	
ELK Stack	
TheHive and Cortex	
Security Onion	
Invoke-AtomicRedTeam	
Yara rules	
Sigma rules	

There are many excellent technologies available to improve the capacity to detect threats and efficiently respond to security incidents. However, I mainly included open source or free tools in this book instead of commercial tools to make them accessible to everyone, so you can focus on applying the knowledge and concepts that I share in the different chapters.

I invite you to explore and learn about other tools and thus have a broader frame of reference when deciding on a particular one.

All the tools mentioned in the chapters can be used within virtualized environments.

If you are using the digital version of this book, we advise you to type the code yourself or access the code from the book's GitHub repository (a link is available in the next section). Doing so will help you avoid any potential errors related to the copying and pasting of code.

Download the example code files

You can download the virtual machines, lab files, and additional resources from the book's GitHub repository: `https://github.com/PacktPublishing/Incident-Response-with-Threat-Intelligence`. If there's an update to the code, it will be updated in the GitHub repository.

You can use the password, `[P4cktIRBook!]`, to access the link for downloading the virtual machines for this book.

Download the color images

We also provide a PDF file that has color images of the screenshots and diagrams used in this book. You can download it here: `https://static.packt-cdn.com/downloads/9781801072953_ColorImages.pdf`.

Conventions used

There are a number of text conventions used throughout this book.

`Code in text`: Indicates code words in text, database table names, folder names, filenames, file extensions, pathnames, dummy URLs, user input, and Twitter handles. Here is an example: "To start using this virtual pre-installed version of TheHive, you need to import the downloaded `.ova` file using VMware Workstation Player."

A block of code is set as follows:

```
detection:
  selection1:
    EventID: 1
  selection2:
    Image|contains:
```

When we wish to draw your attention to a particular part of a code block, the relevant lines or items are set in bold:

```
import "pe"
rule procdump_tool {
    meta:
        description = "Simple YARA rule to detect the presence
of Sysinternals Procdump"
        version = "1.0"
```

Any command-line input or output is written as follows:

```
sudo so-status
```

Bold: Indicates a new term, an important word, or words that you see onscreen. For instance, words in menus or dialog boxes appear in **bold**. Here is an example: "On TheHive's main dashboard, click on the **New Organization** button."

> **Tips or Important Notes**
> Appear like this.

Get in touch

Feedback from our readers is always welcome.

General feedback: If you have questions about any aspect of this book, email us at customercare@packtpub.com and mention the book title in the subject of your message.

Errata: Although we have taken every care to ensure the accuracy of our content, mistakes do happen. If you have found a mistake in this book, we would be grateful if you would report this to us. Please visit www.packtpub.com/support/errata and fill in the form.

Piracy: If you come across any illegal copies of our works in any form on the internet, we would be grateful if you would provide us with the location address or website name. Please contact us at copyright@packt.com with a link to the material.

If you are interested in becoming an author: If there is a topic that you have expertise in and you are interested in either writing or contributing to a book, please visit authors.packtpub.com.

Share Your Thoughts

Once you've read *Incident Response with Threat Intelligence*, we'd love to hear your thoughts! Scan the QR code below to go straight to the Amazon review page for this book and share your feedback.

https://packt.link/r/1801072957

Your review is important to us and the tech community and will help us make sure we're delivering excellent quality content.

Section 1: The Fundamentals of Incident Response

This first part of the book introduces you to the different angles of the cyber threat landscape and how they affect organizations of all sizes, as well as individuals. It also addresses the basic concepts of digital forensics and incident response, and you will learn some of the first response procedures to follow when a cybersecurity incident occurs.

This section comprises the following chapters:

- *Chapter 1, Threat Landscape and Cybersecurity Incidents*
- *Chapter 2, Concepts of Digital Forensics and Incident Response*
- *Chapter 3, Basics of the Incident Response and Triage Procedures*
- *Chapter 4, Applying First Response Procedures*

1
Threat Landscape and Cybersecurity Incidents

Cyber attacks against organizations worldwide, regardless of their size or geography, are growing in a sustained way, and every day we see more news about security breaches.

According to a study of the Identity Theft Resource Center, between January 1, 2005, and May 31, 2020, there were 11,762 recorded breaches, and just in the first half of 2020, about 36 billion records were exposed according to a report from the company Risk Based Security.

In the ninth annual study of the cost of cybercrime, elaborated by The Ponemon Institute and the firm Accenture, security breaches have increased by 67% in the last 5 years, and according to the security company, McAfee, in their report entitled *The Hidden Costs of Cybercrime*, the monetary loss was around 1 trillion dollars.

The significant impact that cyber attacks have on a world in which we increasingly rely on technology to do business, keep the industry running, or in terms of national security, and our daily activities, is clear. Unfortunately, many organizations are not prepared to deal with a security incident and, in many cases, react when it is too late.

There is a whole ecosystem around cyber attacks and it will depend on the motivation and skills of the attackers so that they can be realized. That is why it is important to understand that beyond a conventional risk assessment, it is necessary to know the potential threats to which the particular organization is exposed.

A proactive posture on cybersecurity involves focusing on monitoring and detection by betting everything on the front line of defense and developing an ability to identify and respond early to a cybersecurity incident by minimizing its impact.

In this chapter, we're going to cover the following topics.

- The current threat landscape
- The motivations behind cyber attacks
- The emerging and future threats

Knowing the threat landscape

When a cybersecurity strategy is based solely on a defensive posture, without an understanding of current threats and the capabilities of adversaries to achieve their goals by evading security controls and avoiding detection, there is a risk of developing very limited capabilities that will rarely be efficient. It is the equivalent of being in a completely dark room, without being able to see anything, knowing that at some point, someone could try to hurt us, but without knowing the exact moment or the way in which this will happen. It's like walking blind without seeing the way.

The increase in the number of cyber attacks in the world on major sectors such as government, finance, manufacturing, health, education, critical infrastructures, small and medium-sized enterprises, and individuals, finally turned on the alert for strategies and investments needed to raise the level of protection and response of organizations to the possibility of becoming the next target.

In that sense, one of the biggest challenges for cybersecurity professionals is first to evolve and create protection and response strategies at the same speed with which new threats appear and then go one step further using threat intelligence information. The threat landscape is changing every day, cyber threats are evolving and becoming more dangerous, and the forms of protection that worked before may not be efficient enough today, which is why organizations need to develop the ability to adapt and switch from a reactive posture to a proactive attitude. Any regional or global context or situation can generate new risks and change the threat landscape drastically.

Is COVID-19 also a cyber-pandemic?

The COVID-19 outbreak completely changed the course of things and showed that countries around the world were not in a position to deal with it, and although scientific and technological advances enabled the development and manufacture of a vaccine in record time, the coordination and budgets required failed to solve the problem in the short term. This incident, in the same way as a cybersecurity incident, shows us once again the importance of being prepared and having a plan in case a threat materializes.

This global health crisis formed the perfect storm, many things changed in the workplace and at home, more people started using their digital devices, made online purchases, used financial apps instead of going to the bank, subscribed to streaming services, and took their classes online. The companies sent their employees and collaborators to work at home and, in some cases, asked them to use their own devices to do their job.

Cybercriminals and **Advanced Persistent Threat** (**APT**) groups know how to find and use the time and circumstances to launch their offensive campaigns and operations successfully, and this was an amazing opportunity for them.

In August 2020, Interpol published the report *Cybercrime: COVID-19 Impact* about the increase in cyber attacks, especially against individuals, companies, government, and healthcare infrastructure. According to this report, in the period January-April, the key cyber threats were phishing and scam fraud, accounting for 59% of incidents, malware and ransomware – 36%, malicious domains – 22%, and the dissemination of fake news – 14%. In all cases, the common factor was content or topics related to COVID-19. Meanwhile, according to the FBI, the number of complaints in relation to cyber attacks stood at 4,000 per day, roughly a 400% increase since the start of the pandemic:

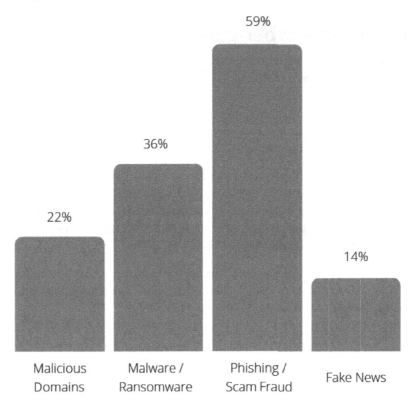

Figure 1.1 – Distribution of the key COVID-19 inflicted cyber threats based on member countries' feedback (source: Interpol's Cybercrime COVID-19 Impact report)

In the words of Jürgen Stock, Secretary-General of INTERPOL, "*Cybercriminals are developing and driving their attacks on people in an alarming way, and they also exploit the fear and uncertainty caused by the unstable social and economic situation created by COVID-19.*"

Cyber espionage against pharmaceutical companies

The urgency of developing a COVID-19 vaccine began a race against time in the pharmaceuticals industry. Unsurprisingly, these companies became a natural target of threat actors. Kaspersky discovered in late September 2020 that a group known as **Lazarus** had started a cyber espionage campaign against a pharmaceuticals company and a health ministry. Although **different tactics, techniques, and procedures (TTPs)** were used in both attacks, common elements were found that could attribute the attack to that group.

Cyber attacks targeting hospitals

Although some cybercriminal groups reported that they would not attack health organizations at the beginning of the pandemic, some of them did attack hospitals, including the Department of Health and Human Services.

In October 2020, the **Department of Homeland Security (DHS)** and the FBI issued an alert about an imminent threat of ransomware attacks on the U.S. healthcare system.

In the Czech Republic, a COVID-19 testing center hospital was compromised by a cyber attack, affecting its systems and disrupting the normal functioning of its operations, so that some urgent surgeries had to be postponed and several patients had to be sent to nearby hospitals.

Insecure home office

The need to adopt a home office model as a preventive measure to reduce the expansion of the pandemic surprised many organizations and their employees. According to the Kaspersky study *How COVID-19 changed the way people worked*, 46% of respondents said that had never worked from home before and 73% of workers did not receive security awareness training about the risks of working from home.

This scenario increased the demand for remote working applications and services such as video conferencing, collaboration, file sharing, and remote connection. Employees also began to perform a practice known as Shadow IT, which involves the use of unauthorized or company-evaluated applications; for example, 42% of respondents said that they were using their personal email accounts for work and 38% used personal instant messaging apps, making it a security problem because, according to Kaspersky's telemetry, there were 1.66 million Trojans detected related to such applications.

Additionally, IT teams had to adapt their infrastructure in some cases in an impromptu manner and without considering the security measures. For example, enabling remote connections directly to the company's servers from the internet opened a potential attack vector that was at once exploited by cybercriminals. According to Kaspersky, the number of brute-force attack attempts on the **Remote Desktop Protocol (RDP)** has soared significantly since the beginning of March 2020, reaching 3.3 billion attempts, compared to 969 million in the same period of the previous year.

Supply chain attacks

Supply chain attacks have been increasing in recent years. The main reason is that organizations have not considered these attacks within their threat modeling and cannot visualize them as a relevant attack surface.

The main risk of this threat is that it is difficult to detect. Usually, third-party services or tools are considered part of the company's ecosystem and are reliable, having a high trust level. Hence, the levels of security assessment and monitoring are more relaxed.

There are several cases related to supply chain attacks, including the compromise of the application CCleaner, which is a tool used by many companies around the world, or the attack known as ShadowHammer, where the ASUS live utility that comes pre-installed on that brand's computers and serves to update various components such as firmware, UEFI BIOS, drivers, and some applications, was compromised.

Without a doubt, however, one of the supply chain attacks that has had the most impact was the attack on the SolarWinds company discovered in December 2020. On December 8, the FireEye company revealed that they had been the victims of a cyber attack. The attackers had stolen tools that their Red Team teams used to conduct security assessments, and the attack vector was a SolarWinds tool installed in the company.

The attack's impact is unprecedented and affected even large technology companies such as Microsoft, Intel, Nvidia, Cisco, VMware, and at least 18,000 other companies worldwide and changed the threat level of this kind of attack for organizations.

Understanding the motivation behind cyber attacks

Each action taken by a threat actor has a motivation behind it, as it requires time, planning, and resources to launch offensive activities against a target.

This motivation can often be financial when it comes to cybercriminal groups. Still, there are scenarios when sponsored state threat actors or industry competitors look to gain a position of power or a competitive advantage over an adversary by spying and stealing information.

There are also groups of cyber-mercenaries who sell their services to the highest bidder and use their resources and skills to perform offensive actions. In this case, the motivation is mainly financial.

The ransomware that was not

In May 2017, the entire world was shocked when news broke that ransomware had disrupted the operations of several major companies in Spain, as well as the British health service. In a single day, more than 140,000 computers had been affected. It was the first time that malware of those features had self-replicated without control across networks:

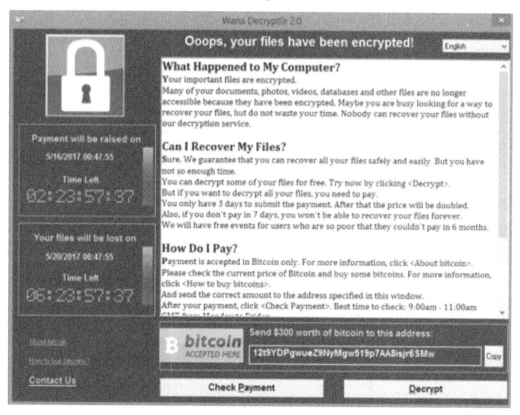

Figure 1.2 – Ransom note left on an infected system (source: Wikipedia)

This malware exploited a vulnerability known as *EternalBlue* related to a failure in the implementation of the **Server Message Block (SMB)** protocol labeled CVE-2017-0144, and particularly affected Microsoft Windows operating systems and could self-replicate without control and without the need for human interaction.

In the following days, this ransomware began to replicate around the world, becoming one of the most important threats of recent years. The most ironic thing is that by the time this ransomware appeared, there was already the patch that prevented the computers from being affected.

The world had not yet recovered from the impact caused by WannaCry when, the following month, a ransomware variant appeared that exploited the same vulnerability, but with different behavior, and with some similar aspects in terms of its code, to ransomware known as Petya, which had appeared just 1 year earlier:

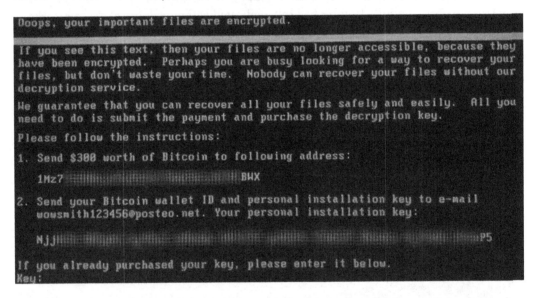

Figure 1.3 – The ID shown in the ransom screen is only plain random data (source: Securelist.com)

A peculiarity of this ransomware discovered by my fellow researchers in Kaspersky's GReAT team, and which they called Petya/ExPetr, was that in the information encryption routines, the creators of the ransomware themselves could not recover the information again, even if the victims paid the ransom.

This is completely unconventional because the reason a threat actor develops ransomware is to get a ransom payment in exchange for handing the key over to the victims to retrieve the information encrypted by the malware, so the motivation behind this campaign was not financial, but was aimed at interrupting business operations of the affected companies.

Another interesting fact about this campaign is that according to the detection telemetries, the most affected victims were companies from Ukraine, Russia, and Eastern Europe:

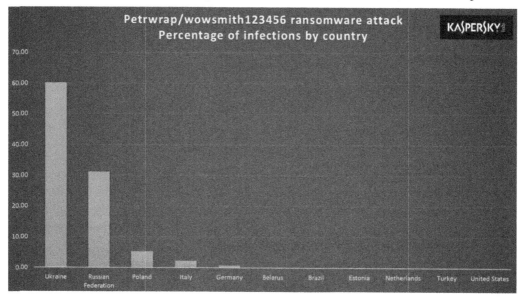

Figure 1.4 – Petya/ExPetr infections by country (source: Securelist.com)

As you can see in the preceding graph, this information is relevant and especially useful to find the specific targets to which a cyber attack was directed and supplies some elements to understand the possible motivations behind it.

Trick-or-treat

In May 2018, unknown threat actors, later linked to the Lazarus group, attacked a South American financial institution. This attack provoked damage by destroying information on 9,000 computers and 500 servers in several of its branches.

In their initial findings, investigators discovered that malware damaged the **Master Boot Record (MBR)** on the hard drive, preventing it from booting and showing the following message on the screen: **non-System disk or disk error, replace and strike any key when ready**.

Trend Micro conducted research on this malware, which was identified as a variant of KillDisk.

In the next hours, the real motive behind the attack would be discovered. Suspicious financial movements began to be detected. The attackers did not seek to disrupt the company's operation or remove information on computers, but to compromise the international transfer system known as SWIFT, which allowed the attackers to make fraudulent transfers of about $10 million to multiple accounts in Hong Kong.

Nothing is what it seems

But what do these cyber attacks have in common? Clearly, the attribution points to different threat actors and both operations were carried out in different contexts and places. The key elements here are **distraction** and **deception**.

In the first case, the threat actors used the ransomware as a front to make the affected companies believe that they were being attacked by such malware, when the real reason was to completely remove the information from their computers without the possibility that it could be recovered; that is, what the attackers were looking for was an interruption of the company's service and operations.

In the second case, the goal was the opposite. The threat actors had a purely financial interest, using malware that prevented computers from continuing to function normally while making money transfers from other computers undetected.

What were the threat actors looking for? Masking their attacks long enough to achieve their goals while confusing investigators to take longer to respond to these incidents.

But why is it so important for an incident response professional to try to find the true intent behind a cyber attack? This is quite simple. As we will see later, when an incident occurs, the nature of the attack must be identified according to the context, motivation, and key indicators to ascertain the type of attack, its characteristics, and scope. This can lead to several hypotheses and define the actions to take to contain the offensive actions and minimize the impact of the attack.

Emerging and future cyber threats

Technology is changing every day, so technological advances allow us to experience new ways of doing things, the way we work, the way we learn, and even the way we relate to other people. These modern technologies are developed to make them more usable and functional so that anyone without having too much technical knowledge can take advantage of them.

However, the architecture, design, and production of these technologies often does not consider the security part and many of the new devices you use daily are unsafe by design and exposed to potential cyber attacks.

Cyber attacks targeting IOT devices

Years ago, few people would have imagined that a simple light bulb, our smart TV, or our toilet could become an attack vector from malicious actors. According to Gartner, there will be 25 billion global Internet of Things (IoT) connections by 2025. The problem is that many devices are manufactured at a low cost to achieve greater market penetration, regardless of the threats to which these devices will be exposed.

Moreover, the risks are not just for home users; in enterprise environments, these devices could be connected within the same network infrastructure of computers and servers, raising the risk of compromising the organization's critical assets and information.

On October 21, 2016, DynDNS (Dynamic Network Services, Inc., a domain name system) was the target of an attack against the infrastructure of its systems. As a result, many Netflix, PayPal, and Twitter users, to name a few, could not access these services for hours.

The attackers provoked a Denial of Service (DoS) using a botnet known as Mirai, which turned millions of IoT devices into zombies that sent traffic in a coordinated manner against specific targets, which primarily affected the operational infrastructure in the United States. The estimated economic impact was $10 million:

Figure 1.5 – Live map of the massive DDoS attacks on Dyn's servers (https://twitter.com/flyingwithfish/status/789524594017308672?s=20)

In November of the same year, several DSL service users in Germany reported problems with their internet connection devices due to traffic saturation on TCP port 7547 by Mirai that affected their access to the network. In January 2018, a variant of the same botnet appeared, targeting the financial sector and affecting the availability of its services.

In that year alone, the percentage of botnet-related traffic for deletions on IoT devices was 78%, according to a NOKIA study. In 2019, Kaspersky detected around 100 million attacks targeting IoT devices using honeypots.

In July 2020, Trend Micro found that Mirai's botnet exploits the CVE-2020-5902 vulnerability on IoT devices, allowing it to search for Big-IP boxes for intrusion and deliver the malicious payload.

The digital evidence generated by these devices is essential to identifying promptly the origin of an attack and to be able to visualize its scope and impact.

Autonomous vehicles

More applications are being integrated with vehicles and can connect with users' mobile devices. These apps often supply access to social networks or payment apps, such as Apple Pay, Samsung Pay, or Google Pay users.

On the other hand, autonomous vehicle manufacturers integrate capabilities that reduce the number of accidents and improve transport infrastructure efficiency. Using the OBD II and CAN bus access points, someone can perform a remote diagnosis of a vehicle's operation or its location, carry out remote assistance, or obtain telemetry information collected from the vehicle.

These capabilities, however, open new attack surfaces, including the following:

- System update firmware manipulation
- Installing malware on the vehicle system
- Interception of network communications
- Exploiting software vulnerabilities

In 2013, security researchers Charlie Miller and Chris Valasek, along with journalist Andy Greenberg, showed how it was possible to hack a vehicle by taking control of the brakes or vehicle speed. In 2015, they met again, and on this occasion, they took control of a Jeep at 70 miles per hour using a zero-day exploit that allowed them to take control of the vehicle remotely over the internet.

These discovered vulnerabilities opened the door to new attack scenarios where sensitive user information can be compromised and even put human lives at risk.

In a short period following a traffic incident, and especially with the increase in the number of autonomous vehicles, it will be necessary to collect evidence from the vehicle's digital devices to investigate the details that will help to identify what caused the accident.

Drones

The global drone market will grow from $14 billion in 2018 to over $43 billion in 2024, with a compound annual growth rate (CAGR) of 20.5%. Their non-military use has shown potential for multiple fields, including engineering, architecture, and law enforcement.

Unfortunately, in many cases, their use is not regulated. In several situations, they have been involved in incidents that have jeopardized the operation of airports or the same plane, as was the case at Heathrow Airport in London, where flights were suspended, causing significant financial losses and inconvenience to passengers.

Other risks relate to organized crime in carrying out drug transfers across the border undetected or even attacking rival groups. Drones can also pose a risk to people's privacy, as a drone could record video, take pictures, or sniff conversations in the distance.

If a drone is used illegally, it is essential to collect the evidence necessary to carry out the investigation, using the appropriate procedures and tools.

Electronic voting machines

The use of digital devices in several countries' electoral processes around the world aims to ensure that the voter registration processes, as well as vote capture and counting, are efficient and reliable.

However, like all digital systems, there are attack surfaces on these systems that an attacker could use to compromise the results of an election and the reliability of the systems themselves. Security researchers have revealed that some voting systems could be vulnerable to distinct types of attacks.

In 2019, in the DefCon Voting Village, several security researchers analyzed more than 100 voting devices, some of them currently in use, and found that they were vulnerable to at least 1 type of attack.

Electoral processes are vital in ensuring not only democracy, but also political and social stability, so it is incredibly important to ensure its reliability and security.

In the event of a security incident occurring on a digital voting device in an election, the Digital Forensics and Incident Response (DFIR) professional's role would be key to quickly and effectively discovering what happened and avoiding further damage to the electoral process.

Cyber attacks on robots

Beyond science fiction, where movies or streaming series show an apocalyptic scenario with robots taking control of humanity, the reality is that robots are already everywhere, whether they are assembling components in a factory or performing high-precision surgeries.

However, the evolution of AI poses new security challenges. What if an attacker compromised a robot and could manipulate it?

There is a category of robots known as social robots; these robots' role is to interact with humans in different ways, such as assisting them or serving as a companion. According to a study by IDLab – imec, University of Ghent, Belgium, regarding the abuse of social robots for use as a means of persuasion or manipulation, they identified the following risks when they performed several proofs of concept:

- Gaining access to protected areas

- Extracting sensitive information

- Influencing people to take actions that put them at risk

In 2018, researchers from the security company IOActive presented the first ransomware attack on robots at the Kaspersky Security Analyst Summit event. In the presentation, they talked about how it was possible to hack social robots known as *Pepper* and *Nao*, showing a proof-of-concept video where they modified the source code and made the robot ask for bitcoins (`https://youtu.be/4djvZjme_-M`).

Considering a robotic-oriented threat landscape, the same scenario could occur with other types of robots and affect a production line in a factory or even a medical surgery, putting people's lives at risk.

For this reason, it is important to identify attack surfaces that could pose a security risk through threat modeling. Currently, there are several related documents with threat modeling for specific models of robots or even for the most well-known robotic operating systems, such as ROS 2: `https://design.ros2.org/articles/ros2_threat_model.html`.

A specialized device called *Black Box* was created by the Alias Robotics company to capture information relevant to robots' activity (`https://aliasrobotics.com/blackbox.php`). In the event of a security incident, this information could be handy in responding and conducting forensic investigations.

The challenge of new technologies for DFIR professionals

Without a doubt, the future looks fascinating for professionals in the incident response field. However, there are many challenges along the way.

The dizzying and constant evolution of technology means that there are more and more digital devices. Although many of them use open and standard technologies, others integrate proprietary components that could make it more challenging to obtain evidence or conduct an investigation.

On the other hand, it is necessary to expand our knowledge into new specialized fields of DFIR and learn about the latest technologies.

Summary

In this chapter, we learned the importance of understanding the threat landscape, with the emergence of new threat actors and how the technical tactics and tools used in cyber attacks have evolved.

Studying the threat landscape is a constant and particularly important activity for an incident response professional and the lack of knowledge will make it more difficult to find the right indicators of compromise when you are responding to a cybersecurity incident.

We also learned how modern technologies bring new risks but also new challenges in responding to incidents.

In the next chapter, we will learn the basic concepts of **DFIR**, the importance of identifying forensic artifacts as evidence, and some of the most important incident response frameworks.

Further reading

- 2020 Q3 Report Data Breach – Quick View: `https://pages.riskbasedsecurity.com/hubfs/Reports/2020/2020%20Q3%20Data%20Breach%20QuickView%20Report.pdf`

- *The cost of cybercrime*, Ninth Annual Cost of Cybercrime study unlocking the value of improved cybersecurity protection – Ponemon Institute: `https://www.accenture.com/_acnmedia/PDF-96/Accenture-2019-Cost-of-Cybercrime-Study-Final.pdf`

- The Hidden Costs of Cybercrime – McAfee: `https://www.mcafee.com/enterprise/en-us/assets/reports/rp-hidden-costs-of-cybercrime.pdf`

- How COVID-19 changed the way people work: `https://media.kasperskydaily.com/wp-content/uploads/sites/92/2020/05/03191550/6471_COVID-19_WFH_Report_WEB.pdf`

- Cybercrime, COVID-19 Impact, Interpol: `https://www.interpol.int/en/content/download/15526/file/COVID-19%20Cybercrime%20Analysis%20Report-%20August%202020.pdf`

- INTERPOL report shows an alarming rate of cyber attacks during COVID-19: `https://www.interpol.int/en/News-and-Events/News/2020/INTERPOL-report-shows-alarming-rate-of-cyberattacks-during-COVID-19`

- Lazarus covets COVID-19-related intelligence: `https://securelist.com/lazarus-covets-covid-19-related-intelligence/99906/`

- FBI warns ransomware assault threatens US healthcare system: `https://apnews.com/article/fbi-warns-ransomware-healthcare-system-548634f03e71a830811d291401651610`

- Czech hospital hit by cyber attack during a COVID-19 outbreak: `https://www.zdnet.com/article/czech-hospital-hit-by-cyber-attack-while-in-the-midst-of-a-covid-19-outbreak/`

- *Inside the Unnerving Supply Chain Attack That Corrupted Ccleaner*: `https://www.wired.com/story/inside-the-unnerving-supply-chain-attack-that-corrupted-ccleaner/`

- Operation ShadowHammer: `https://securelist.com/operation-shadowhammer/89992/`

- The SolarWinds cyber attack: The hack, the victims, and what we know: `https://www.bleepingcomputer.com/news/security/the-solarwinds-cyberattack-the-hack-the-victims-and-what-we-know/`

- ExPetr/Petya/NotPetya is a Wiper, Not Ransomware: `https://securelist.com/expetrpetyanotpetya-is-a-wiper-not-ransomware/78902/`

- KillDisk Variant Hits Latin American Finance Industry: `https://www.trendmicro.com/en_us/research/18/f/new-killdisk-variant-hits-latin-american-financial-organizations-again.html`

- Hackers target payment transfer system at Chile's biggest bank, 'take $10m': `https://www.theregister.com/2018/06/11/chile_bank_wiper_prelude_cyberheaist/`

- Kaspersky Targeted Cyber Attacks Logbook – Lazarus: `https://apt.securelist.com/apt/lazarus`

- IOActive Conducts First-Ever Ransomware Attack on Robots at Kaspersky Security Analyst Summit 2018: `https://ioactive.com/article/ioactive-conducts-first-ever-ransomware-attack-on-robots-at-kaspersky-security-analyst-summit-2018/`

2
Concepts of Digital Forensics and Incident Response

"You know my method. It is founded upon the observation of trifles."

— *Arthur Conan Doyle, The Boscombe Valley Mystery – a Sherlock Holmes Short Story*

One of the fastest-growing cybersecurity fields is **Digital Forensic and Incident Response (DFIR)**. The impact of cybercrime and the reporting of attacks on individuals and organizations have created a significant demand for specialized professionals in these areas to support the investigation of cases from a legal point of view and to ascertain specific details regarding the attacks' context.

Incident response and digital forensic investigation are two activities that are nearly related and should be done in a coordinated manner. Responding to an incident within 72 hours of a security breach is essential for making decisions and taking actions to identify and collect useful information to assist in threat containment.

A typical posture following a cybersecurity incident focuses primarily on ensuring business continuity and acting within the **Recovery Time Objective** (**RTO**). If the company disrupts its operations, it could be significantly affected economically and reputationally. Unfortunately, this can affect the procedures for collecting evidence and reduces the chance of finding indicators and artifacts to help identify attack vectors and activities performed by attackers.

That is why we must look for the middle ground between the urgency of returning to business operations and collecting the evidence necessary for the investigation and align business continuity goals with incident response plans.

Identifying and containing a threat, and having the most information related to the security incident, will make a difference in the organization's final impact.

In this chapter, we're going to cover the following topics.

- Concepts of **digital forensics and incident response** (**DFIR**)
- Digital evidence and forensics artifacts
- Incident response standards and frameworks
- Defining an incident response posture

Concepts of digital forensics and incident response (DFIR)

In this section, we are going to review the basic concepts of DFIR and the main differences between an event and an incident.

Digital forensics

Digital forensics is a field of expertise that integrates components of criminalistics and informatics. According to the **National Institute of Standards and Technology** (**NIST**), *Digital forensics is the application of science to the identification, collection, examination, and analysis of data while preserving the integrity of the information and maintaining a strict chain of custody for the data.*

This definition's basis is relevant as the application of science refers to the use of clear and proven methodologies, procedures, and tools so that the evidence obtained has reliability and validity in the event of a legal process.

Identifying and collecting potential evidence is an essential part of first-response procedures in a cybersecurity incident. Suppose there is no clear identification of incident-related devices or the sources of information that might contain useful artifacts. In that case, there is a risk of not gathering the pieces needed to do the investigation.

Another essential element of digital forensics is preserving the evidence's integrity because digital evidence is fragile by nature and easily manipulated. Therefore, you need to use the right tools and follow established procedures. Part of this procedure is the chain of custody, which retains the integrity in the evidence's management, from acquisition until the processing and analysis.

What is incident response?

Incident response is a series of structured steps that describe the actions to take in the face of a security breach. As I mentioned earlier, threats are continually evolving, and their detection is becoming more difficult. If organizations don't have an efficient identification and response capability, the impact of a cyber attack can be devastating.

Incident response professionals can help organizations improve their maturity level by working with plans to respond to different incidents and align them with the business objectives. The organizations must provide the resources to strengthen their technological capacity and define processes that consider the various attack scenarios they might be exposing.

According to NIST, organizations should build an incident response capacity. This involves the following:

- Creating a policy and plans
- Drawing up incident management procedures and reports
- Establishing communication channels with the internal and external parties involved.
- Creating a structure and work team
- Training the members of those teams

The creation of an incident response program should be comprehensive; for example, if you have plans that do not meet the requirements or have no specific plans for incidents, that could affect the organization. An incident management system will not be sufficient. Besides, if different organization areas do not align with program objectives or staff are not trained, any plan or tool will fail.

Difference between events and incidents

Events and incidents can be confused sometimes. An event is a registered activity as part of the organization's systems operation, such as attempts to log in to the network, connect through a port, or access a resource.

A security incident is when unusual behavior is identified or in clear violation of an acceptable security or use policy. However, this unique action alone might not be enough, as sometimes such behavior could be genuine activities; this is known as a **false positive**.

On the other hand, we should not underestimate threat actors, who sometimes have the skills to go unnoticed with the naked eye and **Living off the Land** (**LotL**) themselves to make their activities seem normal and avoid detection. Remember, just because abnormal behavior isn't detected doesn't mean everything's OK.

Digital evidence and forensics artifacts

The main element of any investigation is digital evidence. **Digital evidence** is information that could be stored or transmitted to other devices. One of the most critical challenges facing a professional investigator is identifying and finding the right evidence that could be relevant to a case.

Edmon Locard, a pioneer in digital forensics, formulated a forensic science principle as this: *Every contact leaves a trace*, which means that in any contact between two items, there will be an exchange. For example, at a robbery crime scene, a supposed offender could leave their fingerprints on several objects, their shoeprints on the floor, or even some hair; this could be enough to identify and find the suspect.

When it comes to digital devices, we can apply the same principle. We use digital devices every day, such as smartphones, wearables, smart homes, and IoT appliances, and any digital device leaves traces behind. For example, when you connect your computer to the internet, it establishes a communication channel through a router or default gateway before reaching a remote server. During this process, multiple resources interact several times and leave information in the device's memory, disk, and logs.

A digital forensic artifact is an object for storing pieces of data or information; for example, the OSes and applications store essential information to work. If you install an application in the Windows OS, this application could create databases and configuration files, or keep crucial data in the system's registry keys.

However, it's essential to not confuse forensic artifacts with **indicators of compromise** (**IoCs**) because they are not the same. Let's take a look at the meaning of forensic artifacts. Forensic artifacts are just the object where you can find specific data relating to an application or system. On the other hand, the IoC is the detailed information stored in the forensic artifact and, from the forensics point of view, could be used to identify the presence of malicious activity.

In this example of research performed by *Kaspersky's GReAT* regarding a malicious campaign that used a multi-platform targeted malware called **Mata**, document several interesting IoCs as registry keys

```
HKLM\Software\Microsoft\KxtNet
HKLM\Software\Microsoft\HlqNet
HKLM\Software\mthjk
```

The Mata malware uses the `lsass.exe` Windows process on infected victims, loads the encrypted configuration data from a registry key, and decrypts it with the AES algorithm:

Victim ID	Random 24-bit number
Internal version number	3.1.1 (0x030101)
Timeout	20 minutes
C2 addresses	108.170.31[.]81:443
	192.210.239[.]122:443
	111.90.146[.]105:443
Disk path or URL of plugin (up to 15) to be loaded on start	Not used in this malware

Figure 2.1 – Information decoded from a victim's registry

This means that if you find those registry keys in a system, indeed the computer was compromised by this malware. Also, if you can decode the content there, you will get other indicators, such as **C2 IP addresses** and **malware configuration data**.

Looking for artifacts and IoCs

Imagine you are doing an investigation, and you know that you can find relevant information related to the case in the Microsoft Teams application. You could start researching the information you can get from this application, the paths where this data is stored, its format, and so on.

Microsoft Teams forensic artifacts

According to Microsoft documentation, you can find information related to the Teams application in Windows Systems on the following path: `C:\Users\%USERNAME%\AppData\Roaming\Microsoft\Teams`.

Please note that this path refers to a Windows installation and may differ in your system, depending on the version of Microsoft Teams you have installed. Therefore, I suggest you consult the official Microsoft documentation to identify the appropriate path:

Name	Date modified	Type	Size
ai_models	2/12/2021 1:58 PM	File folder	
Backgrounds	1/26/2021 2:51 PM	File folder	
blob_storage	2/12/2021 1:57 PM	File folder	
Cache	2/13/2021 3:03 PM	File folder	
Code Cache	1/13/2021 8:05 AM	File folder	
CS_skylib	2/13/2021 3:02 PM	File folder	
databases	1/13/2021 8:07 AM	File folder	
Dictionaries	1/14/2021 10:14 AM	File folder	
GPUCache	2/3/2021 9:55 AM	File folder	
IndexedDB	1/13/2021 8:07 AM	File folder	
Local Storage	2/3/2021 9:55 AM	File folder	
logs	1/13/2021 8:08 AM	File folder	
media-stack	2/12/2021 1:57 PM	File folder	
meeting-addin	2/15/2021 7:35 AM	File folder	
Service Worker	2/3/2021 9:54 AM	File folder	
Session Storage	2/12/2021 1:57 PM	File folder	
SkypeRT	2/13/2021 2:58 PM	File folder	
tmp	2/13/2021 2:57 PM	File folder	
Cookies	2/13/2021 3:06 PM	File	36 KB
Cookies-journal	2/13/2021 3:06 PM	File	0 KB
desktop-config.json	2/13/2021 3:06 PM	JSON Source File	2 KB
installTime.txt	1/28/2021 6:33 PM	Text Document	1 KB
logs.txt	2/13/2021 3:06 PM	Text Document	4,107 KB

Figure 2.2 – Content of the Microsoft Teams folder in Windows

In this folder, you can find metadata information from the specific user and the organization, logs and configuration files, and interesting forensic artifacts, such as calls and message registers. All this is organized and stored in multiple formats such as text, JSON, and binary:

C: > Users > ▓▓▓ > AppData > Roaming > Microsoft > Teams > {} update-telemetry-config.json > ...

```
1   {
2       "UserInfo.TenantId": "▓▓▓▓▓▓▓▓▓▓▓▓▓▓▓▓▓▓▓▓▓▓",
3       "machineId": "▓▓▓▓▓▓▓▓▓▓▓▓▓▓▓▓▓▓▓▓▓▓▓▓▓▓▓",
4       "UserInfo.Ring": "general",
5       "UserInfo.Region": "amer"
6   }
```

Figure 2.3 – Microsoft Teams telemetry configuration file

Each action made when using Microsoft Teams generates information that is recorded in different files. For example, the following illustration shows one of the telemetry files that stores data related to, or associated with, meeting participants, meeting calendars, and the organizations to which they belong:

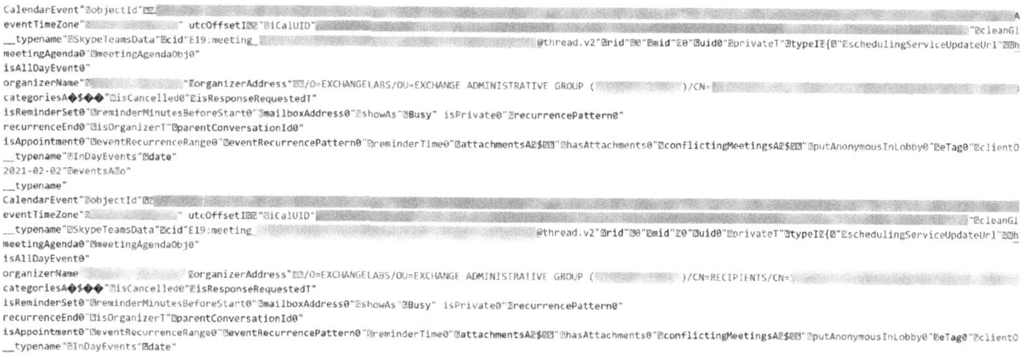

Figure 2.4 – Microsoft Teams session log file

From the forensic investigation point of view, there is more content that can be discoverable using a Microsoft tool called eDiscovery, such as chat messages and links, meeting IM conversations, and metadata, as you can see in the following screenshot:

Content type	eDiscoverable	Notes
Audio recordings	No	
Card content	Yes	See Search for card content for more information.
Chat links	Yes	
Chat messages	Yes	This includes content in Teams channels, 1:1 chats, 1:N group chats, and chats with guest user participants.
Code snippets	No	
Edited messages	Yes	If the user is on hold, previous versions of edited messages are also preserved.
Emojis, GIFs, and stickers	Yes	
Inline images	Yes	
Meeting IM conversations	Yes	
Meeting metadata[1]	Yes	
Name of channel	No	
Private channel messages	Yes	
Quotes	Yes	Quoted content is searchable. However, search results don't indicate that the content was quoted.
Reactions (such as likes, hearts, and other reactions)	No	
Subject	Yes	
Tables	Yes	

Figure 2.5 – Content types to search for evidence using Microsoft eDiscovery tools

You can find valuable information for your investigations identifying the right forensic artifacts from a specific digital device depending on the OS and the applications installed.

Different knowledge bases contain information about forensic artifacts that can be very useful as a digital forensics artifact repository: https://github.com/forensicanalysis/artifacts.

IoCs versus IoAs

As I mentioned earlier, an IoC describes the evidence on a digital device indicating that security has been compromised, but when it comes to an **Indicator of Attack (IoA)**, the goal is to identify the attacker's potential intentions, regardless of the tool they used.

These are two different approaches. From the forensics investigation point of view, the IoCs allow the identification of the traces left behind by the attackers at the time of the attack. On the other hand, IoAs are especially useful in a more proactive approach, such as threat hunting, to identify the threat actors' behavior. IoAs could include unknown attributes, IoCs, and contextual information, including threat intelligence information, even when an attack is still in progress:

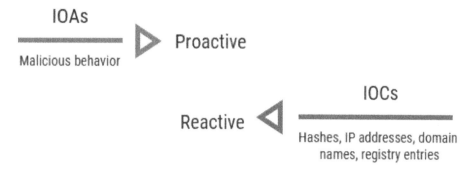

Figure 2.6 – Differences between IoCs and IoAs

An excellent way to identify IoAs is by using the MITRE ATT&CK framework. This framework describes **Tactics, Techniques, and Procedures (TTP)** that an attacker might follow when performing a malicious operation. You can find details of this framework on the MITRE ATT&CK official website: `https://attack.mitre.org/`. We will dig deeper into this framework in *Chapter 6, Understanding the Cyber Kill Chain and the MITRE ATT&CK Framework*.

For instance, think about this scenario. Imagine that you are responding to a ransomware security incident. During the evidence collection stage, you find the following hashes and IP addresses related to the ransomware VHD attack described in this research: `https://securelist.com/lazarus-on-the-hunt-for-big-game/97757/`.

`6D12547772B57A6DA2B25D2188451983`	
`D0806C9D8BCEA0BD47D80FA004744D7D`	
`172.93.184[.]62`	`MATA C2`
`23.227.199[.]69`	`MATA C2`

Now, you can start investigating a little more by checking information related to the TTP used by the threat actor and mapping them with the MITRE ATT&CK matrix to search for specific information that identifies those behaviors in the systems, as shown in *Figure 2.7*:

Chain of infection

1. Gained access to victims' systems by exploiting a vulnerable VPN gateway;
2. Obtained admin rights on the compromised machines;
3. Installed a backdoor;
4. Seized control of the Active Directory server;
5. Infected all computers on the network with the VHD ransomware using a loader specially written for the task.

https://usa.kaspersky.com/blog/lazarus-vhd-ransomware/22905/

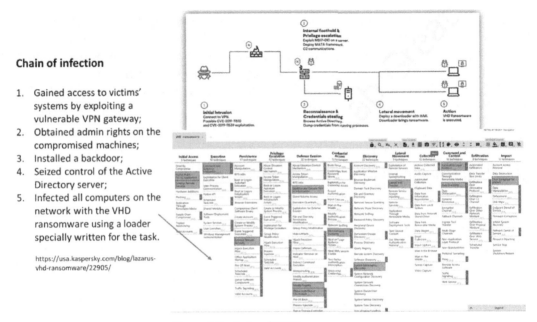

Figure 2.7 – IoAs of VHD ransomware

Using this approach, you can not only look for malicious files or malicious network connections; you can also search for specific behaviors in your infrastructure. This is why in incident response, it is vital to use both IoCs and IoAs.

Incident response standards and frameworks

One of the main problems facing organizations as regards cybersecurity incidents is the lack of plans and procedures available to face the organization's threats because every cyber attack has specific characteristics. You need to understand the nature of these threats, their associated indicators, and the measures you need to follow in order to contain and eliminate them.

Adopting frameworks and standards for creating your *incident response plans* will help you to respond more efficiently and adopt a more proactive posture in the face of cybersecurity incidents. It's essential to adapt these frameworks to the organization's needs because every organization has different business requirements, capacities, and maturity levels in this topic.

The following list includes industry frameworks related to the creation of incident response plans.

NIST Computer Security Incident Handling Guide

This is a practical guide for handling incidents effectively and efficiently, supplying the guidelines to mitigate cybersecurity incidents. This document focuses on these steps:

1. Preparation
2. Detection and analysis
3. Containment, eradication, and recovery
4. Post-incident activity

These steps can be recurrent. For example, if you have detected an IoC on a device, such as a connection to a particular IP address categorized as malicious, you can apply containment actions by blocking communications or identifying all devices connected to that address. Then you could go back and look for new indicators, as shown in the following diagram:

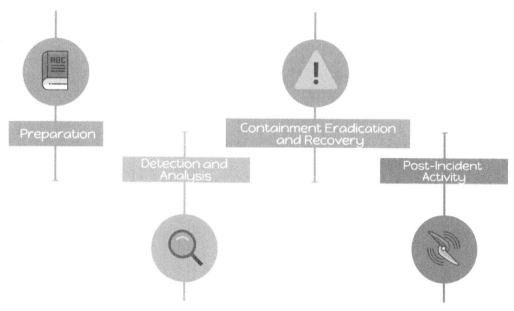

Figure 2.8 – Incident response life cycle

The document also includes guidelines and recommendations for developing an incident response capacity to create an incident response team, as well as develop policies, plans, and procedures, and the steps for communicating with third parties for coordination and sharing information with third parties:

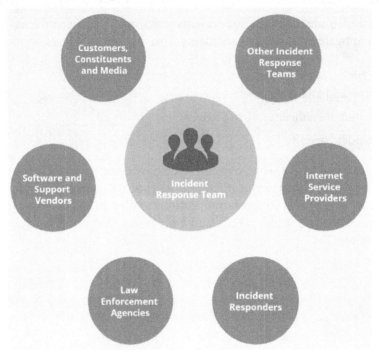

Figure 2.9 – Communications with outside parties

It also includes appendices that raise different hypothetical scenarios to apply the principles of the framework practically.

SANS incident response process

The SANS Institute has published its document, a handbook that defines six structured steps to respond to cybersecurity incidents:

1. Preparation
2. Identification/Scoping
3. Containment/Intelligence Development
4. Eradication/Remediation
5. Recovery
6. Lessons Learned

The SANS handbook establishes a more detailed perspective regarding the distinct phases to respond to a security breach. Even though it has specific similarities with the NIST Computer Security Incident Handling Guide, it does retain some differences.

One of these differences is that the phases of Containment, Eradication, and Detection are independent processes in the SANS handbook in the same way as Recovery and Lessons Learned:

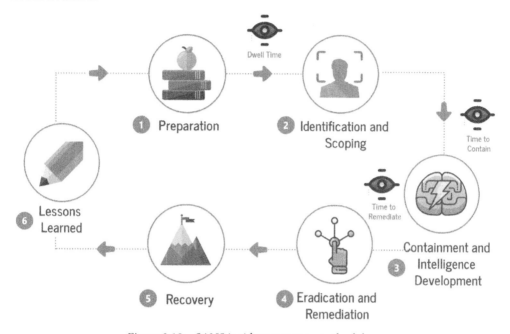

Figure 2.10 – SANS incident response methodology

A particularity of the SANS six-step process focuses on the scope and contention of threats in an agile way. According to SANS, there are three critical time frames for responding successfully to a security breach:

- **Time to detect**: The length of time between the initial compromise and its detection (How long does it take to find it?)

- **Time to contain**: The length of time between detection and containment (How long to limit or control the damage?)

- **Time to remediate**: The time between containment and remediation (How long to remove the threat?)

According to IBM, the average time to identify a breach in 2020 was 207 days, so you cannot contain a threat if you don't know that it exists; the faster you detect a threat, the more likely you are to stop it in time and avoid a more significant impact.

It is not just about identifying threats; we need to know how many assets are compromised; this is about defining the scope. There is no point in removing a computer threat if it stays persistent on other devices and allows attackers to stay with access to the organization's network.

Another essential element of the SANS methodology is the integration of intelligence development in the step of contention. Threat intelligence is vital for incident response because it provides actionable information for hunting threats and provides indicators for real-time detection to the SOC.

Once you identify the threats, you can apply the controls to reduce the attack surfaces and limit the compromise's impact.

NIST Guide to Integrating Forensic Techniques into Incident Response

Another interesting document is the NIST Guide to Integrating Forensic Techniques into Incident Response. I find this guide especially useful because this document's approach is from the technological point of view and not a law enforcement view.

The purpose of this guide is to integrate the forensic procedures in the incident response phases and perform forensics activities, providing information about different data sources, including files, OSes, network traffic, and applications.

Like the *NIST Computer Security Incident Handling Guide*, this document supplies the guidelines to develop a forensic capability in the organization and the forensic process:

Figure 2.11 – The forensic process

The concept and the approach integrating these two disciplines is the basis of the idea of DFIR. To collect the evidence, you need to follow the first response procedures. To process and analyze the evidence, you need to identify the forensic artifacts, and to identify IoCs, you need the threat intelligence information.

Defining an incident response posture

The incident response posture has changed radically in recent years. Today, we should be using more than just a conventional approach to fight these cyber threats. We need to create specific plans to deal with threats; for example, you need to use different methods to respond to an information leak or ransomware incident other than a denial-of-service.

Another important thing is that you need to align the DFIR strategy with the organization's business objectives and vision. Every organization is different. You should not implement generic plans just from a compliance posture; you need to *test the plans* and be sure that they will work in a real-life cybersecurity incident.

The organizations' size doesn't matter. Even medium-sized or small enterprises can adopt a preventive-proactive security posture that includes incident response plans according to their budget and requirements.

In a world where digital transformation has allowed companies to develop and make them more competitive, the difference between surviving a cyber attack and not having the ability to continue their operations is to have plans to respond appropriately and efficiently to these incidents.

Summary

In this chapter, we covered the basic concepts of digital forensics and incident response and learned the difference between events and incidents. We also learned the concept of digital evidence and the importance of forensic artifacts. We identified the differences between IoCs and IoAs. This will be very useful for conducting forensic investigations and identifying the persistence of a threat actor.

We reviewed three of the most important frameworks and guidelines regarding incident response and digital forensics and learned the importance of defining an incident response strategy.

In the next chapter, we will learn how to perform first-response procedures and collect evidence using triage.

Further reading

- MATA: Multi-platform targeted malware framework: `https://securelist.com/mata-multi-platform-targeted-malware-framework/97746/`

- Conducting an eDiscovery investigation of content in Microsoft Teams: `https://docs.microsoft.com/en-us/microsoftteams/ediscovery-investigation`

- Looking at Microsoft Teams from a DFIR perspective: `https://cyberforensicator.com/2020/04/16/looking-at-microsoft-teams-from-a-dfir-perspective/`

- Digital forensics repository: `https://github.com/ForensicArtifacts/artifacts`

- IOC security: Indicators of Attack versus Indicators of Compromise: `https://www.crowdstrike.com/blog/indicators-attack-vs-indicators-compromise`

- NIST Computer Security Incident Handling Guide: `https://nvlpubs.nist.gov/nistpubs/SpecialPublications/NIST.SP.800-61r2.pdf`

- NIST Guide to Integrating Forensic Techniques into Incident Response: `https://nvlpubs.nist.gov/nistpubs/Legacy/SP/nistspecialpublication800-86.pdf`

- It's Awfully Noisy Out There: Results of the 2018 SANS Incident Response Survey: `https://www.sans.org/media/vendor/noisy-there-results-2018-incident-response-survey-38660.pdf`

- 2021 Incident Response Steps for NIST and SANS Framework | AT&T Cybersecurity: `https://cybersecurity.att.com/blogs/security-essentials/incident-response-steps-comparison-guide`

3
Basics of the Incident Response and Triage Procedures

"There is nothing more deceptive than an obvious fact."

— Arthur Conan Doyle, The Boscombe Valley Mystery – a Sherlock Holmes Short Story

When responding to a cybersecurity incident, there are three essentials to consider:

- Response time
- Following appropriate procedures depending on the type of incident
- Using the right tools

Every incident is unique and has very particular challenges...

We reviewed some cases in the first chapter where attackers used deception to make the response and investigations more difficult. For example, in the cyberattack against Banco de Chile, the attackers used the distraction to compromise around 9,000 devices using the KillMBR malware. The threat actors' real objective was to transfer money to another country, abusing the SWIFT money transfer system, to avoid the security staff figuring out what was happening.

An incident response professional needs to have the ability to understand the context of a security breach and identify the key elements to act in the shortest possible time.

In this chapter, you will learn about the following:

- Principles of first response

- Triage's concept and procedures

- First response procedures in different scenarios

- First response toolkit

Technical requirements

In case you haven't already done, you need to download and install VMware Workstation Player from this link `https://www.vmware.com/products/workstation-player/workstation-player-evaluation.html`.

You'll also need to download the following from the book's official GitHub repository `https://github.com/PacktPublishing/Incident-Response-with-Threat-Intelligence`:

- Virtual machines:

  - IR-Laptop

  - IR-Workstation

- Lab file:

  - Chapter03

Principles of first response

At the time of an incident, things happen quickly, and you need to act efficiently and assertively. It is therefore imperative to follow the correct procedures.

In many cases, the problem is that organizations do not have the staff with the skills, knowledge, or tools to perform the activities associated with first response or documented procedures. This obviously results in improvised actions that increase the risk of errors that can negatively affect an investigation's outcome.

Each incident is different and cannot be handled in the same way; however, there are basic standard procedures to follow. It is crucial to document these procedures and make them accessible to first responders.

First response guidelines

One of the basic principles of incident response is to preserve and protect the evidence's integrity, so the first responder must identify and evaluate the context of the incident and the environment around the scene to define the best approach to get the necessary information to investigate the incident without compromising the evidence:

- **Evaluating the context and the scene**: Before taking any action, the first responder must know the nature and context of the incident; there are differences between the procedures to follow when responding to an incident related to an information leak to another where the attackers exploit a vulnerability that can compromise the organization's infrastructure.

  The environment around the scene is also relevant for defining the procedures to follow; for instance, in a production environment, sometimes you need to be careful to not interrupt the business process or take away the devices.

- **Securing the scene**: As mentioned, the integrity of the evidence must always be ensured, even before its acquisition. It is vital to secure the scene and prevent, as much as possible, anyone, even employees of the company, from using suspicious devices unless it is indispensable.

  When you respond to a cybersecurity incident, you must act similarly to what would be done at a crime scene. Police secure the area and control all access to where the evidence is located.

  This procedure must prevent someone from intentionally or accidentally contaminating the evidence, causing evidence to be lost. If the incident requires law enforcement intervention, this evidence could not be valid in court.

- **Identifying the sources of the evidence**: Like a crime scene, the first responder must identify which elements can be useful as evidence based on the incident type. For example, if you respond to an incident where an insider is involved and their workspace is being insured, you should consider collecting information from their computer, USB devices, external hard disks, and everything that could contain relevant evidence for the investigation.

- **Volatile and non-volatile information**: As I mentioned earlier, most digital information is volatile by nature, so you should try to recover as much evidence as you can before it is lost. The prioritization at this point is essential; you must first acquire the evidence considered volatile, such as RAM, and then what is stored in files or databases.

  RFC 3227 defines the *Guidelines for Evidence Collection and Archiving* and describes how the evidence must be acquired following a particular order according to its volatility (`https://tools.ietf.org/html/rfc3227`).

  Fortunately, some tools collect numerous pieces of evidence at once, reducing the chance of making mistakes or losing relevant evidence.

- **Establishing the legal admissibility of the evidence**: Depending on the case's nature, sometimes cybersecurity incidents require following legal procedures. If this is the case, it is necessary to act following the procedures established by international laws or the country's laws where the incident happened; in some cases, it is even necessary to notify the judicial authorities to continue the procedure.

  However, many cybersecurity incidents do not follow legal courses of action, sometimes for reputational reasons or to maintain the case's confidentiality, and do not require judicial handling.

- **Chain of custody**: Part of the procedure to ensure the integrity of the evidence is related to chronological documentation of each part of the evidence transportation process, from the moment of the evidence acquisition until it is stored or until the investigation is completed. This is known as the chain of custody:

DIGITAL EVIDENCE
CHAIN OF CUSTODY FORM

Case No:	Page:	of:

ELECTRONIC MEDIA/COMPUTER DETAILS

Item/Tag No:	Description		
Manufacturer:	Model No:		Serial No:
Obtained From:		Date/Time:	Obtained By:

IMAGE DETAILS

Date/Time:	Created By:	Method Used:	Image Name:
Storage Drive:	HASH:		

CHAIN OF CUSTODY

Tracking No:	Date/Time:	FROM:	TO:	Reason:
	Date:	Name/Org:	Name/Org:	
	Time:	Signature:	Signature:	
	Date:	Name/Org:	Name/Org:	
	Time:	Signature:	Signature:	
	Date:	Name/Org:	Name/Org:	
	Time:	Signature:	Signature:	
	Date:	Name/Org:	Name/Org:	
	Time:	Signature:	Signature:	
	Date:	Name/Org:	Name/Org:	
	Time:	Signature:	Signature:	
	Date:	Name/Org:	Name/Org:	
	Time:	Signature:	Signature:	
	Date:	Name/Org:	Name/Org:	
	Time:	Signature:	Signature:	

e-fense, Inc.   05/01/09 v1.5

Figure 3.1 – Example of a chain of custody form

The goal of the chain of custody is to prevent the tampering or contamination of evidence.

As you may realize, first response procedures are critical in a cybersecurity incident as the quality of this work can determine the direction of an investigation.

Triage – concept and procedures

The amount of evidence around a cybercrime scene can be overwhelming, and the time available to perform first response procedures is limited. We also need to consider containment of the attack, and ensuring business continuity is vital for organizations. That's why the incident responder needs to identify and prioritize which forensic artifacts can provide useful information to the case.

The process of classification and prioritization is known as **triage**, and according to Oxford Languages, triage (from the French *trier*, which means to *separate out*) is defined as *the action of sorting items according to quality*. This term is used regularly in some professional fields such as healthcare.

In digital forensics, this prioritization is known as *forensic triage*. It refers to identifying, classifying, prioritizing, and acquiring evidence relevant to investigate the case. Doing it properly can be the difference between an investigation being successful or unsuccessful.

In first response procedures, the triage begins at the time when potential sources of evidence are identified; for example, in an incident related to information leakage, the data sources could be database servers, computers that might contain files with sensitive information, active directory servers with user activity logs, network traffic captured at any given time, network devices, or even USB devices or external hard drives.

Once the sources of information have been identified, it should be determined which techniques and tools to use to make the evidence acquisition as efficient as possible, reducing the risk of loss or contamination.

The triage process ends when the acquisition of images or forensic artifacts is completed and delivered for investigation.

First response procedures in different scenarios

The incident response professional plays a key role in supporting organizations in developing first response processes to address cybersecurity incidents. These processes cannot be developed generically and must be based on an evaluation and analysis of the organization where they need to be implemented.

This is a basic example of what the general steps might be in a first response procedure for a particular case of a ransomware attack:

1. The incident is reported via the help desk platform, by email or by phone.
2. The information provided by the user is evaluated to confirm the incident.

3. A ticket is generated on the incident response platform.

4. The device is requested to be secured.

5. First response staff is assigned to respond to the incident.

6. The chain of custody process begins.

7. Photos of ransom messages are taken on the screen.

8. Acquisition of the RAM on the affected computer or computers is carried out.

9. Forensic copying of the hard drive is made.

10. If making a forensic copy of the disc is not possible, the main artifacts are extracted from the device.

11. The scope of the incident is evaluated to validate whether more equipment is affected.

12. The evidence obtained is delivered for investigation.

During first response activities, it is likely that the environment's conditions could change. For example, you get intelligence information regarding certain communication to the internet from the affected computers. This can lead to the need to adapt the procedures to these new conditions, so the first responder must have the flexibility to make the necessary changes.

It is important to mention that once investigators receive forensic images or information extracted from the artifacts, they will start in parallel with the investigation, and the findings can lead to starting other activities such as threat containment, acquiring new evidence, or threat hunting.

First response toolkit

As I mentioned before, tools are a vital part of first response procedures. Their proper use will help obtain the evidence required for the investigation without compromising information or systems' integrity.

It is essential to know the technical details of the tools you will use, how they work, and how they interact with the target systems; this will prevent contamination, leading to invalidating it in a legal case or making it unusable when analyzing it.

The goal of these tools is to obtain a forensic image of the device to be investigated. The first responder must integrate these tools into their toolkit to always be prepared.

Fortunately, there are not just commercial tools for first responders; there are also many free and open source reliable options. We will mention and use a few of them in the practical labs for this book's purposes.

There are two categories of tools that are used: those to obtain forensic images and then analyze them with specialized tools in a *post-mortem* stage and those that allow the acquisition of particular forensic artifacts, such as information from Windows registry keys, web browsing history, network connections, or processes, regularly obtained in a *live* environment.

There are excellent commercial and free tools for the **Digital Forensics and Incident Response (DFIR)** investigations field, many of them even open source.

To make it easier for you to learn how to use the tools and perform the practical labs in this book, we will use **Free and Open Source Software (FOSS)**, although we will also mention commercial tools.

Forensic image acquisition tools

Forensic evidence acquisition tools make a bit-to-bit copy of the devices to ensure the integrity of the information to be analyzed post-mortem without affecting the conditions that exist when taking the image.

Tools for memory acquisition

As we learned earlier, it is imperative to consider that it is a priority to collect volatile information that could be lost if the environment's conditions change, or you need to restart or disconnect the device you want to analyze.

Magnet RAM Capture

Magnet RAM Capture is a tool that makes a physical acquisition of the suspicious computer's memory in a raw format, which means that the resulting file size will be equal to the RAM the device has.

One of the advantages of this tool is that it does not require installation and can be run from a pen drive without the risk of contaminating the evidence:

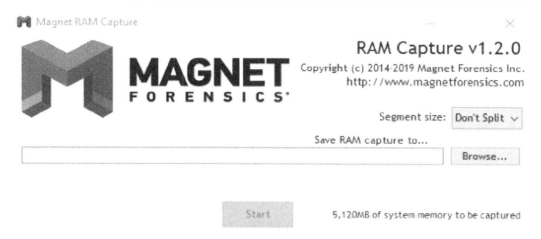

Figure 3.2 – Magnet RAM Forensics GUI interface

This tool only works in Windows environments and is supported from Windows XP to Windows 10 (works even with Virtual Secure Mode enabled) in desktop and Windows 2008 to 2012 Server (32 and 64 bits).

You can download this tool from here: `https://www.magnetforensics.com/resources/magnet-ram-capture/`.

Belkasoft Live RAM Capturer

Belkasoft Live RAM Capturer is also a tool to acquire the device's RAM content even if the system is protected by anti-debugging or anti-dumping, and you can run it from a pen drive.

When you download the tool, you will get the 32-bit and 64-bit versions separately:

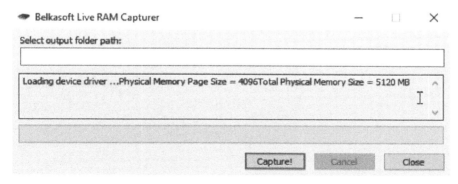

Figure 3.3 – Belkasoft Live RAM Capturer GUI interface

This tool supports all Windows versions from Windows XP to Windows 10 and Windows 2003 to 2008 Server.

You can download this tool from here: `https://belkasoft.com/ram-capturer`.

Linux Memory Extractor (LiME)

On modern Linux systems, restrictions on virtual devices only allow access to a subset of memory, which is why it is no longer an option to use tools built into the system such as dd.

LiME is a **Loadable Kernel Module (LKM) tool**, which allows the full acquisition of memory from Linux and Android-based devices. Similarly, as with the tools mentioned previously, it does not significantly modify the memory's contents during its acquisition:

Figure 3.4 – Example of Linux memory acquisition using LiME

Unlike the other tools, LiME also allows remote memory acquisition over the network.

You can download this tool from here: `https://github.com/504ensicsLabs/LiME`.

Acquire Volatile Memory for Linux (AVML)

This is a volatile memory acquisition tool developed by Microsoft that supports the x86_64 architecture. An interesting functionality is that you do not need to know the target OS and you can compile it in a single binary:

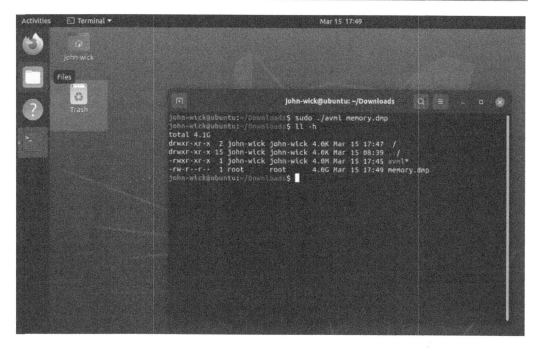

Figure 3.5 – Example of Linux memory acquisition using AVML

AVML uses the LiME output format. You can download this tool from here: `https://github.com/microsoft/avml`.

Disk acquisition

Sometimes, the information in memory won't be enough, and you will need to get forensic artifacts from the disk. In that case, you can use acquisition tools that follow the same principle and make bit-to-bit copies.

Here are some useful and free disk forensic acquisition tools.

Forensic Toolkit® (FTK) Imager

FTK Imager is a data preview and disk acquisition tool; you can use it to get an image of the device's local hard drives, folders, or individual files; you can also preview and analyze the content and even mount forensic images for analysis in a forensic way without the risk of compromising the original image:

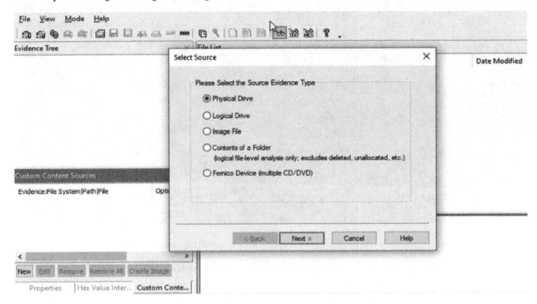

Figure 3.6 – FTK Imager GUI interface

You can select different output formats that are compatible with the major industry standards (Raw DD, SMART, E01, or AFF) supported by almost any forensic analysis tool.

You can download this tool from here: `https://accessdata.com/product-download/`.

USB acquisition

Sometimes you will need to get evidence from USB devices; remember that it's imperative to do it forensically to reduce the possibility of compromising its integrity.

ImageUSB

ImageUSB is a tool to create **USB Flash Drive (UFD)** forensic bit-to-bit and master boot records:

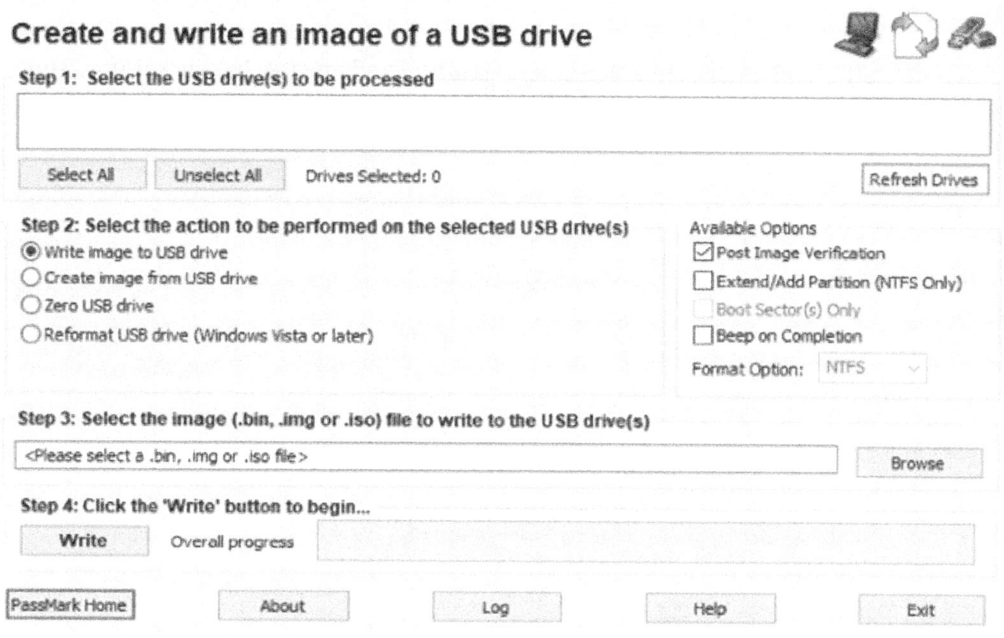

Create and write an image of a USB drive

Step 1: Select the USB drive(s) to be processed

| Select All | Unselect All | Drives Selected: 0 | | Refresh Drives |

Step 2: Select the action to be performed on the selected USB drive(s)

- ◉ Write image to USB drive
- ○ Create image from USB drive
- ○ Zero USB drive
- ○ Reformat USB drive (Windows Vista or later)

Available Options
- ☑ Post Image Verification
- ☐ Extend/Add Partition (NTFS Only)
- ☐ Boot Sector(s) Only
- ☐ Beep on Completion

Format Option: NTFS ⌄

Step 3: Select the image (.bin, .img or .iso) file to write to the USB drive(s)

| <Please select a .bin, .img or .iso file> | Browse |

Step 4: Click the 'Write' button to begin...

| Write | Overall progress | |

| PassMark Home | About | Log | Help | Exit |

Figure 3.7 – ImageUSB GUI interface

It's important to mention that if you use a USB device to output the forensic image, the developer recommends using a USB with a similar storage capacity; thus, you will optimize the space.

You can download this tool from here: `https://www.osforensics.com/tools/write-usb-images.html`.

Network package acquisition

Sometimes you need to correlate information from different sources; for example, if you find some suspected connections in memory analysis, it would be useful to have a capture of the traffic that provides more information.

Wireshark

Wireshark is free and an extraordinary tool to capture and analyze network traffic. You can install the tool or just use the portable version; all you need is to connect the device with Wireshark to a span port of a network device and filter to capture the specific information you need:

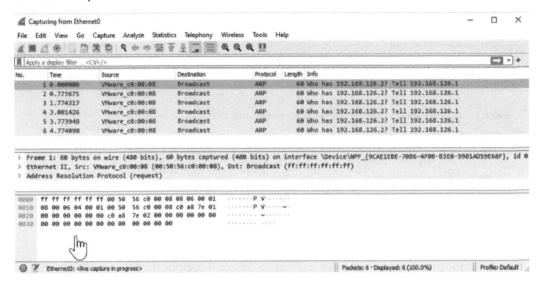

Figure 3.8 – Screenshot of a Wireshark network traffic capture

Wireshark is multiplatform and you can use the GUI version or the command line version using TShark. You can download this tool from here: https://www.wireshark.org/download.html.

Artifact collectors

Artifact collectors are tools that extract specific information from a system that can be useful in an investigation.

It is estimated that less than 5% of the information will be useful in 99% of an investigation, so it is extremely important to identify not only the best way to get that information but also what could be the most accurate sources to obtain it, especially when time is limited, and we do not have a guarantee that we will be able to access this source again.

Kroll Artifact Parser and Extractor (KAPE)

KAPE is a Windows artifact collector tool. This tool collects different artifacts from a target system and processes the information using different integrated tools. You can run this tool from a USB drive because it doesn't need any installation:

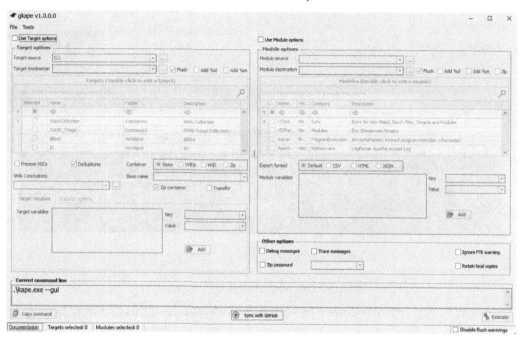

Figure 3.9 – Screenshot of KAPE GUI

KAPE is modular, so you can select what modules you want to run to do the triage. You can use the GUI or the command-line version. You can download this tool from here: https://www.kroll.com/en/services/cyber-risk/incident-response-litigation-support/kroll-artifact-parser-extractor-kape.

MAGNET Web Page Saver (WPS)

Magnet **Web Pager Saver** (**WPS**) is a tool to capture web page content to collect evidence of the content at a specific time. WPS supports snapshots using scrolling functionality and you can save the captured data in a SQLite database file:

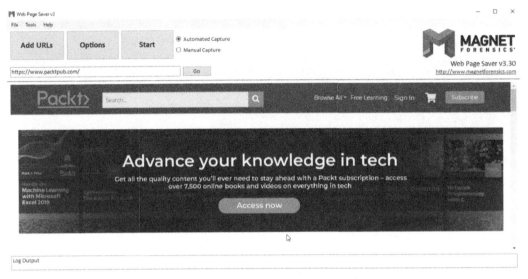

Figure 3.10 – Magnet WPS GUI interface

Magnet WPS supports Windows 7 or higher. You can download this tool from here: `https://www.magnetforensics.com/resources/web-page-saver/`.

DFIR-O365RC

This tool for Office 365 log collection works using PowerShell and PowerShell Core. You can get data from Azure **Active Directory** (**AD**) sign-in and audit logs and from Office 365 unified audit logs:

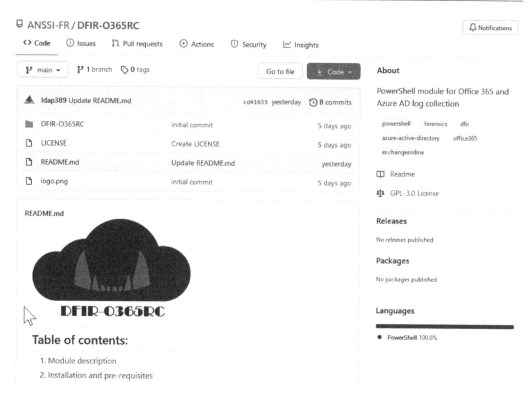

Figure 3.11 – GitHub repository of the DFIR-O365RC Project

DFIR-O365RC is a multiplatform tool that works on Windows, Linux, and macOS. You can download this tool from here: `https://github.com/ANSSI-FR/DFIR-O365RC`.

Summary

In this chapter, we learned the importance of first response procedures when addressing a cybersecurity incident. We also reviewed the concept of chain of custody and prioritizing the acquisition of evidence based on the order of volatility.

We also learned about the concept of triage and the different tools we can use to collect evidence from forensic artifacts.

In the next chapter, we will apply the concepts learned in the first three chapters to work on practical labs based on scenarios.

Further reading

- *What is Forensic Triage?* https://www.adfsolutions.com/news/what-is-forensic-triage

- *Triage and Basic Incident Handling Handbook*: https://www.enisa.europa.eu/topics/trainings-for-cybersecurity-specialists/online-training-material/documents/triage-and-basic-incident-handling-handbook/at_download/file

- *Electronic evidence - a basic guide for First Responders*: https://www.enisa.europa.eu/publications/electronic-evidence-a-basic-guide-for-first-responders/at_download/fullReport

- *Cyber Security Incident Response Guide*: https://www.crest-approved.org/wp-content/uploads/2014/11/CSIR-Procurement-Guide.pdf

- *First Responders Guide to Computer Forensics*: https://resources.sei.cmu.edu/asset_files/Handbook/2005_002_001_14429.pdf

- *Roles of First Responder in computer forensics*: https://info-savvy.com/roles-of-first-responder-in-computer-forensics/

- *Ransomware First Response Guide – What to do in the 'Oh $#@t' moment*: https://securityboulevard.com/2019/05/ransomware-first-response-guide-what-to-do-in-the-oh-t-moment/

4
Applying First Response Procedures

In this chapter, we will have the opportunity to apply the concepts learned in the previous chapters in a very practical way, using scenarios of cases related to cybersecurity incidents. As mentioned in the previous chapters, one of the main objectives of first-response procedures is to get useful information to investigate a cybersecurity incident.

So, there are several things that we must ask ourselves based on the information we have on the case:

- What are the possible sources of data?

- What kind of technology is behind the device from which I should get the information?

- How volatile is the data?

- Can I take the device into custody if necessary, or is that device required for business continuity?

These questions will help you make the best decision about what could be the most appropriate methodologies, procedures, and tools to perform first-response procedures in a particular case.

In this chapter, you'll begin your journey into the fascinating field of **incident response** (**IR**). You will analyze a case study related to a cybersecurity incident of a fictitious company and use some tools to perform first-response and triage procedures covering the following topics:

- Case study—a data breach incident
- Following first-response procedures

Technical requirements

In case you haven't done already, you need to download and install VMware Workstation Player from here: https://www.vmware.com/products/workstation-player/workstation-player-evaluation.html.

You'll also need to download the following from the book's official GitHub repository, https://github.com/PacktPublishing/Incident-Response-with-Threat-Intelligence:

- Virtual machines:
  - IR-Laptop
  - IR-Workstation
  - Corp-Laptop
- Lab file:
  - Chapter04

Additionally, you will need a completely clean pen drive with at least 16 gigabytes (GB) of capacity.

Case study – a data breach incident

Michael Smith, the **chief executive officer** (**CEO**) of a global energy company, traveled to Asia a couple of months ago to attend one of the industry's most important events. Recently, confidential and strategic information from the company that was only accessible to a very few people, including the CEO, began to circulate publicly.

This leak of information has impacted many different areas of the business and has affected some negotiations that were taking place with different companies around the world. Some of the published information was on the CEO's computer, and now, there are suspicions that his computer was hacked on the last trip.

You were assigned as the lead investigator of the case, so now, you need to carry out first-response procedures and get the necessary information from the CEO's computer to start the investigation.

Analyzing the cybersecurity incident

According to this scenario, several elements need to be considered. The initial point of our analysis is about the identification of places where the information is stored and which people have the privileges to access that information.

In this case, within the circle of people who have that information in their possession is just the CEO, and there are suspicions that he may have been one of the targets of this security compromise.

Depending on the circumstances and information we got, the first device to review is the CEO's computer, without ruling out that it may be necessary to review other devices.

As a first step, we must have a meeting with the CEO to get as many details as possible that will allow us to have a clearer context and focus on the type of information we are looking to obtain.

Once we have interviewed the CEO, we must request his computer to perform first-response procedures.

Selecting the best strategy

Considering the circumstances of the case, it would be very useful to perform procedures to obtain disk and memory forensic images from the CEO's computer. In this way, we would be able to review all the information and have evidence that it could have happened in the period from his trip abroad to the time when the information leak was discovered.

In addition, it would be very valuable to obtain specific artifacts of programs installed on the computer and preprocessed information of timelines, executed applications, information about requests to domains or **Internet Protocol** (**IP**) addresses, and some other data that would allow us to speed up the investigation so that we could use tools allowing us to obtain this information.

Next steps

We now have some context information and the CEO's computer. The first thing we need to do is identify the type of information and forensic artifacts we will need in order to start the investigation. You can download a template to do this from here: `https://github.com/PacktPublishing/Incident-Response-with-Threat-Intelligence`.

Which forensic artifacts could be key pieces to find the evidence you need for the investigation? Think about it—what could have been the compromise vector? Are there any new programs that the user installed on their trip?. Might the user have navigated to malicious sites? Where could this information be found?

Once you have identified the information you need for the investigation, the next step will be to select the appropriate tools according to the environment and the particular circumstances of the scene.

To perform the practical exercises of this chapter, we will use first-response tools to get the evidence we need from the suspect computer.

Following first-response procedures

Before starting with the first-response procedures, you will need to prepare a **Universal Serial Bus** (**USB**) device to create your kit with all the tools and configuration necessary to perform the exercises of this chapter. This is the equivalent of having a first aid kit to use in case of an emergency.

For this exercise, you will need your pen drive ready and then follow these steps:

1. Right-click the mouse button, select the disk drive of your pen drive to open the context menu, and then select the **Format...** option.

2. In the **Format** dialog box, on the **File system** option, select **NTFS** or **exFAT** (this format is useful in environments different from Windows, such as macOS or Linux, providing full read-write support), as shown in the following screenshot:

Figure 4.1 – Preparing the first-response toolkit USB

> **Note**
>
> Pen drives are usually formatted as **FAT32** filesystem by default. The problem with this filesystem format is that it restricts the maximum size of a file to 4 GB and, in our case, this will not be convenient as sometimes we will need to save larger files than that.

3. Press the **Start** button to initialize the pen-drive formatting. It's important to note that during this process, the disk will be formatted, and all the information will be erased, as illustrated in the following screenshot:

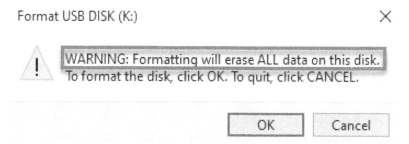

Figure 4.2 – Warning message displayed after clicking on Start

4. Once your pen drive is ready, open the drive and create a folder called `FirstResponseTools` (this is where we will save all our tools).

5. Then, create a folder called `Evidence` (this is where we will save the acquired files from the suspect devices).

6. Inside the `FirstResponseTools` folder, we will create a new folder called `Installers`.

7. Inside the `Evidence` folder, we will create two more folders—one called `MemDump` and another one called `Artifacts`.

Now that we have our pen drive ready, it's time to start adding our tools and performing first-response procedures to collect evidence from the compromised device, starting with the volatile information.

Memory acquisition

There are several advantages of acquiring the full memory; for instance, we should not worry about maintaining the volatility order since we are capturing everything at a specific point in time. Remember—we will have an exact *picture* of everything that is happening on the device at that very moment.

Another advantage is that we will not lose any of the information, and if the environment changes, that will not affect us since we will be able to access it as many times as necessary without risking it.

Capturing memory using MAGNET RAM Capture

In the investigator VM, proceed as follows:

1. Navigate to the MAGNET RAM Capture tool, found at `https://www.magnetforensics.com/resources/magnet-ram-capture/`.

2. Provide the information required in the web form and press the **GET FREE TOOL** button.

3. You will receive an email with instructions and a link to download the tool.

4. On your first-response toolkit pen drive, create a new folder under the `FirstResponseTools/Installers` folder, called `MagnetRamCapture`.

5. Download the executable program and save it in the folder you created for this tool.

You now have the tool that you will use to dump the memory from the suspect computer. Now, let's prepare the practice environment.

Simulating the scene

In this case, we will simulate the scene using our VMs so that you can start with the memory acquisition procedure.

In the Corp-Laptop VM, proceed as follows:

1. Connect the pen drive to the VM by right-clicking on the top right of the virtualization console, selecting the name of your pen drive, and then selecting **Connect (Disconnect from host)**, as shown in the following screenshot:

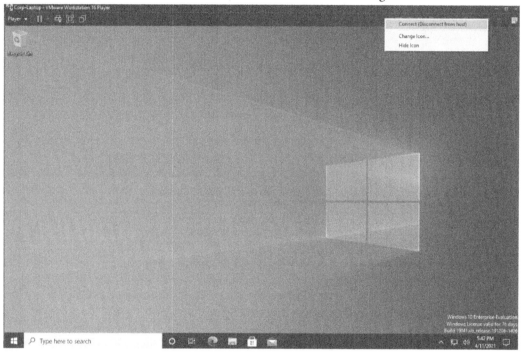

Figure 4.3 – Connecting an external pen drive to the VM

2. Once the pen drive is connected to the VM, just double-click on the MAGNET RAM Capture executable file, and the program will open a dialog box (this program does not need to be installed).

3. For the **Segment size:** option, open the list to select if you want to split the image into several files according to its size; otherwise, keep the default option **Don't split**.

4. For the **Save RAM capture to....** option, press the **Browse** button and navigate to the directory where you want to save the file (in this case, on Evidence\ MemDump) and write the name to identify the image file (in this case, Corp-LT-Mem-01).

5. Press the **Start** button to initialize the memory acquisition.

The process is illustrated in the following screenshot:

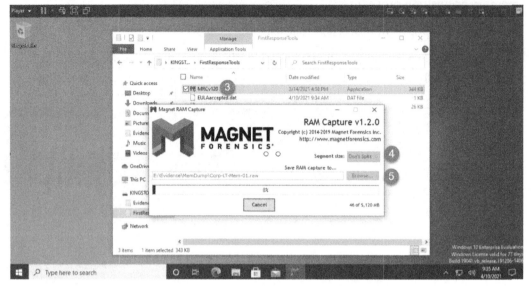

Figure 4.4 – Using MAGNET RAM Capture

> **Note**
>
> If you receive an error message that the filesystem is FAT, just ignore it. This is because you formatted your pen drive as exFAT and the memory size is 4 GB (unless you didn't format your pen drive beforehand and it's still FAT32). In this case, you need to format your pen drive beforehand. This message will not appear if you formatted your pen drive as NTFS.

Once the process is complete, a forensic image will be saved in the Evidence\ MemDump directory.

6. Disconnect the pen drive from the VM by right-clicking on the top right of the virtualization console, selecting the name of your pen drive, and then selecting **Disconnect** in the same way as you previously connected.

Remember—it is very important that you interact as little as possible with the suspicious computer because there is a risk of contaminating the evidence. Once the memory-capture process is complete, you must disconnect your device and analyze the information later in your own computer or laboratory. In this case, you can use the investigator VM to analyze the evidence.

Memory capture and artifacts acquisition using Velociraptor

When we have the opportunity to obtain forensic artifacts in addition to a memory image, we can speed up the process of analyzing the evidence, since we will have accurate and first-hand information that will help us to have a clearer idea of what to look for and where to look on the memory or hard drive.

Velociraptor gives us that possibility as it allows us to get a memory capture using the WinPmem tool, and we can also define the artifact collectors that we need in each case.

In the investigator VM, follow these next steps:

1. As in the previous exercise, we will follow the procedures to connect our pen drive to the VM.

2. Create a folder inside the `FirstResponseTools` directory called `velociraptor` to download the tool there.

3. Navigate to the Velociraptor website, `https://github.com/Velocidex/velociraptor/releases/`, and click on the **DOWNLOAD LATEST** button, as shown in the following screenshot:

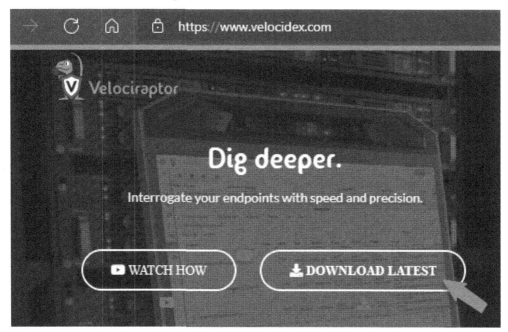

Figure 4.5 – Official website for downloading Velociraptor

Depending on the architecture of your operating system, you can download the 32-bit or 64-bit versions. In this case, we will download the 64-bit version for Windows.

4. Click on the most recent stable release to download the following executable files:

    - `velociraptor-vx.x.x-windows-amd64.exe` to use on interactive mode

    - `velociraptor-vx.x.x-windows-amd64.msi` in case you need to install the tool as an agent

    Save both files inside the `velociraptor` folder.

5. Change the name of the `velociraptor-vx.x.x-windows-amd64.exe` file to `velociraptor.exe`.

6. Press the *Shift key, right-click* on the Windows terminal icon on the taskbar, and select Run as administrator option to open a new Windows terminal with admin privileges..

7. Change to the USB drive unit using the corresponding letter and switch to the `FirstResponseTools | velociraptor` directory.

8. In the console, run the `velociraptor.exe artifacts list > artifacts.txt` command. This will send to a text file the different forensics artifacts supported by Velociraptor.

    Now, we are going to create a batch file where we'll define which artifacts we want to get from the computer to investigate.

9. Using Windows Explorer, double-click on the `artifacts.txt` file to open it on Notepad and review the list of artifacts.

10. Open a new instance of Notepad and create a new file with the name `triage.bat`, making sure you select from the **Save as Type:** list. Choose the `All Files` option and the file will be saved in the same directory as the `artifacts.txt` file.

11. From the `artifacts.txt` file, copy the following artifacts to the `triage.bat` file:

    - `Windows.Memory.Acquisition`

    - `Windows.Forensics.Timeline`

    - `Windows.Applications.Edge.History`

    The previous steps are shown in the following screenshot:

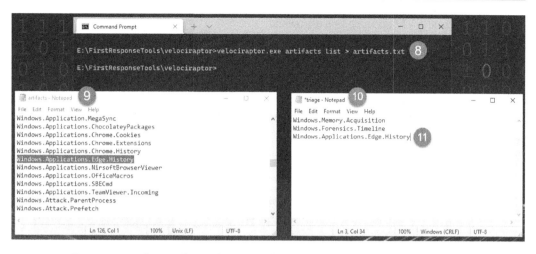

Figure 4.6 – Selecting the artifacts we will use and copying them to the batch file

For this lab, we want to collect a memory dump image, the forensics timeline activity on the suspicious computer, and the browsing history from Microsoft Edge.

To do this, we will write the following sentences in the `triage.bat` file:

- For the memory acquisition, we will write this:

```
velociraptor.exe artifacts collect -v <artifactname>
--output ..\..\Evidence\MemDump\<outputfilename.zip>
```

- For the forensic timeline and the browsing history from Microsoft Edge, we will write this:

```
velociraptor.exe artifacts collect -v <artifactname>
--output ..\..\Evidence\Artifacts\<outputfilename.zip>
```

Once finished, optionally add the following sentence at the top of the `@echo off` file to indicate the command lines will not be displayed when you run the batch file, as shown in the following screenshot:

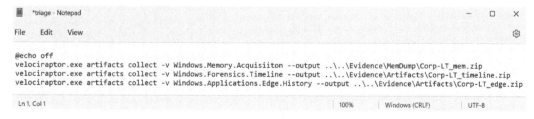

Figure 4.7 – Creating a triage.bat file

Save the file. Disconnect the pen drive from the VM.

In the Corp-Laptop VM, proceed as follows:

12. Connect your first-response toolkit pen drive to the VM.

13. Open a command-line console using admin privileges.

14. Run the `triage.bat` batch file from the `E:\FirstResponseTools\velociraptor\` directory, as shown in the following screenshot:

Figure 4.8 – Executing the triage.bat file

Once the process has finished, the files containing the forensic artifacts obtained from the compromised device will be created in their respective directories.

15. Disconnect the pen drive from the VM.

You can now analyze the content of the artifact files and memory in the investigator VM, as shown in the following screenshot:

Figure 4.9 – Content of a forensic timeline file

We already have valuable information to start the analysis, such as the timeline of executed applications, details about the user's navigation using Microsoft Edge, and the dump of the **random-access memory (RAM)** of the suspicious device. In this case, we assumed that we performed the process directly; let's see how we can create preconfigured files for someone else to run.

Creating artifact collectors

Sometimes, it will not be possible to perform these procedures in person, and the people we can rely on to perform them do not have the technical knowledge necessary to complete these tasks.

In such cases, Velociraptor is an ideal tool because it allows us to create an executable file that will perform all the procedures in an automated way just by running it.

In the IR-Workstation VM, proceed as follows:

1. Open a Linux Terminal.

2. In the home directory, create a new directory called DFIR_Tools, and under this directory, create a new one called velociraptor.

3. Navigate to the website `https://github.com/velocidex/velociraptor/releases`.

4. Click and download the newest stable Linux version, `velociraptor-vx.x.x-x-linux-amd64`, and save it inside the `velociraptor` directory.

5. Change the name of the file to `velociraptor`.

6. Change the permissions of the file to be executable by running the following code:

```
$ sudo chmod +x velociraptor
```

7. Generate the configuration server and client configuration files by running a `$ sudo ./velociraptor config generate -i` command, as shown in the following screenshot:

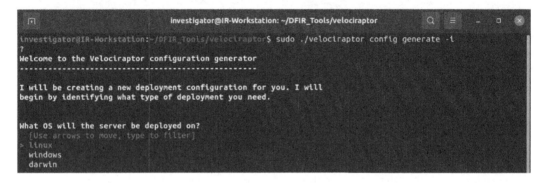

Figure 4.10 – Configuring the Velociraptor client and server files

If you select all the default options, the `server.config` and `client.config` files will be created in the same working directory and the server will be configured with the address `127.0.0.1`, using a self-signed certificate to allow connections using the **HyperText Transfer Secure (HTTPS)** protocol.

8. It's necessary to create a new user to operate the server. We can do that by running the following command:

```
$ sudo ./velociraptor --config server.config.yaml user
add investigator --role administrator
```

9. Assign the following password: `L34rn1ng!`

10. Now, we can start running the server just by executing a `$ sudo ./velociraptor --config server.config.yaml frontend -v` command, as shown in the following screenshot:

Figure 4.11 – Running the Velociraptor server

11. Open Firefox and navigate to `https://127.0.0.1:8889` to access the web interface of Velociraptor.

12. A warning message will appear because we are using an auto-signed certificate. Just press the **Advanced…** button, and a new message will appear at the bottom. Then, press the **Accept the Risk and Continue** button, as shown in the following screenshot:

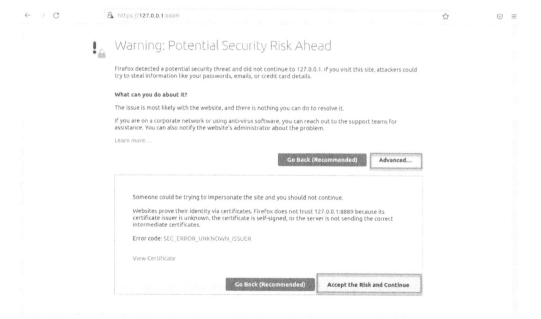

Figure 4.12 – Warning message when you access the Velociraptor user interface (UI)

13. To log in to the server, use the credentials created in *steps 8* and *9*.

14. In the left sidebar, expand the sidebar by clicking on the upper button, before clicking on the Velociraptor logo.

15. Select the **Server Artifacts** option.

16. Press the **Build offline collector** button, as shown in the following screenshot:

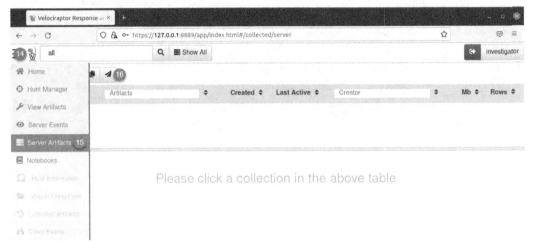

Figure 4.13 – Interface to generate the collector file

A new window will be opened. You can select the artifacts and configurations that you want to include for the generation of the executable file; to do so, you must follow the next steps.

17. Select the following forensic artifacts:

- `Triage.collection.upload`

- `Windows.Applications.Edge.History`

- `Windows.Attack.Prefetch`

18. Next, press the **Configure Parameters** button to define parameters for every artifact; each artifact may require different configuration parameters. In this case, just press on the artifact to review the parameters, but we will not change any of these.

19. Press the **Configure Collection** button to define additional configuration parameters such as the password, the collection type, the `temp` directory, the level of compression, and any others. In this case, we will use the default options without changes.

20. Press the **Review** button to view a summary of the selected options and configurations.

21. Finally, press the **Launch** button to create an executable file.

The preceding steps are illustrated in the following screenshot:

Figure 4.14 – Configuration options to create a collector file

22. Once the process has finished, the window will be closed, and you just need to click the name of the FlowId collector created. Details of this will appear at the bottom of the screen.

23. Select the **Uploaded Files** tab.

24. Finally, click on the link of the generated executable file, as shown in the following screenshot:

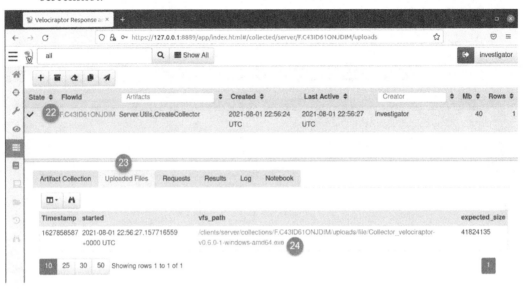

Figure 4.15 – Download of the collector file

25. Copy the downloaded file to your first-response toolkit pen drive in the velociraptor directory.

26. Connect your pen drive to the Corp-Laptop VM and open the velociraptor directory.

27. Right-click on the Collector_velociraptor-vx.x.x-x-windows-amd64 file and then select **Run as administrator** because you need to execute this file with Administrator privileges.

28. The collector will now retrieve the previously configured artifacts, as we did earlier with the triage.bat file, as shown in the following screenshot:

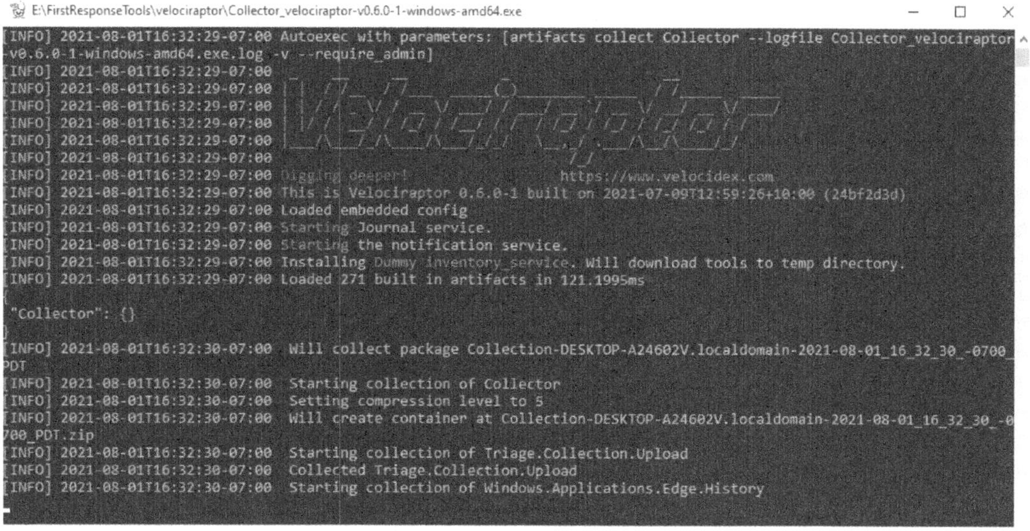

Figure 4.16 – Executing the collector file

At this point, we have learned how to generate forensic artifact collectors using Velociraptor. Now, let's see how we can do it using another amazing tool.

Memory capture and artifacts acquisition using KAPE

Another very powerful tool is **Kroll Artifact Parser and Extractor** (**KAPE**). With this tool, we can obtain a lot of forensic artifacts and preprocessed information that can significantly reduce the collection and analysis time.

Additionally, KAPE not only integrates the possibility to capture memory but also includes preprocessing modules and memory analysis that will allow us to find valuable information at the early stage of an investigation.

In the investigator VM, proceed as follows:

1. Connect your first-response toolkit pen drive.

2. Under the `FirstResponseTools` directory, create a folder named `KAPE`.

3. Under the `Evidence` directory, create a folder called `KAPE` as well.

4. Under the `Evidence\KAPE` directory, create two folders: `Target` and `Module`.

5. Navigate to the website `https://www.kroll.com/en/services/cyber-risk/incident-response-litigation-support/kroll-artifact-parser-extractor-kape`.

6. Fill in the web form with your information and then press the **Download Now** button.

7. Save the `.zip` file in the KAPE folder and unzip it.

8. Disconnect your pen drive from the VM.

In the Corp-Laptop VM, proceed as follows:

1. Connect your pen drive to the VM.

2. Navigate to the `FirstResponseTools\KAPE` folder and execute the `gkape.exe` file (this will start the **graphical user interface (GUI)** version of KAPE).

   Once opened, you can configure the information you want to collect from the compromised computer.

   In this process, we must select from the left-side column the disk drive from where we want to obtain the information and the place where we want to store the obtained forensic artifacts. We will also select from the list the artifacts we are interested in and choose how we want to save them locally or remotely, following the steps shown in the following screenshot and described next:

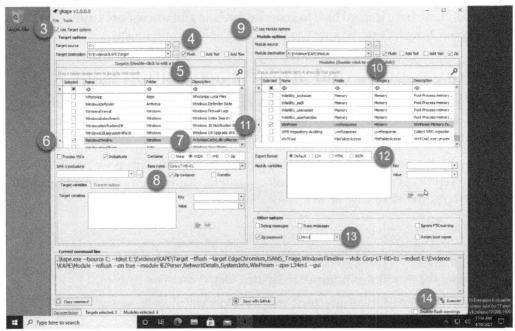

Figure 4.17 – Configuring artifact acquisition options in KAPE

3. Select the **Use Target options** checkbox.

4. For the **Target source** option, select `C:\`.

5. For the **Target destination** option, select the E:\Evidence\KAPE\Target directory.

6. For the **Targets** option, select the following artifact collectors:

   - !SANSTriage

   - EdgeChromium

   - WindowsTimeline

7. For the **Container** option, select **VHDX** (this will create a virtual disk in this format).

8. For the **Base name** option, enter the name of the **virtual hard disk (VHD)** to create.

   From the right-side column, we are going to select modules to preprocess the information we will need—for instance, the network connections, the system information, and memory acquisition.

9. Select the **Use Module options** checkbox.

10. For the **Module destination** option, select the E:\Evidence\Kape\Module directory.

11. in the **Modules** list, select the following checkboxes:

    - !EZParser

    - NetworkDetails

    - Systeminfo

    - WinPmem

    As in the previous exercise with Velociraptor, we will be able to get an image of the memory, and additionally, we will obtain important forensic artifacts.

12. For the **Export format** option, keep the **Default** option.

13. Under **Other options**, select the **Zip password** checkbox and write the following password: L34rn1.

14. Press the **Execute** button.

15. A warning message will appear telling you that all the `Target` and `Module` folders' content will be deleted, as shown in the following screenshot. Just press the **OK** button:

Figure 4.18 – Data destruction warning message

Now, KAPE will start processing the information and create files with the artifacts obtained from the compromised device, as shown in the following screenshot:

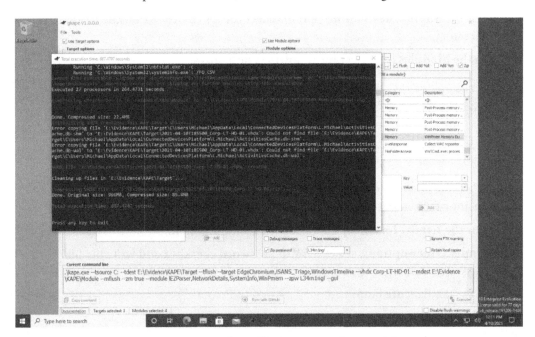

Figure 4.19 – Artifact collection process from KAPE

Once the procedure is complete, you will be able to disconnect your pen drive from the Corp-Laptop VM and connect it to your investigator VM to analyze the information obtained.

Disk drive acquisition procedures

Sometimes, the acquisition of memory or forensic artifacts will not be enough in an investigation, especially if the scenario is complex or limited information is available.

Also, in situations where legal procedures are followed, it may be required that in addition to the procedures described earlier, a forensic acquisition of storage units or disks should also be made.

This procedure can be performed in two ways, as outlined here:

- Using specialized software along with disk connectors such as the Tableau Forensic USB 3.0 Bridge (`https://www.forensiccomputers.com/tableau-t8u.html`), which provides write protection when you connect the disks directly to your computer

- Using a hardware device that allows you to create forensic images directly and without the need for a computer

In both cases, the computer is required to be powered off and the disk from the compromised device needs to be extracted. Now, let's see how we can get a forensic image copy from a hard disk.

Hard drive acquisition using AccessData FTK Imager

In this case, to simplify our hands-on labs, we are going to use a VMware virtual disk to simulate the process of connecting the hard drive to our investigator VM, following these steps.

In the investigator VM, proceed as follows:

1. Connect your pen drive to your VM.
2. Navigate to `https://www.exterro.com/ftk-imager` to download FTK Imager.
3. Fill in the web form with your information and press the **Download** button.
4. Save the installer file in the `FirstResponseTools\Installers` directory.
5. Double-click the file to begin the installation of the program and keep the default options.

6. Once the program is installed, an icon will appear on the desktop. Double-click it to open the program, as shown in the following screenshot:

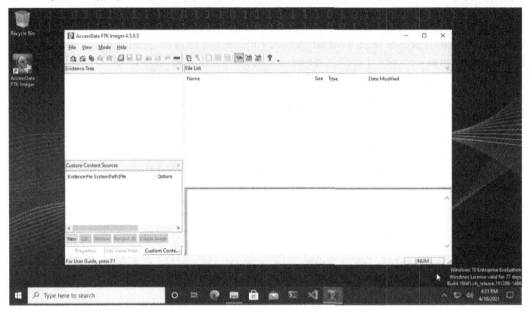

Figure 4.20 – Access Data FTK Imager GUI

Let's now simulate the connection of the suspicious computer hard drive to our IR laptop.

To do this, follow these steps:

1. In the computer where you have your VMs, create a new directory called HD_Acquisition_simulation.

2. Go to the Corp-Laptop VM directory and copy the Corp-Laptop-cl1.vmdk file to the HD_Acquisition_simulation directory.

3. Open the IR-Laptop VM and open the **Player** menu, select **Manage**, and then **Virtual Machine Settings**.

4. In the **Virtual Machine Settings** dialog box, press the **Add** button.

5. In the **Add Hardware Wizard** functionality, select **Hard Disk**, and then press the **Next** button.

6. In the **Select a Disk** dialog box, select **Use an existing virtual disk** and then press the **Next** button, as shown in the following screenshot:

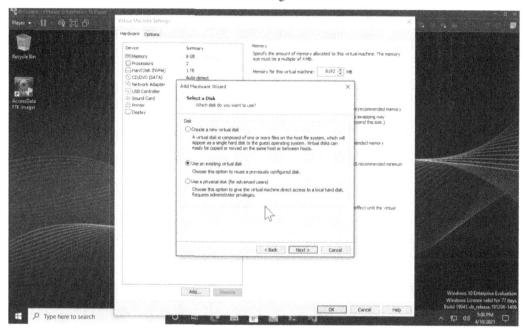

Figure 4.21 – Adding an existing virtual disk

7. Select the `Corp-Laptop.vmdk` file from the `HD_Acquisition_simulation` directory and then press the **Open** button.

At that point, the hard drive would appear as a new drive, just as if we had externally connected it to our computer. In real life, it is very important to use cables that integrate write protection, as mentioned earlier, and preferably, we should not interact with the disk to avoid contaminating the evidence.

Now, we will be able to carry out the forensic acquisition on the hard drive and the compromised computer, as follows:

1. From the Access Data FTK Imager program, select the **File** menu and then the **Create Disk Image...** option, as shown in the following screenshot:

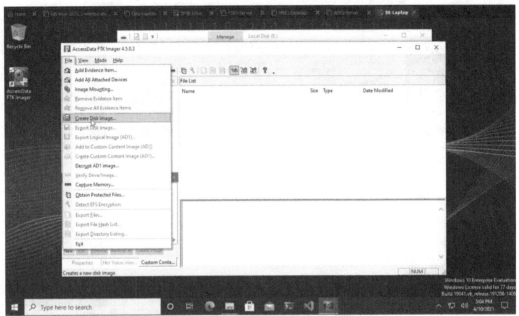

Figure 4.22 – Creation of a disk image

2. In the **Select Source** dialog box, select **Physical Drive** and press the **Next** button, as shown in the following screenshot:

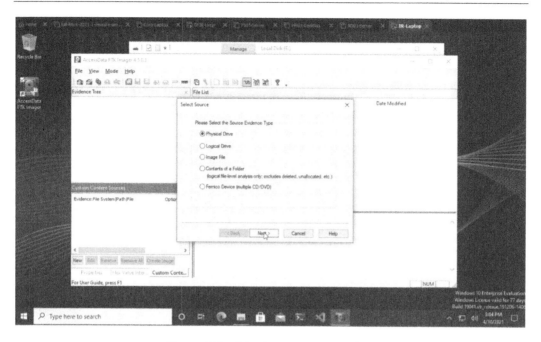

Figure 4.23 – Selecting a source to analyze

3. In the **Select Drive** dialog box, select the second disk that appears in the list that corresponds to the hard drive we added earlier, and press the **Finish** button, as shown in the following screenshot:

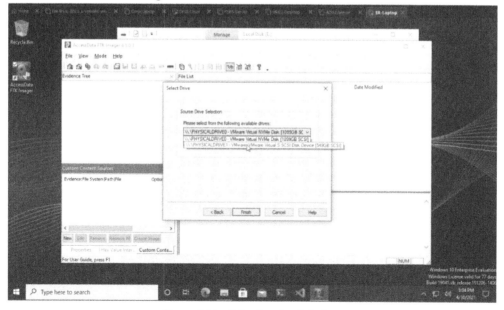

Figure 4.24 – Selecting the disk drive

4. In the **Create Image** dialog box, press the **Add** button and select the **Destination Image Type** format as **E01 (Expert Witness Format (EWF)** or Encase Image Format) and press the **Next** button, as shown in the following screenshot:

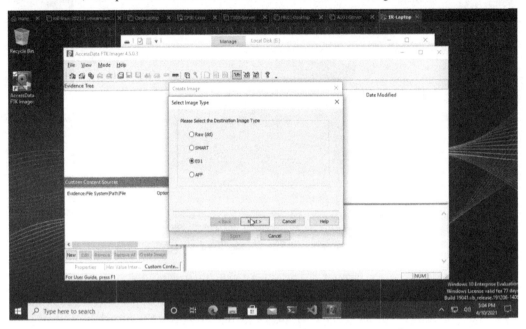

Figure 4.25 – Selecting the image type

5. In the **Evidence Item Information** dialog box, fill in the appropriate information and press the **Next** button.

Follow the next steps to configure the rest of the image parameters, as shown in the following screenshot:

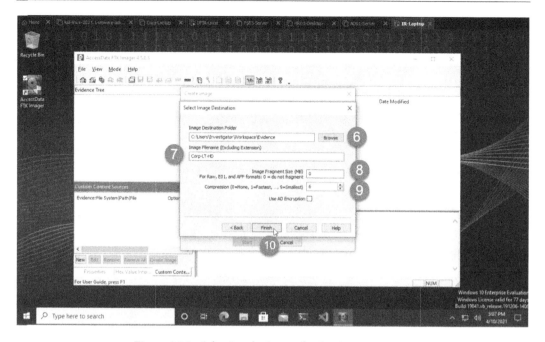

Figure 4.26 – Selecting the image destination parameters

6. Select the directory where you will save the disk image.

7. Enter the name of the image file—in this case, `Corp-LT-HD`.

8. Write the value of 0 so as not to fragment the file into multiple files.

9. Leave the value of 6 for the compression level so that the disk image size is smaller than the original size.

10. Press the **Finish** button.

Now, the disk image creation process starts. This can take quite a while, depending on the size of the disk.

Hard drive acquisition using a hardware duplicator

The process of disk images using hardware devices that do not require a computer is faster and more efficient.

This is because they have complete autonomy and are specifically designed for this purpose, in addition to the great processing capacity. These devices have a touchscreen and several ports to connect different types of storage units.

While copy processing an image can take several hours using software and a computer, these devices can process copies in less than 1 hour, depending on the disk capacity.

To create a forensic copy of a disk using a hardware device, simply connect the hard drive to this device using the appropriate connection cable and start the forensic imaging process using the front panel. The following figure shows a photo of Logicube's Forensic Falcon device that is used for the acquisition of forensic images from hard drives:

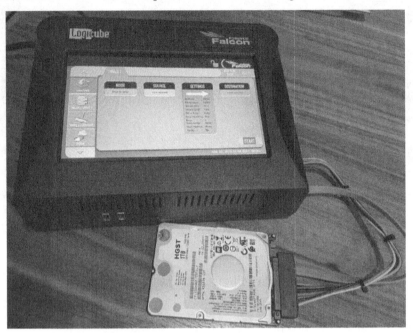

Figure 4.27 – Logicube's Forensic Falcon device

Once the forensic copy of the disc is complete, you can fill in the chain of custody form with the procedure's details and then perform an analysis on the created image. Again, remember that you should never work on the original disc because you can compromise or contaminate the evidence.

Summary

In this chapter, we learned how to identify from a practical case the best strategy for performing first-response procedures.

We also learned in a very practical way how to perform first-response procedures using different tools to obtain images of memory, disk, and forensic artifacts.

In this first part of the book, we learned the fundamentals of the threat landscape and IR procedures. In the next part, we will learn about the different types of adversaries, their **modus operandi** (**MO**), and some frameworks that will help us identify their **tactics, techniques, and procedures** (**TTPs**) to look for specific artifacts or evidence.

Further reading

You can find out more about DFIR distributions with preinstalled tools for IR and forensics at the following links:

- Tsurugi Linux DFIR open source project: `https://tsurugi-linux.org/`

- **Sans Investigative Forensics Toolkit (SIFT)** workstation: `https://digital-forensics.sans.org/community/downloads`

- CSI Linux: `https://csilinux.com/`

Section 2: Getting to Know the Adversaries

In this section, you will learn to understand different threat actors, their motivations, capabilities, and attack vectors. You will also learn to use and apply frameworks such as MITRE ATT&CK and models such as the Cyber Kill Chain framework to map malicious behaviors in incident response. Afterward, you will know the importance of using threat intelligence to identify threats during the initial stages of an investigation.

This section comprises the following chapters:

- *Chapter 5, Identifying and Profiling Threat Actors*
- *Chapter 6, Understanding the Cyber Kill Chain and the MITRE ATT&CK Framework*
- *Chapter 7, Using Cyber Threat Intelligence in Incident Response*

5
Identifying and Profiling Threat Actors

Identifying the potential kind of threat actor behind a cyberattack is one of the most important things you need to pay attention to when responding to a cybersecurity incident, and you can achieve this by analyzing in detail the characteristics and context of the attack.

Knowing in advance the different attackers' profiles and their intentions behind an attack is a big help because you can anticipate their moves, and it is also helpful in developing strategies to respond to and contain these attacks efficiently.

Knowledge of adversaries is very important in incident response; when you have information about them, including their profile, capabilities, techniques, and tools, you can use it as intelligence that can be actionable in multiple ways.

In this chapter, we will study the different types of threat actors, and we will learn how to profile them based on their behavior, motivations, and mode of operation. This information will be useful when we get evidence and want to consult our intelligence base to identify potential adversaries behind an attack.

In this chapter, you will cover the following topics:

- Exploring the different types of threat actors
- Researching adversaries and threat actors
- Creating threat actor and campaign profiles

Technical requirements

In case you haven't already done, you need to download and install VMware Workstation Player from this link `https://www.vmware.com/products/workstation-player/workstation-player-evaluation.html`.

You'll also need to download from the book's official GitHub repository `https://github.com/PacktPublishing/Incident-Response-with-Threat-Intelligence` the following:

- Virtual machine:

  - IR-Laptop

Exploring the different types of threat actors

There are specific categories of threat actors, and their characteristics and motivations mainly define these categories. Different attackers can pose a risk to the organization at particular times. Therefore, according to the circumstances, it is imperative to know their categories and interests. Let's look at the main types of threat actors.

Hacktivists

The term *hacktivism* is a portmanteau of the words *hacker* and *activism*. These actors are related to movements that look to get attention using digital tools in a non-violent way for their ideological interests.

The motivations behind hacktivism are more related to social struggles, the search for justice, defiance of political and economic powers, and even in some cases with a certain sense of the search for anarchy, but rarely with malicious intentions.

What makes these groups dangerous is that they can sometimes be infiltrated or manipulated by people or groups outside the causes that undermine the movement's actual goals.

There is also the possibility that these groups are too heterogeneous with different views and objectives, causing some participants to act independently by applying their own agendas.

The roots of hacktivism date back to the 1980s–1990s when the internet emerged, with devices interconnected through a global network.

The potential risk of this type of threat is that it can occur at any time, due to a geopolitical or socio-economic event, or even simply by having a relationship or link with a targeted third party. Another important aspect is that it is difficult to associate the specific capabilities of these groups beyond their characteristics; they can only be people or groups that want to send a message or state actors with high skills and sufficient economic and technological resources.

Script kiddies

Script kiddies are a particular category within groups that can pose a threat to organizations. Unlike hacktivists, they do not have a clear motivation; sometimes, they will do it for money, for fun, to compete with their peers, or to gain recognition and notoriety within their circles.

They have basic technical skills and often learn how to use tools without fully knowing how they work; this would be the equivalent of having a weapon and not knowing how to use it, with the risks that this poses.

Usually, they prefer to work individually rather than collectively and pose a risk to organizations precisely because they can turn an organization into a target incidentally and provoke a more significant impact unexpectedly, making them a potentially dangerous threat.

In 2015, a 15-year-old script kiddie was arrested in the UK for unauthorized access to systems and theft of information from a telecommunications company called TalkTalk Telecom Group Limited. The teenager managed to access the systems through a **SQL Injection** (**SQLI**) attack. It is no secret that many websites share cheat sheets, instructions, or even tools that automate SQL injection, and some people abuse these tools for unethical or non-professional purposes.

Script kiddies are dangerous because, most of the time, they do not have a specific, defined goal and lack the technical knowledge or skills with the tools they use, so they can turn any organization into an involuntary target.

Insiders

This group of adversaries represents one of the greatest threats to organizations because it involves employees, collaborators, or business partners who regularly have access to the physical facilities of corporate systems.

The problem is that they have the privileges and permissions necessary to carry out different activities. Therefore, they often go unnoticed, so their malicious actions are not detected in time, as it is all based on trust.

Sometimes, these threat actors act on their own, and their motivations may be the theft of confidential information for their benefit to use or sell, or sabotage for a personal vendetta.

Another significant risk may occur when the company's internal staff is threatened or extorted by third parties who force them to perform malicious activities, which may include the actions described previously or the installation of malicious code that implants a backdoor or rootkit.

Insiders can be divided into three categories – malicious, accidental, or negligent – and are classified according to their motivations and behaviors, as described in the following diagram:

Figure 5.1 – The categories of insiders

In August 2020, Egor Igorevich Kriuchkov, a 27-year-old Russian citizen and a member of a criminal group, contacted an employee of Tesla, the car manufacturer, asking them to install a ransomware program on the company's devices in exchange for a significant sum of money.

Fortunately for the company, the employee decided to report the incident, and they, in turn, reported it to the authorities. After agreeing to cooperate with the **Federal Bureau of Investigation (FBI)**, they managed to arrest Kriuchkov.

If this attempt had succeeded and information had leaked, the disruption of Tesla's operations would have resulted in the company losing millions, affecting its reputation; this demonstrates the potential risk and threat of insiders.

Cybercriminals

Cybercrime could not survive without the ecosystem that supports it. This ecosystem has allowed the interconnection of various actors and components that depend on and correlate with each other, with related interests, which guarantees their survival.

Cybercriminals use technology and financial resources to break into organizations' information systems or against ordinary users illegally to get profits. They organize into groups that sometimes focus only on technology-related activities and are sometimes part of organized crime groups that decide to expand their *cyber*-field of action to increase their profits.

A characteristic of these groups is that they often recruit members with high technical skills and pay them considerable amounts of money to keep them motivated. The money they get from their illegal activities is what also allows them to maintain technological infrastructures.

The types of cybercrime activities relate to, among other things, identity theft, email and internet fraud, cyber extortion, banking fraud, theft of financial data, and the robbery and sale of corporate information and industrial secrets. Cybercrime threat actors use different techniques and tools where the main element is social engineering, such as phishing and malware.

They even extend their cheating techniques to a third party – for example, there is an attack called SIM swapping. This consists of tricking the operators of a mobile company into reactivating a cell line on attacker's own devices, thus having access to the information of their victims and their **Two-Factor Authentication** (**2FA**) mechanisms that use SMS messages.

The main motivation of cybercriminals is obviously financial, and their main targets are users with little knowledge of the risks to which they are exposed when using technology, as well as any company or organization that they can take money from. With a very robust and mature ecosystem, it is a growing threat.

Ransomware gangs

Without a doubt, ransomware has become one of the biggest threats today to individuals and businesses worldwide. Moreover, this extortion-based activity is one of the most lucrative for cybercriminal groups, which make millions of dollars with every successful operation.

Behind these groups, there are people with skills and knowledge in different areas who plan their campaigns in detail and carefully choose their potential targets, as described in the findings of the security company Kaspersky, shown in the following diagram:

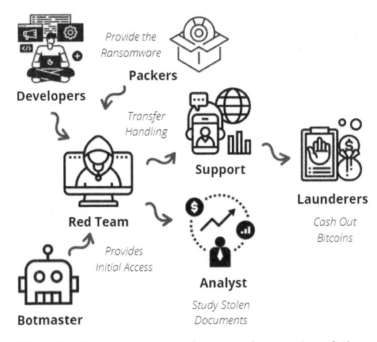

Figure 5.2 – The ransomware group's structure (source – Securelist)

Their victims are companies, such as hospitals, schools, governments, financial institutions, and energy companies. In addition, they now must deal with the theft of information, which cybercriminals use as an additional form of extortion or to make greater profits by selling it to the highest bidder.

Return on investment and million-dollar profits have caused these groups to consolidate and new groups to appear. The business is extensive and works through different operational models, such as ransomware as a service or affiliate programs, where ecosystems facilitate the distribution of profits among groups that play different roles.

According to estimates from different studies, more than half of companies pay the requested ransom to retrieve their information or resume their business operations.

In December 2020, at the **Remote Chaos Communication Congress (RC3)**, a research team presented an exciting study. In their investigation, they analyzed cybercriminal campaigns, following the footprints they left in cryptocurrency transactions.

One of the most important findings was that, over 2 years, 19,750 victims transferred about $16 million to a small number of traders, concentrating almost 90% on only two of the most active ransomware families at the time, Locky and Cerber.

According to DarkTracer, there was leaked information from more than 2,000 companies on the dark web in April 2021. However, just 30 ransomware cybercriminal groups controlled those operations, as shown in the following screenshot:

Figure 5.3 – The affected organizations and ransomware gangs

This growth in ransomware-related threats and the evolution in attackers' techniques and procedures make responding to these incidents successfully a challenge. The early identification of attacks and the ability to contain a threat are essential to reduce the impact on an organization.

Threat actors behind ransomware attacks must be considered high-risk for any organization, and it is essential to know their capabilities, modes of operation, and the tactics and techniques they use before the ransomware is deployed.

Advanced Persistent Threats (APT) groups

It is more common within targeted attack groups to find threat actors who have enough resources and skills to direct those attacks toward very high-profile targets, such as diplomats, politicians, governments, financial institutions, and security and energy companies.

Regularly, their attacks are more elaborate and tend to be harder to detect, usually being successful. Thus, the challenge in addressing such threats is to develop the capacity for early identification and detection capabilities to improve the effectiveness of an incident response of this type.

One feature that defines an attack as *advanced* is that it has components that require careful planning and execution. To achieve this, threat actors go through a phase of gathering detailed information about their targets to identify potential attack surfaces and weaknesses; otherwise, these attacks might not be as successful.

Sometimes, these groups develop sophisticated malicious code that exploits zero-day vulnerabilities, which is challenging to detect. Furthermore, these groups also use open source programs created by third parties, which reduces the time and the cost of an operation.

Persistence is undoubtedly an essential component in this category of attacks. A cyberattack can hardly succeed in the short term because each company's environment and infrastructure are complex and different, so attackers must know and adapt their attack strategy.

Even if they have managed to gather sufficient information from their targets' infrastructure, they may encounter elements that require adapting their strategies and selecting which tools to use.

No company should be considered exempt from becoming a target of these threat actors, as we have seen APT attacks on organizations of any size, from family businesses to large corporate companies, including governments.

Cyber-mercenaries

Cyber-mercenaries are individuals or groups of malicious actors who offer their services to perform specific actions. These threat actors act under contract from a third party that pays them to achieve a goal, and they rarely have any direct motivation related to their victim.

Some of these threat actors offer their services openly in darknet markets, while others handle lower profiles, and their customers must contact them through very closed channels.

The way these groups operate is known as *hit and run* – that is, persistence is less important because instead of maintaining the compromise of their victims for a long time, once they achieve what they are looking for, they end the operation.

In 2011, my colleagues on Kaspersky's **Global Research and Analysis Team (GreAT)** opened an investigation into a malicious actor called **Icefog**, also known as **Dagger Panda** according to CrowdStrike.

Icefog/Dagger Panda is a small group of attackers whose objective was to compromise supply chains related to government institutions, the defense sector, telecommunications, and high technologies in South Korea and Japan.

As in any other field, a mercenary is a high potential risk mainly because they have different capacities, a clear monetary interest, and no direct link to their targets, so they have little to lose.

As you can see, threat actors have different interests and can pose different levels of risk to an organization. This is why it is essential to know them with a mindset of developing better defense capabilities and responding to an incident; the more you know the adversaries, the greater the chance you have of understanding how to follow the investigation of a case.

Researching adversaries and threat actors

It would be challenging to know who the actor is behind an attack in the first security incident. However, the more you know about different adversaries, the more information you will have to assess the incident and decide how best to act when considering the characteristics of a security breach.

Fortunately, there is a lot of threat intelligence information about different malicious campaigns and the threat actors behind them. Some security companies have documented details behind high-profile cyberattacks and the groups related to these attacks. You can consult this information on sites such as MITRE ATT&CK (`https://attack.mitre.org/groups/`), Kaspersky (`https://apt.securelist.com/`), and Mandiant (`https://www.mandiant.com/resources/apt-groups`), among others.

However, sometimes, it is handy to create your own intelligence documentation with specific threat actors' profiles. The key elements to consider when profiling threat actors and their capabilities are as follows:

- The name of the threat actor

- A suspicious origin

- The category or type

- Victimology and target countries

- Campaigns related to this actor

- Associated **Tactics, Techniques, and Procedures (TTPs)**

- The malware used

Integrating this information will help us to create intelligence, correlate actors with campaigns and malware or the tools used by them, join the dots, and have access to a fuller context when responding to an incident.

STIX and TAXII standards

STIX and TAXII are two open source standards developed to create and share cyberthreat intelligence information. In this chapter, we will focus specifically on **Structured Threat Information eXpression (STIX)**. Alternatively, **Trusted Automated eXchange of Intelligence Information (TAXII)** defines the standard and protocols needed to carry out the transport and exchange of intelligence information. According to its official website, STIX is a standardized language created by MITRE and the OASIS committee for cyberthreat intelligence to describe threat information.

STIX version 2.1 defines 18 objects known as **STIX Domain Objects (SDOs)** and 2 **STIX Relationship Objects (SROs)**, described here: `https://oasis-open.github.io/cti-documentation/stix/intro`. An example of how they integrate is shown in the following diagram:

Figure 5.4 – A STIX threat description example

The basic structure of an object represented in JSON is shown in the following screenshot:

```
{
    "type": "indicator",
    "spec_version": "2.1",
    "id": "indicator--71312c48-925d-44b7-b10e-c11086995358",
    "created": "2017-02-06T09:13:07.243000Z",
    "modified": "2017-02-06T09:13:07.243000Z",
    "name": "CryptoLocker Hash",
    "description": "This file is a part of CryptoLocker",
    "pattern": "[file:hashes.'SHA-256' = '46afeb295883a5efd6639d4197eb18bcba3bff49125b810ca4b9509b9ce4dfbf']",
    "pattern_type": "stix",
    "indicator_types": ["malicious-activity"],
    "valid_from": "2017-01-01T09:00:00.000000Z"
}
```

Figure 5.5 – An example of the JSON representation of a STIX object

You can interconnect different objects through "relationships" to establish a context that describes threats, considering their abilities, motivations, and capacities.

Working with STIX objects

You can work with STIX JSON files using several tools, including Microsoft Visual Studio Code, Sublime, and Atom, in a very simple way. In the following screenshot, you can see the structure of a STIX bundle object:

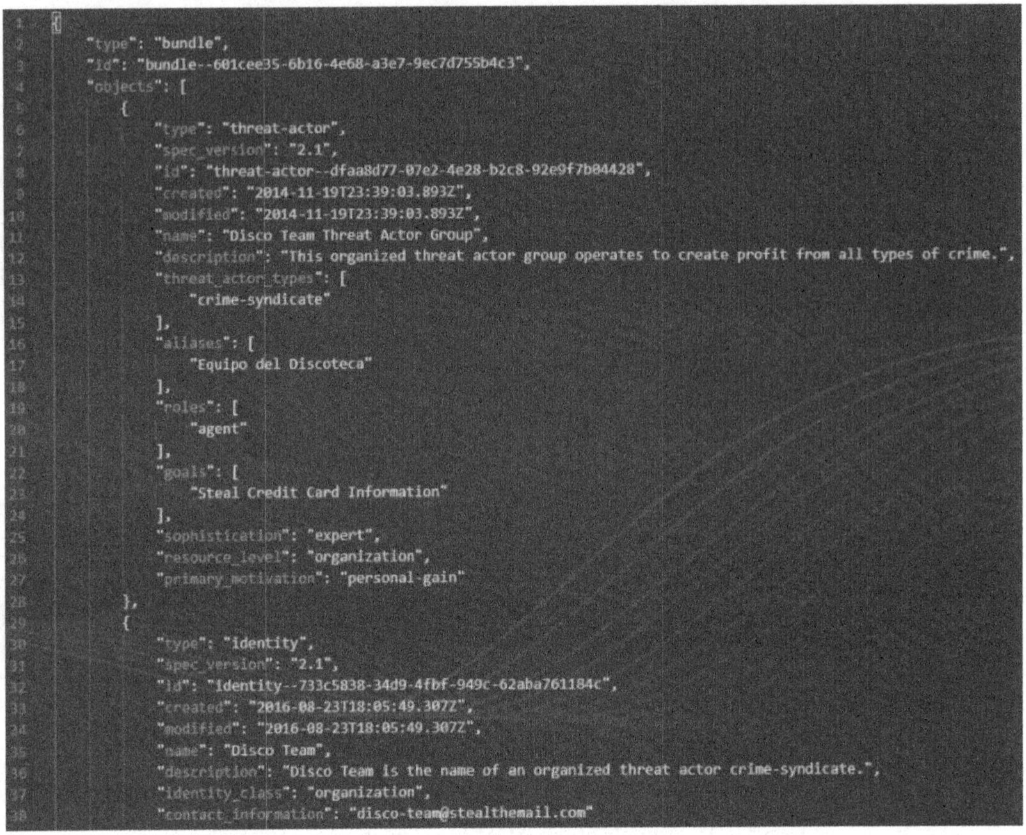

```json
{
  "type": "bundle",
  "id": "bundle--601cee35-6b16-4e68-a3e7-9ec7d755b4c3",
  "objects": [
    {
      "type": "threat-actor",
      "spec_version": "2.1",
      "id": "threat-actor--dfaa8d77-07e2-4e28-b2c8-92e9f7b04428",
      "created": "2014-11-19T23:39:03.893Z",
      "modified": "2014-11-19T23:39:03.893Z",
      "name": "Disco Team Threat Actor Group",
      "description": "This organized threat actor group operates to create profit from all types of crime.",
      "threat_actor_types": [
        "crime-syndicate"
      ],
      "aliases": [
        "Equipo del Discoteca"
      ],
      "roles": [
        "agent"
      ],
      "goals": [
        "Steal Credit Card Information"
      ],
      "sophistication": "expert",
      "resource_level": "organization",
      "primary_motivation": "personal-gain"
    },
    {
      "type": "identity",
      "spec_version": "2.1",
      "id": "identity--733c5838-34d9-4fbf-949c-62aba761184c",
      "created": "2016-08-23T18:05:49.307Z",
      "modified": "2016-08-23T18:05:49.307Z",
      "name": "Disco Team",
      "description": "Disco Team is the name of an organized threat actor crime-syndicate.",
      "identity_class": "organization",
      "contact_information": "disco-team@stealthemail.com"
```

Figure 5.6 – The structure of a STIX object in JSON format

For the visualization of STIX JSON files, you can use the STIX Visualizer tool, https://oasis-open.github.io/cti-stix-visualization/; you just need to upload a file or copy and paste the code directly, and you will see the graphic representation of this code, as shown in the following screenshot:

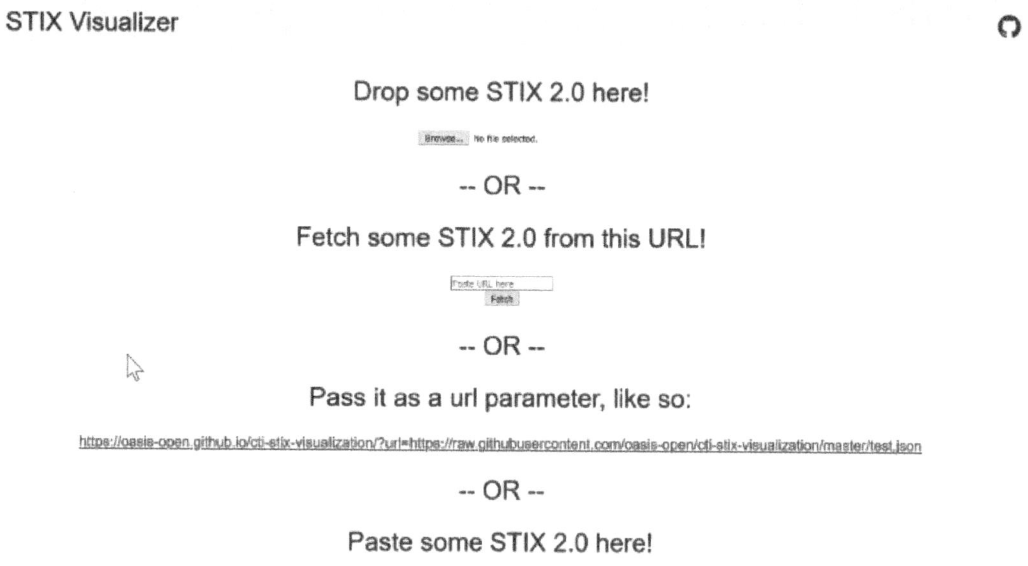

STIX Visualizer

Drop some STIX 2.0 here!

Browse... No file selected.

-- OR --

Fetch some STIX 2.0 from this URL!

Paste URL here
Fetch

-- OR --

Pass it as a url parameter, like so:

https://oasis-open.github.io/cti-stix-visualization/?url=https://raw.githubusercontent.com/oasis-open/cti-stix-visualization/master/test.json

-- OR --

Paste some STIX 2.0 here!

Figure 5.7 – The STIX Visualizer tool

Once you provide the information, a graph will show the relationship between the different objects; thus, you will get a clearer idea about the threat, as shown in the following diagram:

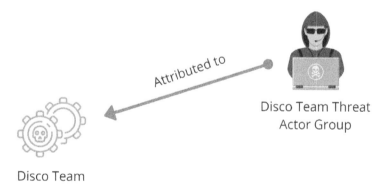

Figure 5.8 – The visualization of STIX objects and relations

In the next section, you will learn how to create profiles of threat actors and malicious campaigns.

Creating threat actor and campaign profiles

Usually, **Threat Intelligence Platforms (TIPs)** have a section with the profiles of different threat actors, their characteristics, the campaigns attributed to them, and their main TTPs.

If you do not have access to a TIP, you can still consult the information about threat actor profiles and their malicious campaigns from public sources such as **MITRE ATT&CK** (`https://attack.mitre.org/groups/`), **AT&T OTX** (`https://otx.alienvault.com/browse/global/adversaries`), or this compilation created by industry colleagues: `https://apt.threattracking.com`.

However, these information sources cover only threat actors with a specific visibility level due to the nature of their attacks or the relevance of their targets. So, there will be many others that do not appear there, but they threaten organizations nonetheless.

Sometimes, organizations should create their own internal threat actor profiles and campaigns from their incident response teams or other organizations. In practice, this is within the remit of the threat intelligence area, but it is beneficial to familiarize yourself with this process.

In the following section, you will learn how to create threat actors' profiles from intelligence collected from a fictitious company's incident response team.

Creating threat actors' profiles using Visual Studio Code

If you have used **Microsoft Visual Studio Code (VS Code)** (`https://code.visualstudio.com/`) previously for software development, you might not have imagined that it can be a practical tool to create threat actor profiles.

The security company *Red Canary* did an extraordinary job developing an open source extension for VSCode called **VSCode ATT&CK**. This extension allows you to research and directly add MITRE ATT&CK TTPs from VSCode.

Let's learn how to create threat actor profiles using this extension:

1. On the IR-Laptop virtual machine, open VS Code, clicking on the control panel icon, as shown in the following screenshot:

Figure 5.9 – Opening VS Code

2. Once VS Code is open, click on the extensions icon.

3. In the **Search Extensions in Marketplace** text box, type ATT&CK.

4. On the **VSCode ATT&CK** extension, press the **Install** button, as shown in the following screenshot:

Figure 5.10 – Installing the VSCode ATT&CK extension

Now, we need to add another extension to export our reports in different formats.

5. As we did in the previous step, in the search textbox, type `Yzane Markdown PDF`, and then click on the **Install** button, as shown in the following screenshot:

Figure 5.11 – Installing the Yzane Markdown PDF extension

You are ready to start creating threat profile reports using VS Code. We will use the **Markdown** format (`.md`) as the default format, since the VSCode ATT&ACK extension recognizes this format, to map the MITRE ATT&CK TTPs (we will learn more about MITRE ATT&CK in the following chapters).

To create the threat actor's profile, we are going to use a fictitious security incident:

1. In VS Code, open the **File** menu and select **New File**.

2. Save the new file in the `C:\Users\Investigator\Workspace\Labs\Chapter-5` directory as `TA-INT0012_OctopusBlack.md`, as shown in the following screenshot:

Figure 5.12 – Creating the threat actor's profile file

At the bottom of VS Code, you will see how the VSCode ATT&ACK extension recognizes the Markdown format, and the first time the **Yzane Markdown PDF** extension is used, it will create a Chromium plugin, as shown in the following screenshot:

Figure 5.13 – The Markdown PDF Chromium plugin installation and loading VSCode ATT&CK

> **Important Note**
> In case you are not familiar with the Markdown language format, you can learn more here: https://www.markdowntutorial.com/.

3. To enable and test dynamic previews, do the following:

    • Write the following text in the VS Code editor: # This is a title

    • Press *Ctrl* + *K*, release the keys, and then press *V*.

    You will see the **Editor** and the **Preview** panels alongside each other, as shown in the following screenshot:

Figure 5.14 – Activating the Preview panel

4. Write the following text in the VS Code editor:

```
# OctopusBlack
```
```
## Threat Actor profile
```
```
#### **#ID: TA_Int-I0012**
```

```
OctopusBlack is a financially motivated Threat Group that
operates mainly in *Latin America*.
```

```
OctopusBlack group has been active since at least
**2020** and was responsible for attacks on **small and
medium-sized companies**.
```

```
The malware used by this group is related to similar
attacks on multiple countries from *Latin America*.
```

```
## Associated Group Descriptions
 | Name        | Description                                          |
 |-----------|---------------------------------------------------
 -|
 |Deathfish  | Related to similar attacks in South America
 |
```

You should see results similar to what is shown in the following screenshot:

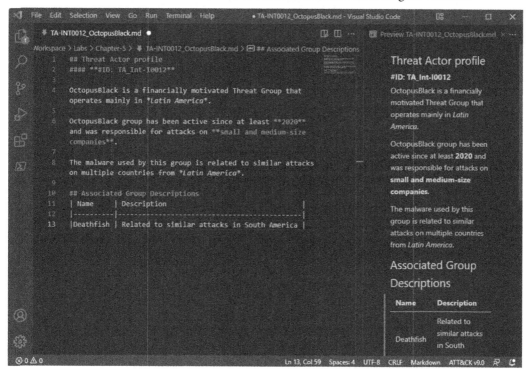

Figure 5.15 – Editing the threat actor's profile report

5. Save the changes using *Ctrl + S*.

6. To export the report to multiple formats, use the *Ctrl + Shift + P* shortcut, and then search for and select the **Markdown PDF: Export (all: pdf, html, png, jpeg)** option from the list, as shown in the following screenshot:

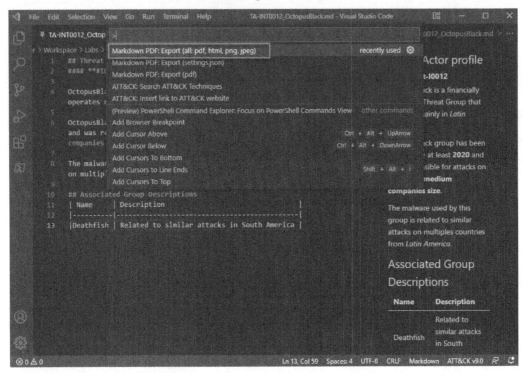

Figure 5.16 – Exporting the report to multiple formats

7. On Windows Explorer, navigate to the `C:\Users\Investigator\Workspace\Labs\Chapter-5` directory, and you will see the report created in multiple formats, as shown in the following screenshot:

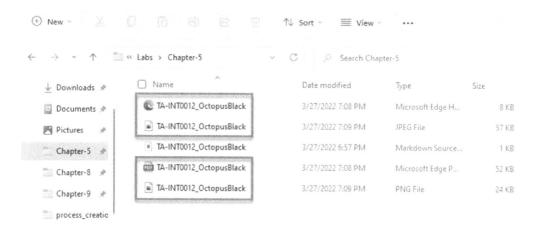

Figure 5.17 – Opening the threat actor's profile in multiple formats

8.   Open the report in every format to compare the different files.

The best option is to create threat actor profiles on a centralized TIP such as the **Malware Information Sharing Platform** (**MISP**) (`https://www.misp-project.org/`) where the information can be consulted and managed more efficiently.

But VS Code is also a great tool and an alternative way to create threat actor profiles, since the VSCode ATT&CK extension has complete integration with the MITRE ATT&CK framework.

An incident response professional must have as much information as possible about threat actors on hand at the time of a security breach, and these tools and frameworks are useful to help them act more efficiently and accurately.

Summary

In this chapter, you learned about the different categories of threat actors and the importance of knowing your adversaries and their capacities to have a better level of contextual understanding when responding to an incident.

You learned how to analyze threat profiles from different sources and the basic concepts of the STIX and TAXII standards.

You also learned how to start documenting a threat actor's profile report using VS Code, the Markup language, and the VSCode ATT&CK extension.

In the next chapter, you will learn about the different stages of an attack using the Cyber Kill Chain model, how to identify attacker TTPs using the MITRE ATT&CK framework, and how to create threat intelligence documentation for incident response.

Further reading

For more information on the topics covered in this chapter, you can refer to the following links:

- *Threat Actor Basics: The 5 Main Threat Types*: https://www.sentinelone.com/blog/threat-actor-basics-understanding-5-main-threat-types/

- *Hacktivism*: https://en.wikipedia.org/wiki/Hacktivism

- *Hacktivism 101: A Brief History and Timeline of Notable Incidents*: https://www.trendmicro.com/vinfo/us/security/news/cyber-attacks/hacktivism-101-a-brief-history-of-notable-incidents

- *15-year-old script kiddie arrested in TalkTalk hacking investigation*: https://siliconangle.com/2015/10/27/15-year-old-script-kiddie-arrested-in-talktalk-hacking-investigation/

- *Insider Threat*: https://www.imperva.com/learn/application-security/insider-threats/

- *A Closer Look at the Attempted Ransomware Attack on Tesla*: https://www.tripwire.com/state-of-security/featured/closer-look-attempted-ransomware-attack-tesla/

- *Ransomware's cryptofootprint*: https://www.kaspersky.com/blog/rc3-bitcoin-ransom-tracing/38488/

- *Threat Actor Type Inference and Characterization within Cyber Threat Intelligence*: https://arxiv.org/ftp/arxiv/papers/2103/2103.02301.pdf

- *The Markdown Guide*: https://www.markdownguide.org/

- *Research ATT&CK techniques from the comfort of your VSCode editor*: https://redcanary.com/blog/vscode-attack/

6

Understanding the Cyber Kill Chain and the MITRE ATT&CK Framework

Cyber-attacks are constantly evolving and becoming more sophisticated due to several reasons, particularly because knowledge is more widely obtainable. There is an entire arsenal of offensive tools available on the internet; these factors significantly reduce the cost of launching a cyberattack.

An incident response professional needs to understand the possible paths an attacker can follow and the tools they could use in a cyberattack. Fortunately, there are handy reference frameworks that detail the actions of adversaries and their tools.

In this chapter, you will learn about some frameworks to analyze attackers' behaviors and the best way to use them when responding to a cybersecurity incident, covering the following topics:

- Introducing the Cyber Kill Chain framework

- Understanding MITRE ATT&CK

- Discovering and containing malicious behaviors

Technical requirements

In case you haven't done already, you need to download and install VMware Workstation Player from this link `https://www.vmware.com/products/workstation-player/workstation-player-evaluation.html`.

You'll also need to download the IR-Laptop virtual machine from the book's official GitHub repository `https://github.com/PacktPublishing/Incident-Response-with-Threat-Intelligence`.

Introducing the Cyber Kill Chain framework

The framework known as Cyber Kill Chain® (`https://www.lockheedmartin.com/en-us/capabilities/cyber/cyber-kill-chain.html`) was developed by Lockheed Martin as part of its model to identify and prevent malicious activities and intrusions, also known as **Intelligence Driven Defense**. The origin of the central concept of this framework is related to the phases that an adversary follows in the stages of a military attack.

The framework consists of seven phases or stages that describe the moments when attackers perform different actions to pursue their goals. This information is handy to identify the possible phase of an attack in a cybersecurity incident, as is depicted in the following diagram:

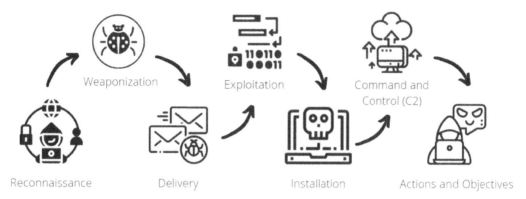

Figure 6.1 – Lockheed Martin's Cyber Kill Chain® framework

The seven phases seen in the preceding diagram are described as follows:

1. **Reconnaissance**: Attackers gather information to profile the target.

2. **Weaponization**: The attackers develop their own malicious code or customize tools created by others to gain initial access.

3. **Delivery**: Threat actors select the best way to distribute or use the malicious code.

4. **Exploitation**: In this phase, the malicious code is executed to exploit a vulnerability.

5. **Installation**: The attackers install programs to maintain persistence.

6. **Command and Control (C2)**: Malicious code communicates with the threat actor's infrastructure and provides remote access and control to the attackers.

7. **Actions and Objectives**: The attackers achieve their goal, which may be information exfiltration, ransomware installation, denial of service, and so on.

Knowledge of the different phases of this framework help defenders to identify an attack in the early phases by designing detection and protection strategies for each stage. However, cyberattacks are not linear, and you can't always anticipate the attacker's actions as they can take different paths, depending on the environment and the specific objective they are pursuing.

There is no exact formula for detecting and containing an attack, but you can narrow attackers' range of motion in advance and limit the impact by anticipating the opponent's actions and successfully disrupting the attack's flow.

As I mentioned at the beginning of this chapter, you can identify a specific phase in developing an attack from an incident response perspective. The starting point will be to analyze the nature of the attack according to the incident and use the information collected in the field. Next, you can use this information and correlate it with any **Indicator of Compromise (IoC)**, and **Indicator of Attack (IoA)** found; this will provide valuable information to establish the starting point for the investigation and assess possible attack containment strategies.

For instance, imagine an incident related to a human-operated ransomware attack. Because of its characteristics, this type of attack could originate from an external attack surface to the internal network so multiple attack vectors could exist, not just by email. At best, the attack can be detected before valuable company information is exfiltrated and encrypted.

Suppose the SOC team detects an alert due to an irregular flow of traffic from the internal network to the internet. At that moment, we don't know what's going on; we only have information about suspicious behavior.

If we use the Cyber Kill Chain as a model, at what stage would the attack be? The answer is: it depends. For example, suppose one of the attacker's goals is to **exfiltrate information**. In that case, the attacker is now in **stage 7**, this would be one of the main objectives in a targeted ransomware attack before encrypting the data, so maybe they would have to go back to **stage 4 (Exploitation)** or **stage 5 (Installation)** to achieve their second goal. That means the Cyber Kill Chain involves phases of a cyclic process and those phases could occur several times while developing the cyberattack as you can see in the following diagram:

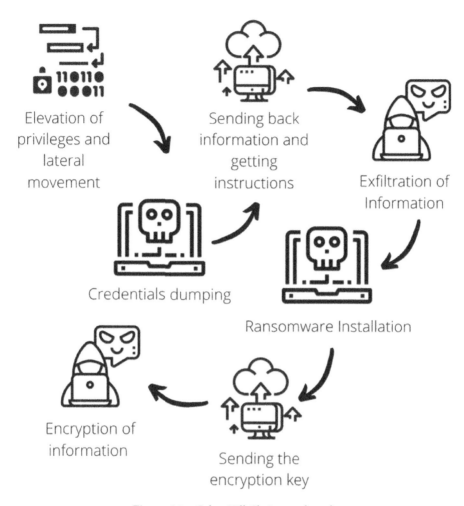

Figure 6.2 – Cyber Kill Chain attack cycle

It's time to start with the incident response and triage procedures. Our first objective here is to identify the potentially compromised devices, asking the monitoring team for a list of those who are sending unusual network traffic to suspicious IP addresses and domains.

Following the **National Institute of Standards and Technology (NIST)** Incident Response framework, we are working in the **Detection and Analysis** phase, and according to the Escal Institute of Advanced Technologies or **SysAdmin, Audit, Network, and Security (SANS)**, this is the phase of **Identification**, as shown:

Incident Response Steps

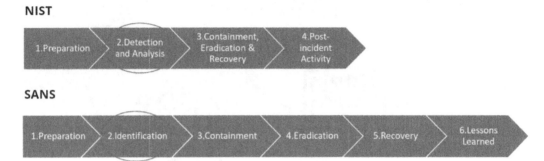

Figure 6.3 – NIST and SANS incident response steps

Once we identify as many compromised devices as possible, the next step is to obtain the memory-disk forensic images from these computers or search for the specific artifacts that provide us with helpful information for the investigation.

Sometimes, when we examine the evidence, we may find new IoCs that will help us identify other devices compromised in previous stages of the attack, even if they do not exfiltrate information to the internet.

Depending on the context of the attack, you can start with containment actions. For instance, you can ask the monitoring team to block traffic to the **Command and Control (C2)** related IP addresses and domains; this will be very useful to interrupt the information leak and avoid the attacker completing stage 7 of the Cyber Kill Chain.

As you can see, the Cyber Kill Chain model can be handy as a reference to identify the stage of an attack when responding to a cybersecurity incident.

Understanding the MITRE ATT&CK framework

MITRE **Adversaries Tactics, Techniques, and Common Knowledge (ATT&CK)** (`https://attack.mitre.org/`) is a knowledge base created by MITRE in 2013 and maintained by multiple organizations and the security community to identify the tactics and techniques used by malicious actors in different real-life attacks. The information of the **ATT&CK Matrix for Enterprise** is organized into 14 tactics divided into techniques and sub-techniques based on the phases presented in an attack as shown in the following screenshot:

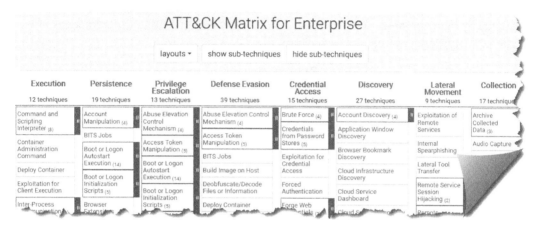

Figure 6.4 – The ATT&CK Matrix for Enterprise

There are currently three categories of ATT&CK matrices:

- **Enterprise**: Describes the actions that a threat actor can use on corporate networks that include Windows, macOS, Linux, PRE, Azure AD, Office 365, Google Workspace, SaaS, IaaS, network, and container platforms: `https://attack.mitre.org/matrices/enterprise/`

- **Mobile**: Describes threat actors' actions on Android and IOS mobile platforms: `https://attack.mitre.org/matrices/mobile/`

- **ICS (Industrial Control Systems)**: Describes threat actors' actions in an industrial network: (`https://collaborate.mitre.org/attackics/index.php/Main_Page`)

These matrices are handy tools that provide the necessary information to cybersecurity professionals to improve posture and defense strategies from an offensive or defensive point of view.

In addition, you can find specific and detailed information about the profiles of different threat actors (`https://attack.mitre.org/groups/`) and the software or tools used in different attacks (`https://attack.mitre.org/software/`).

For incident response professionals, this information is precious since it shows possible adversaries' actions in a security breach and facilitates identifying IoC or IoA.

Use cases for ATT&CK

Since ATT&CK has become a *de facto* framework and is supported, updated, and adopted by many organizations, its use is increasingly widespread in different areas of cybersecurity; some examples are shown in the following diagram:

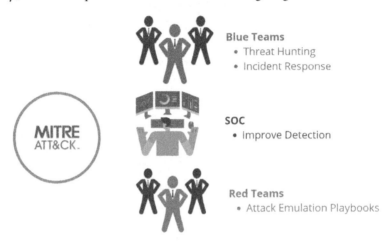

Figure 6.5 – Examples of use cases for ATT&CK

In this way, the different techniques could be used proactively:

- **Incident response**: Mapping intelligence information for the identification of IoC or IoA

- **Threat hunting**: Mapping intelligence information to proactively search for threats

- **SOC monitoring**: Providing information to the monitoring area to improve the detection capacity

- **Red teaming**: Mapping intelligence information for the emulation of adversary behaviors and activities

But let's look at an example of using ATT&CK in incident response. In the early hours of a Saturday, the SOC team received an alert triggered by an attempt to query a database from an unauthorized device. Your incident response team acts and performs the first response and triage procedures.

By analyzing the image of the device's memory, you find a Visual Basic script scheduled to execute the queries to the database and store the results in raw text format in a false `.dll` file (attackers sometimes use this technique to hide the information obtained).

At this point, you can identify the tactic as **Execution** and the technique/sub-technique as **Command and Scripting Interpreter | Visual Basic | ID: T1059.005** as shown in the following screenshot:

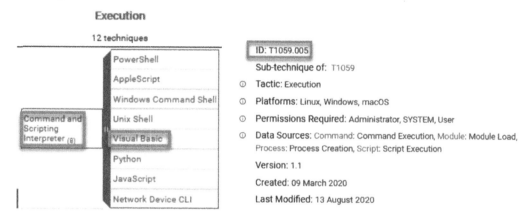

Figure 6.6 – Technique and sub-technique of the execution of a Visual Basic script

On the other hand, the storage of the exfiltrated data is identified as the tactic as **Collection** and the technique as **Automated Collection | ID: T1119**. In this case, there are no associated sub-techniques, as shown in the following screenshot:

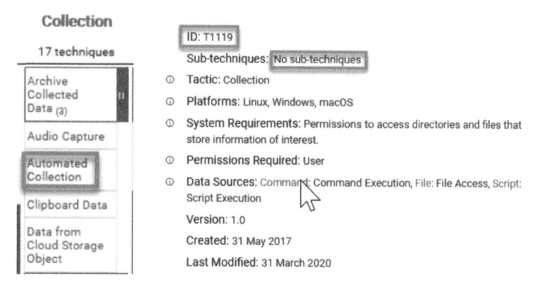

Figure 6.7 – Technique and sub-technique of the collection of information

As part of the investigation, it would be essential to determine how the script got there since this device could not necessarily be the initial vector of the attack, and maybe there was a previous lateral movement. The identification of additional IoC and IoA will be of vital importance, so if we use ATT&CK, we could, for example, search for initial access techniques before the execution of the script, or lateral movement techniques such as those shown in the following screenshot:

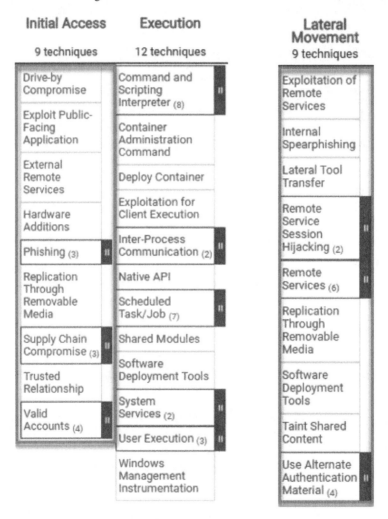

Figure 6.8 – Possible techniques around the execution of a script

As I mentioned at the start of this topic, ATT&CK is a very useful tool for incident response professionals as it provides very valuable information about the possible behaviors of an attacker and helps us to search for and find evidence very efficiently.

Using the ATT&CK Navigator

The ATT&CK Navigator is a tool to visualize and work with the different tactics and techniques of ATT&CK matrices. You can use the ATT&CK Navigator in two ways, directly from the MITRE ATT&CK official GitHub repository `https://mitre-attack.github.io/attack-navigator/` or you can set it up locally on your computer. You will learn how to install it in detail in *Chapter 7, Using Cyber Threat Intelligence in Incident Response.*

Let's try the GitHub version to familiarize you with this tool if you don't know it:

1. In your Investigator virtual machine, open a web browser and navigate to `https://mitre-attack.github.io/attack-navigator/`, and you will see the ATT&CK Navigator as shown in the following screenshot:

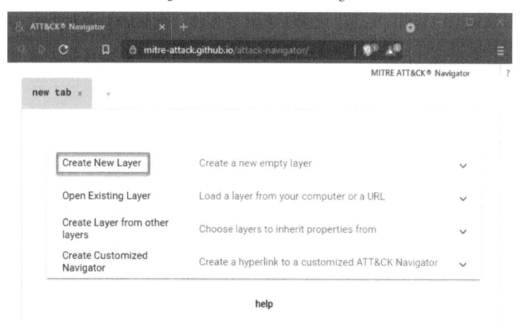

Figure 6.9 – MITRE ATT&CK Navigator main menu

2. Select the **Create New Layer** option and then select the **Enterprise** button as shown in the following screenshot:

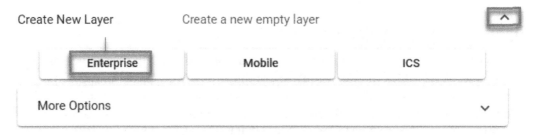

Figure 6.10 – Selection of the type of layer

Now you will see the different tactics and techniques of the Enterprise Matrix as shown in the following screenshot:

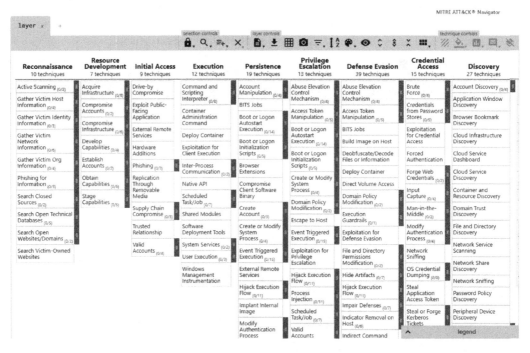

Figure 6.11 – MITRE ATT&CK Navigator tactics and techniques – the Enterprise Matrix

3. Select the desired technique by clicking with the right mouse button to display the contextual menu. Then you can click on the **select** or **add to selection** option to set the selection. If you want to see detailed information on that technique or tactic, select the **view technique** or **view tactic** option, as shown in the following screenshot:

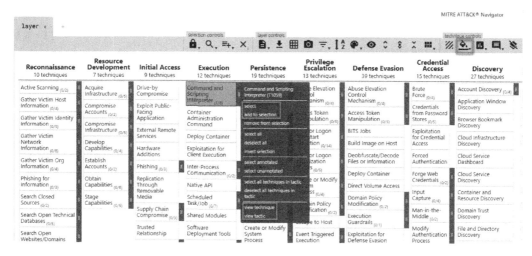

Figure 6.12 – Selection of a specific technique

If the technique contains sub-techniques and you want to select any of them, you must click on the gray bar on the right side of the technique and see the list of related sub-techniques. Then, right-click the sub-technique and select the **add to selection** option, as shown in *Figure 6.13*.

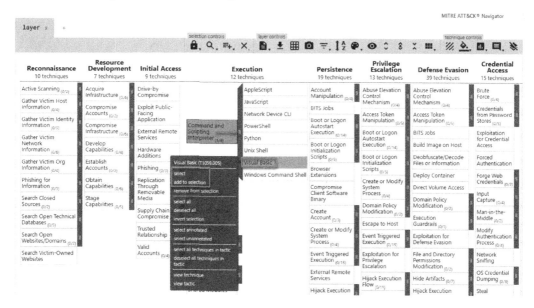

Figure 6.13 – Selection of a sub-technique

4. To change the background color of the technique or sub-technique selected, click the background color button at the top right and then the desired color, as shown in the following screenshot.

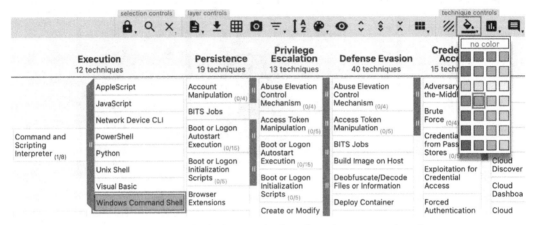

Figure 6.14 – Change the background color of a technique or sub-technique

5. Now you can repeat the same process to add more techniques or sub-techniques.

6. When finished, you can download the created matrix in JSON format, export it to Excel, or download it in SVG format by using the buttons at the top center of the MITRE ATT&CK Navigator:

Figure 6.15 – Exporting the Matrix layer to different formats

These are just some basic concepts to use the tool, and you can explore the rest of its features on your own. I recommend going to `https://attack.mitre.org/resources/training/` where you can learn in depth about the use of MITRE ATT&CK.

Now let's see how we can use ATT&CK in a practical incident response case.

Discovering and containing malicious behaviors

A powerful feature of ATT&CK is making **Cyber Threat Intelligence (CTI)** information actionable to discover and contain malicious actions during incident response.

We are going to use as an example Kaspersky's report on Hakuna MATA, an investigation into a malicious campaign by threat actor Lazarus, published at `https://securelist.com/lazarus-on-the-hunt-for-big-game/97757/`, about the installation of the VHD ransomware and the chain of compromise, as shown in the following diagram:

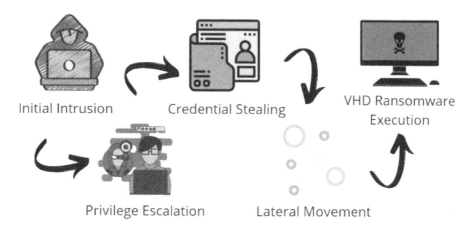

Figure 6.16 – Hakuna MATA VHD ransomware chain of compromise

According to this report, the initial attack vector may have a compromised vulnerable VPN gateway; this allowed attackers to access the network, make lateral movements, elevate privileges, and compromise different services such as Active Directory.

Now, let's assume that your SOC team detects a connection from your network to one of the C2 described in this report. Having the intelligence information on this attack, you can consider the possibility that the organization is under attack by this threat actor.

At this time, we can identify the devices compromised by asking the monitoring team for a list of those making connections to the C2 and perform the first response and triage procedures to obtain the forensic images to get helpful information.

Depending on the circumstances, we may request the blocking of the identified C2 IPs; at this point, there are no encrypted computers, and it's possible that the attacker is still in the Cyber Kill Chain **stages (5) Installation** and **(6) Command and Control**.

Another course of action to identify and contain this threat is adding the hashes to our detection tools or deploy YARA rules to identify compromised computers even if they are not connecting to the C2 (we will learn how to use YARA in *Chapter 13, Creating and Deploying Detection Rules.*

We can now map the behaviors of the threat actor described in the report to create a matrix in MITRE ATT&CK. To do so, we need to identify the techniques used by the attacker and select them in the Navigator as we learned to do previously. For instance, following this matrix, you can search for specific Python scripts, attempts at credential dumping, lateral movement tools, or try to identify the potential initial vector of the attack as shown in the following screenshot:

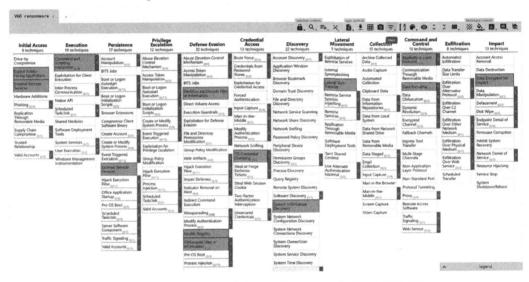

Figure 6.17 – Mapping malicious behaviors to MITRE ATT&CK

As you can see, the Cyber Kill Chain and MITRE ATT&CK frameworks are two handy tools when you are responding to a cybersecurity incident. Rather than having to select one or another, you can use both to get a broader perspective on a cyberattack and be able to identify, contain, or investigate a cybersecurity incident.

Summary

In this chapter, we learned about two frameworks that we can use to respond to cybersecurity incidents and how to apply them.

The Cyber Kill Chain focuses on describing the different phases in which an attack occurs to identify and prevent security breaches.

On the other hand, MITRE ATT&CK helps us identify different tactics, techniques, and tools that an attacker could use in an attack. Thus, the ATT&CK Matrix gives us the advantage of visualizing in a much broader way the possible previous or subsequent actions of an attacker to contain or investigate the details of an attack.

In the next chapter, you will perform several hands-on exercises where you can apply what you learned in the modules of this section.

Through a practical scenario, you will model a potential threat for your organization. Finally, you will identify the IoCs and IoAs in a cybersecurity incident to contain the attack using the CTI provided and create the matrices in the ATT&CK Navigator.

Further reading

- The Cyber Kill Chain Model: A Comprehensive Guide: https://heimdalsecurity.com/blog/cyber-kill-chain-model/

- Cyber Kill Chain & its relevance in Cyber Incident Response Plan: https://www.cm-alliance.com/cybersecurity-blog/cyber-kill-chain-its-relevance-in-cyber-incident-response-plans

- What Is the MITRE ATT&CK Framework? https://www.mcafee.com/enterprise/es-mx/security-awareness/cybersecurity/what-is-mitre-attack-framework.html

- MITRE ATT&CK Framework: Everything You Need to Know: https://www.varonis.com/blog/mitre-attck-framework-complete-guide/

- How to Use the MITRE ATT&CK® Framework and the Lockheed Martin Cyber Kill Chain Together: https://resources.infosecinstitute.com/topic/how-to-use-the-mitre-attck-framework-and-the-lockheed-martin-cyber-kill-chain-together/

7
Using Cyber Threat Intelligence in Incident Response

Every incident is unique and can be approached differently, depending on the context and nature of the attack. You will work in a scenario regarding a fictitious company but use the intelligence information of actual attacks. Surely some colleagues could propose different work paths, and I do not mean to say that there is a unique way to do this. My only interest is to provide you with the means to apply what you have learned.

In this part two of the book, *Knowing the Adversary*, you learned that **Cyber Threat Intelligence (CTI)** is crucial when responding to security incidents. The knowledge you have about threat actors and malicious campaigns gives you a strategic advantage to identify **Indicators of Attack (IoAs)** or **Indicators of Compromise (IoCs)** associated with a security breach faster and more efficiently.

In this chapter, you will learn about the following topics:

- The Diamond Model of Intrusion Analysis
- Mapping **Adversarial Tactics, Techniques, and Common Knowledge (ATT&CK) tactics, techniques, and procedures (TTPs)** from CTI reports
- Integrating CTI into **incident response (IR)** reports

Technical requirements

In case you haven't already, you need to download and install VMware Workstation Player from this link `https://www.vmware.com/products/workstation-player/workstation-player-evaluation.html`.

You'll also need to download the following from the book's official GitHub repository `https://github.com/PacktPublishing/Incident-Response-with-Threat-Intelligence`:

- Virtual machine:
  - IR-Workstation
- Lab file:
  - `Chapter07`

Configuring the lab environment

Before we start with the practical exercises, we will prepare the work environment. In this case, we will use the **IR-Workstation** VM.

Start the IR-Workstation virtual machine and log in using the following credentials:

- **Username**: `investigator`
- **Password**: `L34rn1ng!`

Once you have logged in, you will download, install, and run the Docker containers that contain the tools we will use in this chapter.

Running MITRE ATT&CK Navigator from a Docker container

To install and run MITRE ATT&CK Navigator from a Docker container, follow these steps:

1. Open a new command-line terminal by pressing *Ctrl + Alt + T*.

2. Clone the GitHub project, as follows:

   ```
   git clone https://github.com/mitre-attack/attack-
   navigator.git
   ```

3. Change to the `attack-navigator` directory by running the following command:

   ```
   cd attack-navigator
   ```

4. Build the Docker container, like this:

   ```
   sudo docker build -t attack-navigator .
   ```

   You can see a visual representation of the build process in the following screenshot:

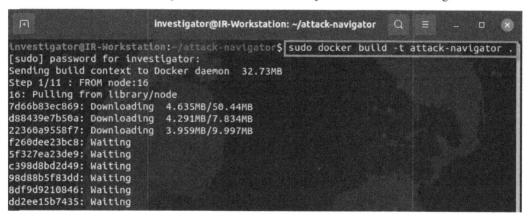

Figure 7.1 – Building the attack-navigator Docker container

> **Note**
>
> If you receive any warning messages through the build, don't worry—it won't affect the practical labs.

5. To run the container, execute the following command:

   ```
   sudo docker run -p 4200:4200 attack-navigator
   ```

6. Finally, when the container is compiled, from the **IR-Workstation** VM, open a web browser and navigate to the following **Uniform Resource Locator** (**URL**): `http://localhost:4200/`.

You will see MITRE ATT&CK Navigator running locally on your VM, as shown in the following screenshot:

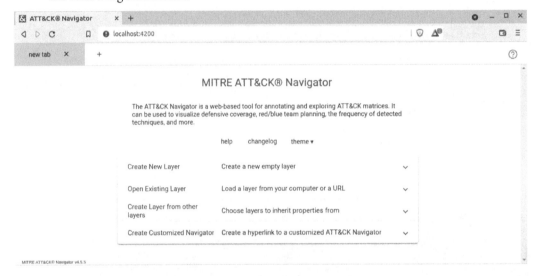

Figure 7.2 – MITRE ATT&CK Navigator running locally

Now that you have a local instance of **MITRE ATT&CK Navigator**, you can use it offline. Next, we are going to install **Threat Report ATT&CK Mapper** (**TRAM**).

Installing TRAM

TRAM is an open source tool created by the **Center for Threat-Informed Defense** (**CTID**) of MITRE Engenuity to automatically map the content of **CTI** reports to **MITRE ATT&CK** TTPs.

The **TRAM** platform uses **machine learning** (**ML**) to identify techniques described in the reports, reducing the time and costs required to identify and classify this information.

To install TRAM on your **IR-Workstation** VM, proceed as follows:

1. Open a new command-line terminal by pressing *Ctrl + Alt + T*.

2. Clone the TRAM GitHub project, as follows:

```
git clone https://github.com/center-for-threat-informed-
defense/tram.git
```

3. Change to the `tram` directory by running the following command:

```
cd tram
```

4. Open the `docker/docker-compose.yml` file using the text editor of your choice, as follows:

```
vim docker/docker-compose.yml
```

5. Under the `environment:` section, change the following parameters to these values:

```
DJANGO_SUPERUSER_USERNAME=analyst
DJANGO_SUPERUSER_PASSWORD=P4cktIRBook!
DJANGO_SUPERUSER_EMAIL=analyst@gosecurity.ninja
```

You can see a visual representation of this in the following screenshot:

```
environment:
 - DATA_DIRECTORY=/tram/data
 - ALLOWED_HOSTS=["example_host1", "localhost"]
 - DEBUG=True
 - DJANGO_SUPERUSER_USERNAME=analyst
 - DJANGO_SUPERUSER_PASSWORD=P4cktIRBook! # your password here
 - DJANGO_SUPERUSER_EMAIL=analyst@gosecurity.ninja # your email address
```

Figure 7.3 – Changing the parameters of the docker-compose.yml file

6. Run the TRAM platform's Docker container, like this:

```
sudo docker-compose -f docker/docker-compose.yml up
```

> **Note**
>
> If you receive any warning messages through the build, don't worry—it won't affect the practical labs.

7. Once the Docker container is up, from your web browser, navigate to the following URL: `http://localhost:8000/`.

8. Sign in to the TRAM dashboard using the following credentials previously defined in the `docker-compose.yml` file:

  - **Username**: `analyst`

  - **Password**: `P4cktIRBook!`

You can see a visual representation of this in the following screenshot:

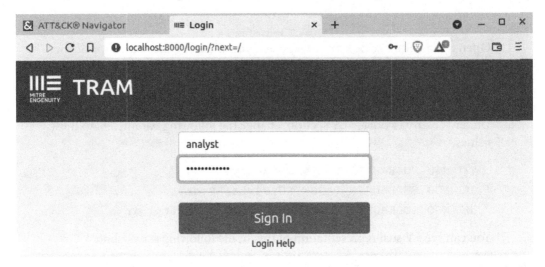

Figure 7.4 – Signing in to the TRAM dashboard

Now that you have prepared your work environment, let's review some TI concepts before starting with the practical exercises.

The Diamond Model of Intrusion Analysis

When we talk about TI, we don't only mean the IoCs integrated into monitoring and detection tools in the form of feeds.

In an IR modern approach, CTI information is vital for the early identification and containment of threats as it provides the necessary context for threat hunting and identifying malicious behaviors.

The Diamond Model of Intrusion Analysis was created by Sergio Caltagirone, Andrew Pendergast, and Christopher Betz from the Center for Cyber Threat Intelligence and Threat Research (http://www.activeresponse.org/wp-content/uploads/2013/07/diamond.pdf).

This model has become one of the pillars for intelligence analysts and is based on four main components, as outlined here:

- **Adversary**: This could be an organization or individual, also known as an adversary or threat actor.

- **Infrastructure**: The threat actor's technology infrastructure could be a domain name, **Internet Protocol (IP)** address, and so on.

- **Capability**: These are the tactics and techniques an adversary uses to achieve their objectives.

- **Victim**: This is an organization or individual of interest that is the target of a cyberattack.

This model is represented in the form of a diamond, as shown in the following diagram:

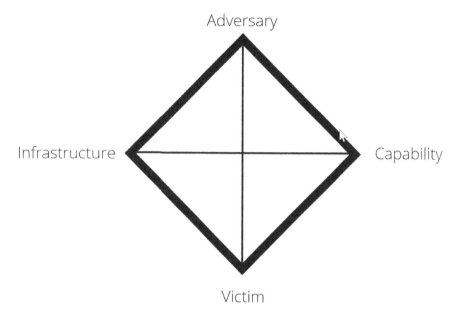

Figure 7.5 – The Diamond Model of Intrusion Analysis

The basis of this model is this: "*For every intrusion, an adversary has the infrastructure and capacity to attack their victim.*"

That means that if we use this model, we will have the ability to know our adversaries better and thus develop robust defense strategies and respond better to security incidents.

In the next diagram, we are analyzing a cybersecurity incident from the perspective of the Diamond Model of Intrusion Analysis:

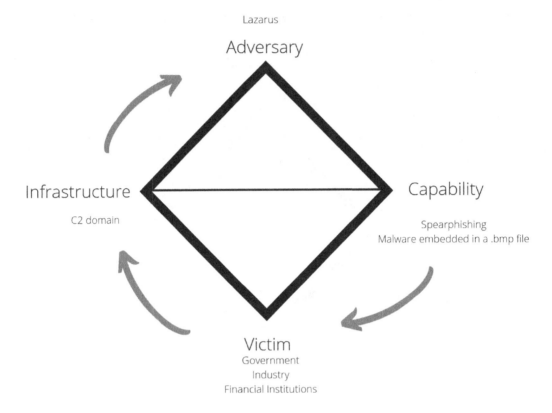

Figure 7.6 – Example of a cybersecurity incident

Once you have TI information about an adversary or a malicious campaign, you can map the diamond model with every stage of the **Cyber Kill Chain** framework, as shown in the following table:

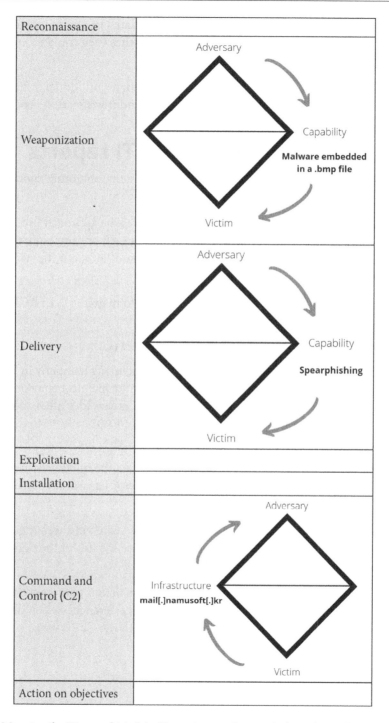

Reconnaissance	
Weaponization	
Delivery	
Exploitation	
Installation	
Command and Control (C2)	
Action on objectives	

Table 7.1 – Mapping the Diamond Model of Intrusion Analysis with the Cyber Kill Chain framework

This approach will allow you to know not just the IoCs related to a security incident but also be able to visualize adversaries' goals, the different routes they could follow, and the tactics and techniques used.

Later in this chapter, you will learn how to integrate the Diamond Model of Intrusion Analysis and MITRE ATT&CK TTPs in the IR analysis and investigation processes.

Mapping ATT&CK TTPs from CTI reports

In the identification stage of responding to a security incident, obtaining enough information about IoCs and IoAs is crucial.

One of the main challenges of mapping CTI to ATT&CK is the approach used to create reports. When analysts document information about an attack or campaign, they focus more on providing technical details regarding the attack and IoCs, but the ATT&CK framework is based more on behaviors or IoAs.

So, let's learn how to identify behaviors from a TI report to map it to ATT&CK TTPs.

Case study – a weaponized document

It is 3 A.M., and you get a call from an important manufacturing company in South Korea. The cybersecurity department reports that there has been suspicious behavior within their corporate network. The **security operations center** (**SOC**) team identified and blocked a connection from the production area manager's computer, PROD-SK07, to the mail[.]namusoft[.]kr domain.

According to the SOC team, the source of information from the intelligence feeds tagged the IoC as a domain related to a campaign of the threat actor Lazarus. For that reason, they opened a security incident ticket.

After the call, you connect to the company's cybersecurity team via a web meeting. They provide you with more details about the incident and share the IoC of the domain that was identified in the connection.

So, you have the connections that were made from the suspicious computer to the malicious domain. Using the Cyber Kill Chain model as a reference, we can determine that the attack is probably in phase 6 (communication with the C2 server).

At this point, you have the following information:

- PROD-SK07: Compromised computer
- mail[.]namusoft[.]kr: C2 server

Responding to the incident

You could start by getting an image of the computer's memory or retrieving forensic artifacts to start the investigation, just as you did in *Chapter 4, Applying First Response Procedures*. However, in this chapter, we will focus on gathering intelligence information, which will help you identify, contain, and eradicate the threat.

From an IR perspective, you can begin validating with the TI area if the IoC is already known or something new.

You can start searching this IoC on **Open Source Intelligence** (**OSINT**) sources, a **Threat Intelligence Platform** (**TIP**), or directly on the **IR system** (**IRS**) with a TI-integrated module, as you will learn in *Chapter 10, Implementing an Incident Management System*.

In this case, we found this IoC was referenced in a published TI report by the antivirus company **Malwarebytes** at the following URL: `https://blog.malwarebytes.com/ threat-intelligence/2021/04/lazarus-apt-conceals-malicious- code-within-bmp-file-to-drop-its-rat/`.

According to this report, the threat actor behind this IoC is Lazarus (`https:// attack.mitre.org/groups/G0032/`), a known state-sponsored cyber-threat group who, among other things, is attributed to attacks such as WannaCry (`https:// securelist.com/wannacry-and-lazarus-group-the-missing- link/78431/`). So, you now have the profile of the potential threat actor, and you can calculate the risk level to which the organization is exposed, as you learned in *Chapter 5, Identifying and Profiling Threat Actors*.

At this time, it is crucial to identify other computers connecting to this C2 server, as you will learn in *Chapter 13, Creating and Deploying Detection Rules*, or find new IoCs related to this malicious campaign.

Using TRAM to map ATT&CK TTPs

As you learned in *Chapter 6, Understanding the Cyber Kill Chain and the MITRE ATT&CK Framework*, ATT&CK is a knowledge base to identify tactics and techniques used by malicious actors in cyberattacks.

Becoming familiar with ATT&CK tactics and techniques takes time and requires dedication and experience. I recommend using ATT&CK in a practical and applicable way instead of just reading the theory.

According to MITRE, the best way to map CTI information to ATT&CK techniques is by following the next steps.

Finding malicious behavior

We need to read the threat intelligence report and identify the techniques used by attackers. Sometimes, you will see a direct reference, but on other occasions, you must read between the lines and understand the context to deduce the possible technique used.

To analyze and find attackers' behaviors using TRAM, proceed as follows:

1. On the **IR-Workstation** VM, go to the web browser and open a new tab to navigate to go the following CTI report: `https://blog.malwarebytes.com/threat-intelligence/2021/04/lazarus-apt-conceals-malicious-code-within-bmp-file-to-drop-its-rat/`.

2. Read about this malicious campaign to familiarize yourself with the context and details of the attack.

   Now, we will import this intelligence report to the TRAM platform to map its content to ATT&CK more efficiently.

3. Save this web page as `Lazarus_Malicious_APT_campaign` in the `/home/investigator/Workspace/Labs/Chapter-7` folder, selecting **Webpage, HTML Only** from the format list at the button of the dialog box.

4. On the web browser, go to the TRAM dashboard and click on the **Upload Report** button, as shown in the following screenshot:

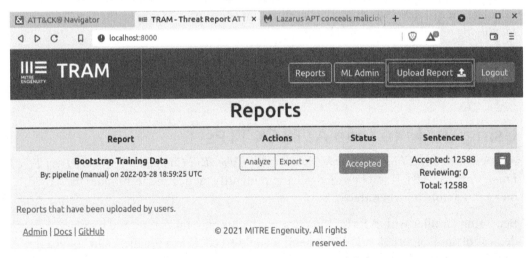

Figure 7.7 – Uploading a new report to be processed

> **Note**
> TRAM supports the following file formats: `.pdf`, `.docx`, `.html`, `.json`, and `.txt`.

5. Go to the `Chapter-7` folder and select the previously saved report, then click on
    the **Open** button.

    You will see a new report imported with a status of **Queued**, as shown in the
    following screenshot:

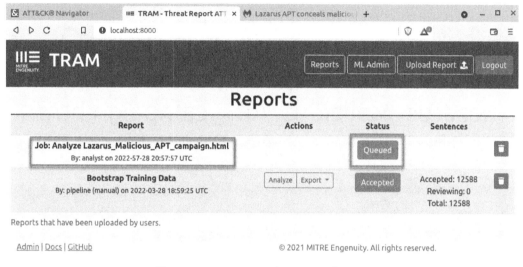

Figure 7.8 – Processing the imported report

After a few seconds, the status will change to **Reviewing**, which means that the
report is ready for processing.

6. Click on the **Analyze** button, as illustrated in the following screenshot, to start
    mapping this report:

Figure 7.9 – Starting the report analysis

You will see the two columns; on the left is the report's content in text format, and on the right are the mappings to the ATT&CK framework, as you can see in the following screenshot:

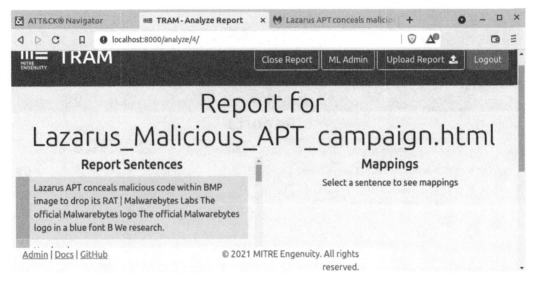

Figure 7.10 – TRAM's report analysis dashboard

7.　Scroll down on the **Report Sentences** column until the following paragraph:

```
In one of their most recent campaigns, Lazarus used
a complex targeted phishing attack against security
researchers.
```

As you can see, *phishing* was one of the threat actor's techniques in this campaign. However, we don't know what kind of phishing this could be, so we will try to get additional information about the specific sub-technique used.

We could assume that phishing was at least one of the attack vectors and start looking for the characteristics and content of emails and the users who received them.

Researching malicious behavior

Sometimes, you may not be familiar with a particular behavior used by attackers, so you should go further and look at additional sources about it and try to figure out how you could better match some technique defined in ATT&CK.

To research malicious behavior, proceed as follows:

1. Continue scrolling down on the **Report Sentences** column until the
    following paragraph:

    ```
    In this campaign, Lazarus resorted to an interesting
    technique of BMP files embedded with malicious HTA
    objects to drop its Loader.
    ```

    This paragraph is shown in the following screenshot:

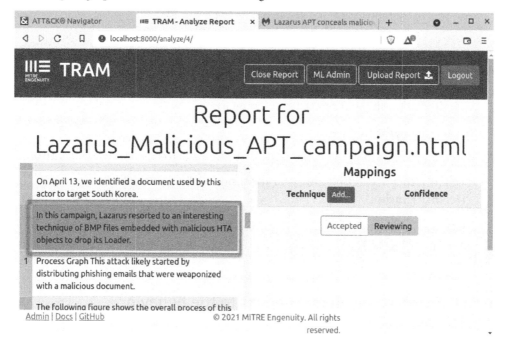

Figure 7.11 – Analyzing an unknown behavior

Suppose that you don't have background knowledge about this technique. In that
case, you could search for sources about the use of **HyperText Markup Language
(HTML) Application** (**HTA**) objects embedded in **bitmap image** (**BMP**) files.

2. Open a new tab in the web browser and use your favorite search engine to find
    information about HTA objects and embedded files on BMP files. Here are a couple
    of sources regarding both topics:

    -   `https://blog.malwarebytes.com/cybercrime/2016/09/`
        `surfacing-hta-infections/`

    -   `https://www.sentinelone.com/blog/hiding-code-inside-`
        `images-malware-steganography/`

Read about this campaign and analyze how the techniques could be used together by attackers to navigate under the radar or avoid detection.

Translating malicious behavior into a tactic

To translate a malicious behavior into a tactic, you need to focus on what the threat actor is trying to accomplish, and which phase the attack is in.

To map a particular behavior into an ATT&CK tactic, proceed as follows:

1. Read this paragraph again:

    > In this campaign, Lazarus resorted to an interesting technique of BMP files embedded with malicious HTA objects to drop its Loader.

2. What do you think the threat actor is trying to do?

    They are doing the following:

    -   First, they are writing malicious code in a `.hta` file to be executed (**Execution**).

    -   Secondly, they are hiding the `.hta` file inside a `.bmp` image file (**Defense Evasion**).

We now have an idea of the attacker's intention and what they were trying to do; if we use the MITRE ATT&CK Navigator tool, we can start looking at which of the possible techniques the attackers used.

Figuring out which technique applies to the behavior

Once you have identified the adversary objectives in the distinct phases of the attack, the next step is to find out which actions they take to achieve them. We could define ATT&CK techniques as the "*what*" and tactics as the "*how*".

Now, the next step will be mapping the behaviors identified in the CTI report to ATT&CK techniques. Proceed as follows:

1. In the web browser, return to the previously opened ATT&CK Navigator tab.
2. Click on **Create New Layer** and then click on **Enterprise.**
3. Review the list of techniques associated with the **Execution** and **Defense Evasion** tactic columns.

If you carefully review the **Execution** techniques, the one that corresponds to the behavior described in the report is the **Command and Scripting Interpreter** technique.

4. On the **Execution** tactic column, select the **Command and Scripting Interpreter** technique and expand it to see a list of associated sub-techniques.

5. Select **JavaScript** as a sub-technique.

6. Click on the background color button (*paint icon*).

7. Select the *green* color from the palette.

The previous steps are shown in the following screenshot:

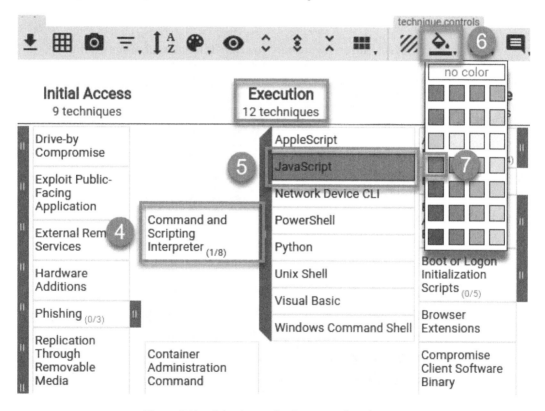

Figure 7.12 – Selecting and coloring a sub-technique

You could save this layer of ATT&CK with the identified techniques to share or consult later.

Next, we will see another way to find a technique or sub-technique in the ATT&CK browser quickly.

One of the attacker's behaviors described in the TI report was the use of a `.hta` file that executes JavaScript code. You can search for this term directly as follows:

1. On ATT&CK Navigator, click on the search and filter button (*magnifying glass icon*).

2. The search panel will open, and then on the **search** textbox, write `hta` and press *Enter*.

   In the **Techniques** section, you will see a list of techniques related to the `hta` search criteria.

3. In **Command and Scripting Interpreter : JavaScript**, proceed as follows:

   - Click on the **view** link if you want to see detailed information about this technique.

   - Click on the **select** button if you want to select this sub-technique on the ATT&CK layer.

   The previous steps are shown in the following screenshot:

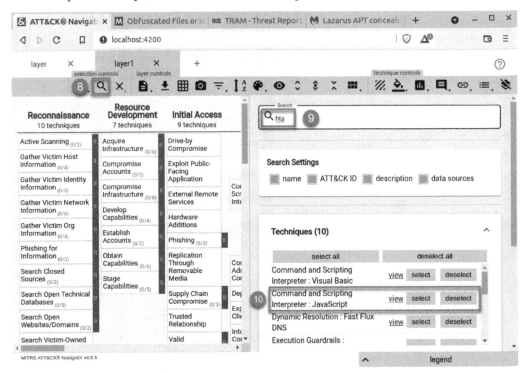

Figure 7.13 – Searching for a specific behavior to correlate with an ATT&CK technique

As you can see, we could find a technique and sub-technique without previously knowing the tactic and using only the method used by the adversary.

Now, go back to the **TRAM** report analysis dashboard to add the following sub-techniques:

- **Command and Scripting Interpreter : JavaScript**
- **Obfuscated Files or Information : Steganography**

4. Click on the **Add...** button next to Technique, as shown in the following screenshot:

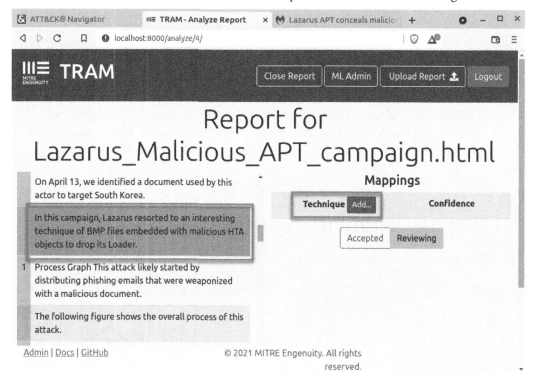

Figure 7.14 – Manually mapping an ATT&CK technique

5. On the **Add Mapping** dialog box, write the word `JavaScript` to return and filter techniques related to this term, then select `T1059.007 - JavaScript/JScript` corresponding to the technique/sub-technique as shown in the following screenshot:

Figure 7.15 – Selecting associated technique sub-technique with the behavior

6. Click on the **Add** button to incorporate this sub-technique in the **Mappings** column, and you will then see the added sub-technique and the confidence level associated with the text in the paragraph, as shown in the following screenshot:

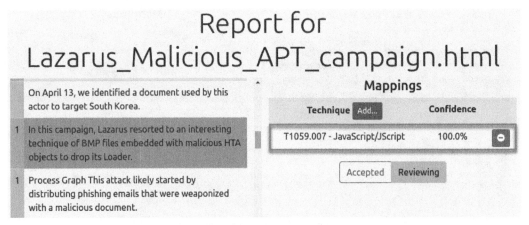

Figure 7.16 – Adding techniques to the Mapping list

In this way, you associated a malicious behavior described in the CTI report with a specific ATT&CK technique.

7. Repeat the same process to add the **T1001.002 - Steganography** sub-technique.

8. Once you have added the two sub-techniques, click on the **Accepted** button to accept the mappings.

Sometimes, the ML functionality of **TRAM** will automatically recognize the behaviors in the CTI report and will assign them an associated technique/sub-technique. You can see an example of this next.

9. Scroll down to the next paragraph, shown here, and select it:

```
Process Graph This attack likely started by distributing
phishing emails that were weaponized with a malicious
document.
```

You will see that **TRAM** recognized the behavior and assigned the **T1566.001** - **Spearphishing Attachment** sub-technique, as you can see in the following screenshot:

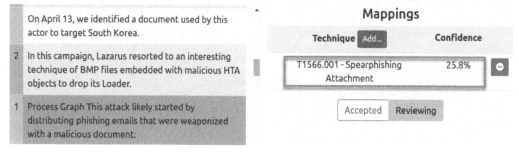

Figure 7.17 – Adding techniques to the Mapping list (continued)

10. If you agree with these criteria, click on the **Accepted** button to accept the mapping.

11. Continue with this process until you cover all the CTI report content and add the technique/sub-technique.

12. Once you have finished analyzing the report, click on the **Close Report** button, as shown in the following screenshot:

Figure 7.18 – Closing the report to finish the analysis

You will see the report status change to **Accepted** (in green). Now, you can export the analysis results in two different formats, **JSON** and **DOCX**, as you can see in the following screenshot:

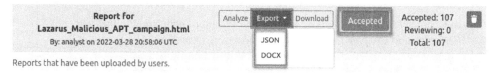

Figure 7.19 – Exporting the analysis results

13. Export the analysis report to **DOCX** format and save it to the `/home/investigator/Workspace/Labs/Chapter-7` folder.

14. Open the exported file in LibreOffice.

   In the first part of the analysis report, you will see a summary of the sentences accepted and reviewed. Additionally, you will find the ATT&CK techniques organized by **identifier (ID)** and the matched sentences, as shown in the following screenshot:

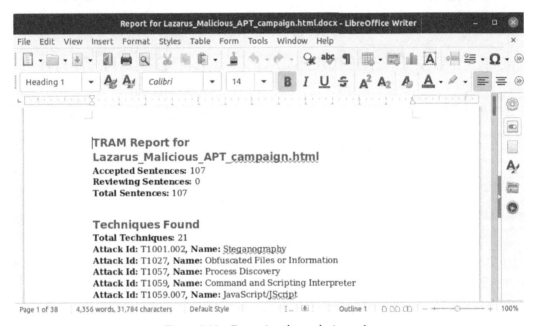

Figure 7.20 – Exporting the analysis results

From an IR point of view and with the information obtained up to now, the chances that the company was the target of the same threat actor and this attack is part of the same campaign launched against other companies, is high.

Now that you have TI information about the potential threat actor and the related campaign, tactics, and techniques, you can start the threat-hunting process to identify compromised assets in the organization.

> **Note**
>
> In *Chapter 12, Working with Analytics and Detection Engineering in Incident Response*, and *Chapter 13, Creating and Deploying Detection Rules*, you will learn more about detection engineering and threat hunting.

Using Visual Studio Code to research ATT&CK techniques and create reports

There is another way to map behaviors from TI to ATT&CK TTPs—you can use **Visual Studio Code** (**VS Code**) with the VSCode ATT&CK extension as a valuable tool for your investigations.

In *Chapter 5, Identifying and Profiling Threat Actors*, you learned how to use this tool to create threat actor profiles using the **Markdown** language.

Before starting, we need to configure the VSCode ATT&CK extension settings. To do so, proceed as follows:

1. First, click on the VS Code button from the Ubuntu taskbar, as shown in the following screenshot:

Figure 7.21 – Opening VS Code in the IR-Workstation VM

2. Open the **File** menu, and then click on **Preferences | Settings**, as shown in the following screenshot:

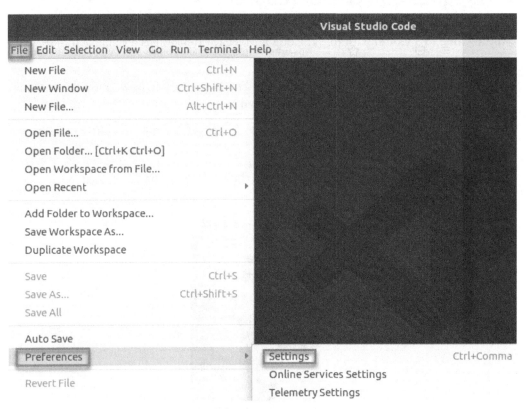

Figure 7.22 – Changing the settings of the VS Code ATT&CK extension

3. On the **Settings** search textbox, write MITRE ATT&CK, and you will then see the parameters related to the **VSCode ATT&CK** extension.

4. Select all the checkboxes to enable code completion, as shown in the following screenshot:

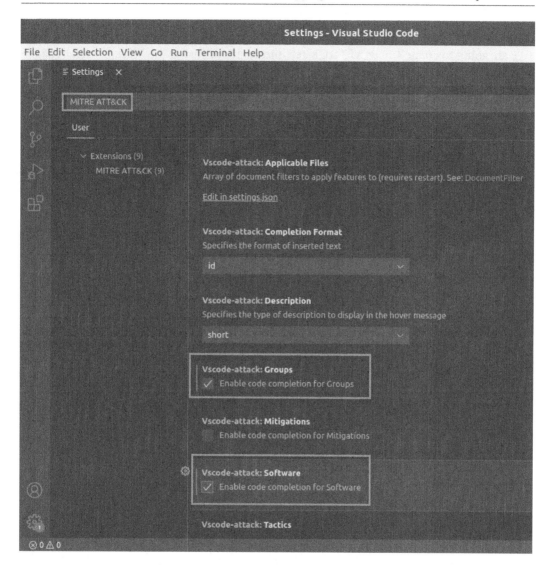

Figure 7.23 – Configuring VSCode ATT&CK extension settings

5.   Close the **Settings** panel to save your changes.

Now that we have configured the VS Code ATT&CK extension, let's begin documenting the techniques we found in various TI sources.

Creating an ATT&CK techniques report

We are going to create a new ATT&CK techniques report using the Markdown language. To do so, proceed as follows:

1. From VS Code, create a new file and save it as `IR-012_22-APT.md` on the `/home/investigator/Workspace/Labs/Chapter-7` folder, selecting **Markdown** from the format list at the bottom, as shown in the following screenshot:

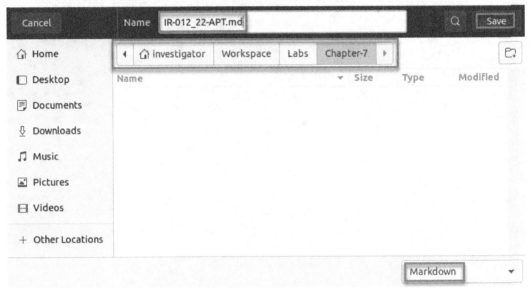

Figure 7.24 – Saving the ATT&CK TTPs report

2. Press *Ctrl* + *K*, release the keys, and then press *V* to see the **Preview** panel.

3. Write the following text in the **VS Code editor**:

```
# Incident Response Investigation - Threat Intelligence
information

#### Report ID: IR-012_22-APT

## Executive Summary

The SOC team of the South Korean branch reported a
suspicious connection from the PROD-SK07 computer to the
domain mail[.] namusoft[.] kr.


According to threat intelligence sources, the domain is
related to malicious campaigns operated by Lazarus's
threat actor.

## Related campaigns
```

```
Lazarus APT conceals malicious code within BMP image to
drop its RAT
https://blog.malwarebytes.com/threat-
intelligence/2021/04/lazarus-apt-conceals-malicious-code-
within-bmp-file-to-drop-its-rat/
## Tactics Techniques and Procedures (TTPs)
```

Your text should look as shown in the following screenshot:

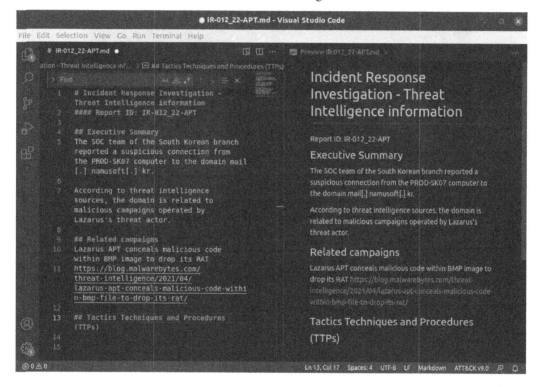

Figure 7.25 – Documenting the report

4. Under Tactics Techniques and Procedures (TTPs) write the word
    Phishing followed by pressing *Ctrl* + spacebar.

You will see the name of the techniques related to the term `Phishing`, as you can see in the following screenshot:

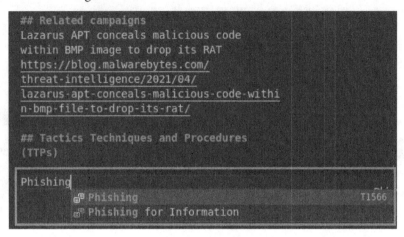

Figure 7.26 – Autocompleting an ATT&CK technique by name

5. Press *Ctrl* + spacebar, and a technique with ID `T1566`, which correspond to `Phishing`, will appear.

6. If you press *Ctrl* + spacebar again and then select the arrow at the right of the technique, you will see the technique description, as shown in the following screenshot:

Figure 7.27 – Autocompleting an ATT&CK technique by ID

Now, let's try providing a technique ID.

7. Write the technique ID `T100` and then *Ctrl* + spacebar, after which you will see a list of sub-techniques related to this technique.

8. From this list, select the `.002` sub-technique.

9. Press *Ctrl* + spacebar, and you will then see a definition of this sub-technique, as shown in the following screenshot:

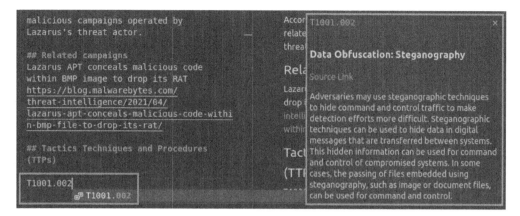

Figure 7.28 – Autocompleting an ATT&CK sub-technique by ID

You can also insert a link associated with a specific technique/sub-technique.

10. Right-click on the technique or sub-technique and select **ATT&CK : Insert link to ATT&CK website**.

11. You will see the technique with an added link to the MITRE ATT&CK website, as shown in the following screenshot:

Figure 7.29 – Inserting a MITRE ATT&CK technique URL

By default, **Markdown** and **YAML Ain't Markup Language** (**YAML**) files support the **VSCode ATT&CK** extension; this is particularly useful for writing Sigma rules, for example. You can also add support to other languages; for more details, consult the official wiki at `https://github.com/redcanaryco/vscode-attack/wiki`.

12. Add the other TTPs related to your investigation and save your work.

Now that you have learned to map TI to ATT&CK techniques, you will next learn how to include CTI information in IR reports.

Integrating CTI into IR reports

You can incorporate TI information into IR reports regarding threat actors and campaigns and correlate it with the **Cyber Kill Chain** framework and the **Diamond Model of Intrusion Analysis**.

There is no doubt that TI and the knowledge of threat actors' behaviors are critical in IR processes, especially in the **Identification** and **Containment** phases, but how can we make it actionable?

Lenny Zeltser (Twitter handle `@lennyzeltser`) created a handy template for the documentation of TI to trigger that information and use it in IR. The *Report Template for Threat Intelligence and Incident Response* is free for use and distributed according to the *Creative Commons Attribution license (CC BY 4.0)*. You can download it from this URL: `https://zeltser.com/cyber-threat-intel-and-ir-report-template/`.

To learn how to use this template, we will use the same hypothetical IR case described in this chapter, whereby we will need to identify critical pieces of information to create a report.

To start collecting intelligence information and create a report, proceed as follows:

1. On the **IR-Workstation** VM, open a web browser and download the Microsoft Word format template directly from this URL: `https://zeltser.com/media/docs/cyber-threat-intel-and-ir-report-template.dotx`.

2. Save the file to the `/home/investigator/Workspace/Labs/Chapter-7` folder.

3. Double-click on the file to open the template in **LibreOffice**.

4. Using the same path as the template, save the file as `IR-012_22-APT` using the **Word 2007–365 (.docx)** format, as shown in the following screenshot:

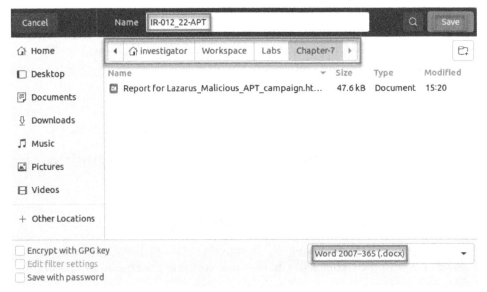

Figure 7.30 – Saving the template in Word 2007–365 (.docx) format

5. When you click the **Save** button, you will see the following warning message. Click on the **Use Word 2007–365 Format** button to use the regular Microsoft Office Word format:

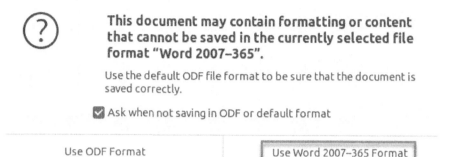

This document may contain formatting or content that cannot be saved in the currently selected file format "Word 2007–365".

Use the default ODF file format to be sure that the document is saved correctly.

☑ Ask when not saving in ODF or default format

Use ODF Format   Use Word 2007–365 Format

Figure 7.31 – Selecting the Microsoft Word 2007–365 format

In the first part of the template, there is a brief description of the frameworks related to this document, as shown in the following screenshot:

Figure 7.32 – Navigating to read about TI

6. Delete the description of the template of the first paragraph, and add the following IR report ID: Report ID: IR-012_22-APT.

7. Selecting the **Styles** menu, change the style of the text in the Cyber Threat Intelligence and Incident Response report to Title.

8. Repeat the process to change the style of the report ID text to `Subtitle`.

9. Fill in the report's header details, providing the following information:

Incident Name: Detection of IoCs related to a Lazarus Threat Actor's Campaign
Report Author: Investigator
Report Date: 05/10/2022

Once you complete the previous steps, your document should look like the following screenshot:

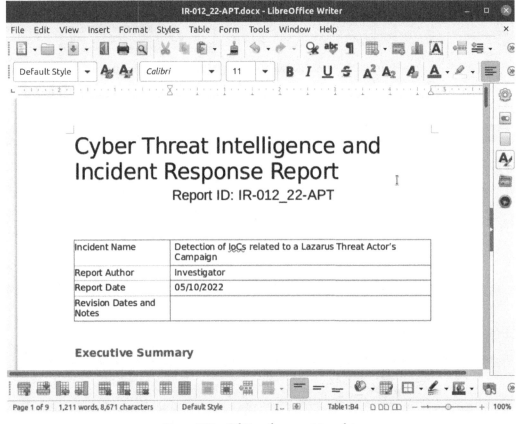

Figure 7.33 – Editing the report template

Next, you will document all the information you can get from different sources. For example, this is another good source with valuable information about this threat actor and the campaigns attributed to them: *Andariel evolves to target South Korea with ransomware* (`https://securelist.com/andariel-evolves-to-target-south-korea-with-ransomware/102811/`—*Kaspersky*).

10. Provide the following information in different sections of the document (you will find detailed instructions on each area of the template):

- In the first part of the report's template, *Executive Summary*, you will provide details about the incident, the adversary's profile (Lazarus), and the related malicious campaigns associated with the IoCs found corresponding to the information you read previously.

- In the second part of the report's template, *The Adversary's Actions and Tactics*, you will be able to document all information related to the adversary, as follows:

  - *Description of the Adversary*
  - *The Adversary's Capabilities*
  - *The Adversary's Infrastructure*
  - *The Victims and Affected Assets*

- In the third part of the report's template, *Course of Action During Incident Response*, you will summarize the steps taken in the different phases of the IR, as follows:

  - *Identify*
  - *Discover*
  - *Detect*

- Actions to **contain** and **eradicate** the detected threats:

  - *Deny*
  - *Disrupt*
  - *Degrade*
  - *Deceive*
  - *Destroy*

- In the last part, *Intrusion Campaign Analysis*, you will summarize the relationship with the information you collected in the IR and other related campaigns, including additional geopolitical or socioeconomic factors.

You will find an example of this report with information in the book's repository in the `Lab-files` section.

As you can see, this template covers different models, such as the **IR** and **Cyber Kill Chain** frameworks, and the **Diamond Model of Intrusion Analysis**.

Also, it is a valuable tool for integrating the profiles of threat actors, malicious campaigns, and TI information into different stages of IR.

Summary

In this chapter, you learned the main concepts of the **Diamond Model of Intrusion Analysis** to create CTI reports.

You learned how to install local instances of MITRE ATT&CK Navigator and TRAM on your VM.

You also learned how to use VS Code with the VSCode ATT&CK extension to research and use ATT&CK techniques interactively.

Finally, you learned how to provide TI information to include it in IR reports.

In the next chapter, you will learn how to develop an IR capacity in an organization to facilitate activities and processes in different IR scenarios.

Further reading

To learn more about the topics that were covered in this chapter, look at the following resources:

- *A Threat-Driven Approach to Cyber Security:* `https://www.lockheedmartin.com/content/dam/lockheed-martin/rms/documents/cyber/LM-White-Paper-Threat-Driven-Approach.pdf`

- *Automating threat actor tracking: Understanding attacker behavior for intelligence and contextual alerting:* `https://www.microsoft.com/security/blog/2021/04/01/automating-threat-actor-tracking-understanding-attacker-behavior-for-intelligence-and-contextual-alerting/`

- *Cyber Threat Modeling: Survey, Assessment, and Representative Framework:* `https://www.mitre.org/sites/default/files/publications/pr_18-1174-ngci-cyber-threat-modeling.pdf`

- *Enriching Attack Models with Cyber Threat Intelligence:* `https://www.diva-portal.org/smash/get/diva2:1477504/FULLTEXT01.pdf`

- *ATT&CK 101:* https://medium.com/mitre-attack/att-ck-101-17074d3bc62

- *Getting Started with ATT&CK:* https://www.mitre.org/sites/default/files/publications/mitre-getting-started-with-attack-october-2019.pdf

- *MITRE ATT&CK®: Design and Philosophy:* https://attack.mitre.org/docs/ATTACK_Design_and_Philosophy_March_2020.pdf

- *Incident Response using MITRE ATTACK:* https://www.huntsmansecurity.com/blog/incident-response-using-mitre-attack/

- *Research ATT&CK techniques from the comfort of your VSCode editor:* https://redcanary.com/blog/vscode-attack/

Section 3: Designing and Implementing Incident Response in Organizations

Designing and implementing an incident response program goes beyond creating a playbook or installing an incident response system. In this part, you will learn how to identify the organization's requirements and maturity, work on incident response plans, and develop an incident response capacity. You will also learn how to integrate different security systems in an ecosystem to improve efficiency in terms of responding to, and investigating, security incidents.

This section comprises the following chapters:

- *Chapter 8, Building an Incident Response Capability*
- *Chapter 9, Creating Incident Response Plans and Playbooks*
- *Chapter 10, Implementing an Incident Management System*
- *Chapter 11, Integrating SOAR Capabilities into Incident Response*

8
Building an Incident Response Capability

Security incidents occur when you least expect them. In a moment, the operation of the business is interrupted, or news about the leak of company information is on social networks and the internet and goes viral. These are times of great uncertainty, and you need to respond quickly and appropriately.

It is a crucial moment, and the clock is ticking fast; there is no time for improvisation, and the only way to succeed is to have a plan and sufficient resources to deal with the security breach. Any organization must have the infrastructure, tools, and staff with the knowledge and skills to respond to and investigate security breaches.

There are several frameworks, such as the **National Institute of Standards and Technology (NIST)** and **SysAdmin, Audit, Network, and Security (SANS)**, that consider the importance of developing an incident response capability, with the first step identified as **preparation**.

You will learn the importance of developing and implementing an incident response capacity for different attack scenarios and creating a program that supports business continuity and actions to identify, contain, and eradicate threats.

In this chapter, we are going to cover the following topics:

- Taking a proactive approach to incident response

- Building an incident response program

- Aligning the incident response plan, the business continuity plan, and the disaster recovery plan

Technical requirements

In case you haven't done already, you need to download and install VMware Workstation Player from this link `https://www.vmware.com/products/workstation-player/workstation-player-evaluation.html`.

You'll also need to download the following from the book's official GitHub repository `https://github.com/PacktPublishing/Incident-Response-with-Threat-Intelligence`:

- Virtual machine:

  - IR-Workstation

- Lab file:

  - `Chapter08`

Taking a proactive approach to incident response

Responding to a cybersecurity incident could be considered a reactive activity since it is done after an offensive action has been detected or identified. So, what does it mean to take a proactive stance? It means that even when you can't avoid incidents, you can have defined procedures for acting in certain circumstances. Also, if you have an infrastructure that supports those activities and the necessary tools to work throughout the life cycle of the incident, you will be better prepared.

Some of the benefits of developing an incident response capability are the following:

- A reduction in the costs and the impact associated with the interruption of business operations of the company

- Faster identification of the nature of the attack, discovery of **Indicators of Attack (IoA)**, and **Indicators of Compromise (IoC)**
- Better management of activities, processes, and documentation improves the organization's ability to protect against future threats

Another vital aspect of adopting a proactive posture for incident management is the organization's ability to adapt to the constant evolution of threats.

The incident response hierarchy of needs

Inspired by the pyramidal hierarchy of needs of the Russian-American Abraham Maslow, Matt Swann from Microsoft developed The Incident Response Hierarchy of Needs: `https://github.com/swannman/ircapabilities`.

This model describes from the base how organizations should develop their levels of maturity and technical capabilities to deal with risks and cyber threats. The main idea is to build solid foundations in each of the layers to build a real capacity for detection and response to cybersecurity incidents, as shown in the following figure:

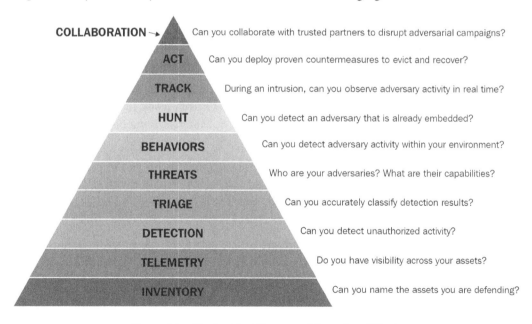

Figure 8.1 – The Incident Response Hierarchy of Needs

Each element from the preceding diagram is described as follows:

- **Inventory**: The same as you would with a risk analysis, you must start with the identification of the main assets of the organization; you cannot protect what you do not know you have.

- **Telemetry**: Having an asset management system in organizations is of great help in incident response. Identifying and containing threats will become more challenging if you do not have up-to-date and accurate information on the assets.

- **Detection**: The sooner a threat is detected, the less impact it will have. The detection and analysis phase in incident response will only be practical if the organization can identify malicious activity before it is too late, as you will learn in *Chapter 11, Integrating SOAR Capabilities into Incident Response*.

- **Triage**: Daily, all digital assets generate a significant amount of information. Your organization needs to develop the capacity to identify and classify what is malicious and what is normal. Also, you will be able to identify the sources of information with helpful evidence for your investigation, as you learned in *Chapter 3, Basics of the Incident Response and Triage Procedures*.

- **Threats**: As you learned in *Chapter 5, Identifying and Profiling Threat Actors*, threat intelligence provides the knowledge of adversaries and their capabilities to improve the identification, containment, and eradication of threats.

- **Behaviors**: One of the steps to making threat intelligence actionable in incident response is to investigate the behaviors of threat actors using frameworks such as MITRE ATT&CK, as you learned in *Chapter 6, Understanding the Cyber Kill Chain and MITRE ATT&CK Framework*.

- **Hunt**: By knowing the **tactics, techniques, and procedures** (**TTPs**) used by threat actors, you can identify the compromised assets and contain the threat; you will learn more regarding threat hunting in incident response in *Chapter 14, Hunting and Investigating Security Incidents*.

- **Track**: Most attacks are non-linear, and threat actors will fly under the radar. Hence, it's essential to use threat intelligence and tools to detect any malicious activity even when it seems "normal," as you will learn in *Chapter 12, Working with Analytics and Detection Engineering in Incident Response*.

- **Act**: In incident response, threat intelligence information is only valuable if it can be made actionable. The goal at this point is to use all resources to contain and eradicate threats, as you will learn in *Chapter 13, Creating and Deploying Detection Rules*.

- **Collaboration**: At the tip of the pyramid is collaboration with other organizations. Collaboration and the exchange of threat intelligence information is a key part of acquiring a proactive posture against threats and responding efficiently to cybersecurity incidents, as you learned in *Chapter 7, Using Cyber Threat Intelligence in Incident Response.*

You can also divide this structure into three stages:

1. Development of technological capabilities to identify and respond to cybersecurity incidents (Inventory, Telemetry, Detection, and Triage.

2. Development of the capacity to detect threats early and proactively (Threats, Behaviors, and Hunt.

3. Development of the capacity to contain and eradicate threats, and also to exchange information with other organizations (Track, Act, Hunt, and Collaborate)

The pyramid showing the three stages is as follows:

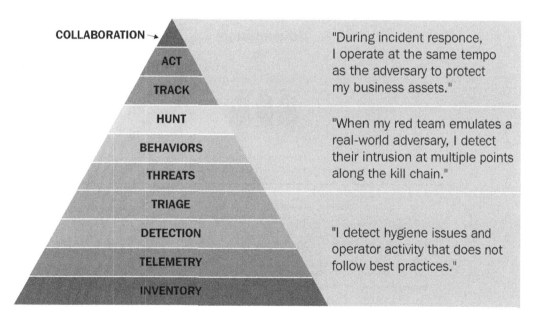

Figure 8.2 – Phases for the development of incident response technical capabilities

This pyramid is a very useful guide and can be applied to the maturity process of any organization to build a better incident response technical capacity.

Developing organizational incident response capabilities

According to the consulting firm Deloitte, the basis for the development of an incident response capacity consists of a strategy developed specifically for the company that includes the following:

- Involvement of different areas of the organization.

- The technologies necessary to perform the triage and investigations.

- Operational resilience to guarantee business continuity and enable recovery from a disaster.

- Risk management and compliance that considers legal and regulatory aspects.

- The remediation of incidents must be related to business processes.

All of this must be orchestrated under a governance structure, as shown in the following figure:

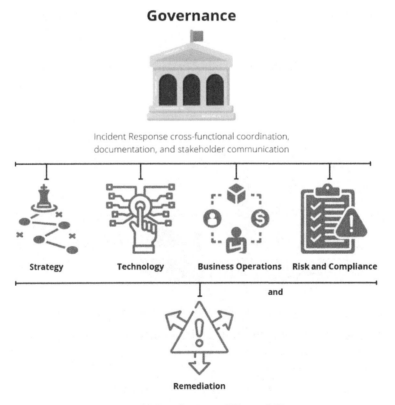

Figure 8.3 – Developing a CIR capability

By integrating the technical and organizational capabilities, not only is it possible to respond effectively to cyber-secured incidents, but you will also guarantee that they are aligned with the business's vision and requirements. In the next part, you will learn how to build a comprehensive incident response program.

Identifying business requirements to create an incident response program

Technology must be a facilitator of the business. The objective of digital transformation is to rely on technology to achieve its goals in the short, medium, and long term, evolving consistently and adapting to the characteristics of the environment.

In the same way, cybersecurity must be a component that, like a bodyguard, helps ensure that the technology meets its objective, anticipating and protecting itself against any risk or threat that could interrupt the business processes or the organization's technological infrastructure.

The challenge is to align technology with business processes and these, in turn, with security; this should be a priority for organizations. The best way to achieve it is by identifying critical business assets, operations, and the associated threats through a risk and threat assessment.

Business knowledge is essential to understand the organization's position around these threats and its risk appetite. For instance, in a company, the leak of internal information can have more business impact than the encryption of the data itself in a ransomware attack. In that case, it probably will not handle the incident as if it identifies it as a more complex threat.

In addition to understanding the critical business processes, it is also crucial to understand the priorities of the C-levels. Each area has different concerns, and therefore, their ways of seeing the business and the associated risks are not necessarily the same.

Keeping this in mind will help align ideas and objectives of all essential business areas to define a unified vision and facilitate the different parties' acceptance.

Some of the priorities from a business perspective can be the following:

- Regulatory and legal compliance
- Cost of implementing controls
- Data protection
- Reputation

It's essential that these concerns help with the optimization of resources that will be allocated and obtain better results.

Another factor to consider is the changing external environment's impact. An example was the COVID-19 pandemic, which forced technology adoption in many businesses. Employees had to work remotely, which represented a real challenge in cybersecurity.

Due to the lack of planning, threat actors attacked many companies and compromised their infrastructures.

Evaluating the incident response maturity level

One of the most important points before starting the implementation process of an incident response program is to understand the organization's position before cybersecurity threats and know its ability to respond to an attack.

The first step is to make a diagnosis of the current capacity of the organization. There are different tools to make this diagnosis, some commercial and others free.

To learn how we can evaluate the maturity level of an organization, we will use a maturity assessment tool created by the international organization **CREST** (a non-profit organization established in the UK in 2006 for accreditations and certifications in security).

To start, follow these steps:

1. Start the **IR-Workstation** virtual machine and log in using the following credentials:

    Username: investigator

    Password: L34rn1ng!

2. Create a new folder under /home/investigator/Workspace/Labs/ Chapter-8 called IR_Maturity_Assessment.

3. Navigate to the CREST website: https://www.crest-approved.org/ cyber-security-incident-response-maturity-assessment/ index.html.

4. Scroll down to the bottom of the web page and find the links to download the assessment tools, as shown in the following screenshot:

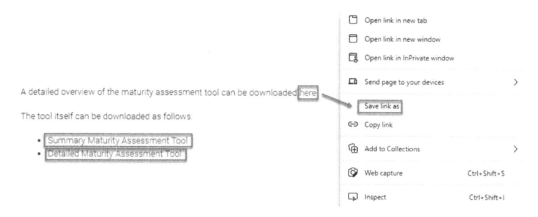

Figure 8.4 – Downloading the maturity assessment tools

5. Right-click on the link **here** after the text **A detailed overview of the maturity assessment tool can be downloaded**, and select the **Save link as** option. After that, provide the path of the `IR_Maturity_Assessment` directory and save the file there.

6. Now, repeat this process to download the files `Summary Maturity Assessment Tool` and `Detailed Maturity Assessment Tool`.

    Once you have downloaded the two documents, you can start the assessment of the maturity level of the organization.

7. Navigate to the `IR_Maturity_Assessment` directory and double-click the `Maturity-Assessment-Tool.xlsm` file to open it on LibreOffice. (You will receive a warning message as shown in the following screenshot; just click the **OK** button because is not relevant for this exercise.)

   Warning loading document Maturity-Assessment-Tool.xlsm: The data could not be loaded completely because the maximum number of columns per sheet was exceeded.

OK

Figure 8.5 – LibreOffice warning message about the limit on the number of columns

8. Next, you will receive another warning message about the macros inside the document, as shown in the following screenshot. Click the **OK** button.

This document contains macros.

Macros may contain viruses. Execution of macros is disabled due to the current macro security setting in Tools - Options - LibreOffice - Security.

Therefore, some functionality may not be available.

OK

Figure 8.6 – LibreOffice warning message about the macros inside the document

For security reasons, the macros are disabled. Always be careful with files downloaded from the internet; it is a tactic widely used by evil actors to compromise users' devices.

In this case, the source is reliable, so we are going to allow the execution of the macros.

9. Open the **Tools** menu and then select **Options…**.

10. In the LibreOffice **Options** dialog box, select **Security** and then the **Macro Security…** button, as shown in the following screenshot:

Figure 8.7 – LibreOffice Options dialog box

11. Next, select the **Medium** option to require confirmation each time you open a file with macros, and then click on the **OK** button, as shown in the following screenshot:

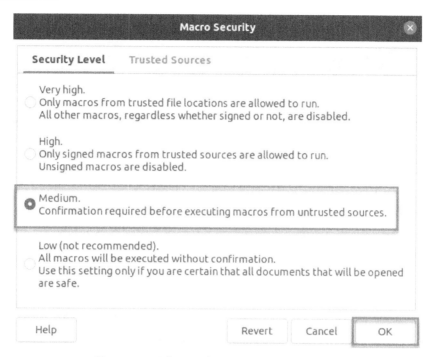

Figure 8.8 – Selecting the security level of macros

12. Finally, click the **Apply** button and then the **OK** button to save the changes.

13. To start using the spreadsheet with the macros enabled, close the file, and open it again. You will see a new warning message about the macros. Just click on the **Enable Macros** button, as shown in the following screenshot:

Figure 8.9 – Enabling the macros of the spreadsheet

Now, to start working with this template, you will need information about a fictitious organization.

14. Download the document that contains information for the company from `https://github.com/PacktPublishing/Incident-Response-for-Cybersecurity-Professionals/tree/main/Lab-Files` and then navigate to the folder `Chapter-8/CompanyInfo.pdf`.

15. Review the content of the `CompanyInfo.pdf` file.

16. Go to the **Guidelines** tab of the `Maturity-Assessment-Tool.xlsm` file, scroll down the sheet, and follow the steps to fill in the fields of the template, as shown in the following screenshot:

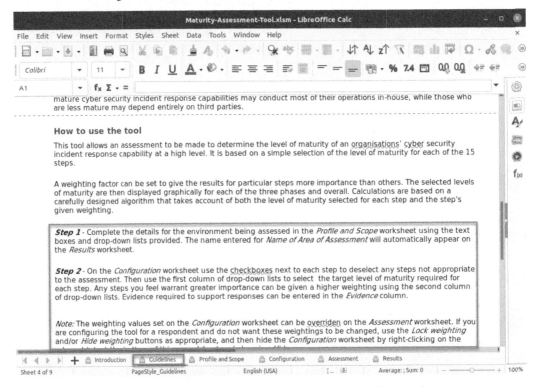

Figure 8.10 – Reviewing the guidelines about the use of the template

The results of this assessment will show the level of maturity of the organization in its security incident response capability and help you identify points for improvement and to develop and plan an efficient strategy.

Building an incident response program

Every organization must define what guidelines will be followed for the preparation to respond to security incidents and the starting point is the evaluation of the level of maturity and the security posture of the organization.

Preparing to respond to cybersecurity incidents should be an ongoing cycle that should consider an up-to-date view of risks and threats.

Incident response is not just about the use of tools or procedures; it requires developing a comprehensive incident response program that helps the organization be more efficient in detecting threats and increasing preparedness to respond to incidents and security breaches.

Incident response procedures and guidelines

Procedures and guidelines should be well documented. Having the procedures documented step by step helps reduce the number of errors and allows the work to be done more efficiently.

Workflows must be documented for the distinct types of incidents or activities; for example, define the actions to be taken if a ransomware incident materializes or if a lateral movement is detected with exfiltration of information from the network.

Activities should be clearly documented so that sometimes the first responder does not necessarily require technical knowledge of incident response.

Integrating people, processes, and technology into the incident response process

As in all aspects related to cybersecurity, it is very important to consider people, processes, and technology in the development of an incident response capacity as shown in the following figure:

Incident Response Capacity

People   Process   Technology

Figure 8.11 – The three pillars of cybersecurity strategies

As you will see later, you cannot respond to cybersecurity incidents efficiently if any of these three elements are missing. For instance, without technology, the response capacity will be insufficient and limited. Technology will not be able to solve the problem without the interaction of qualified personnel. Although the organization has the technology and personnel, the response will not follow any direction without defined processes.

People

There are different criteria for the creation of an incident response team, and much will depend on the characteristics of each organization.

According to **NIST's 800-61** framework of reference, there are different models of incident response teams, and these can be the following:

- **Centralized team**: All incidents are handled by a single team that has its headquarters in a main office. This is mainly recommended in small companies with centralized management.

- **Distributed team**: Unlike the centralized model, in this model, there are several incident response teams according to the geographical and organizational structure of the company. Due to its characteristics, it is recommended in large companies.

- **Coordinated team**: This model is useful when incident response teams do not necessarily belong to the same organization and simply establish a collaboration scheme that benefits them mutually. An example can be financial institutions that decide to create collaboration mechanisms, including information sharing and support when incidents occur that may be of common interest to their industry.

Additionally, these teams can have several working models, such as the following:

- **Employees of the company**: The incident response area is composed of a staff consisting of employees of the company.

- **Hybrid model**: In this model, a part of the processes and work of responding to incidents is carried out by external personnel of the company and the internal staff performs specific and well-defined activities.

- **Fully outsourced staff**: In this model, responsibility for incident management is transferred entirely to an external company and the company's staff only performs specific support tasks.

- **Roles and responsibilities**: The roles and responsibilities will depend to a large extent on the work model adopted in the organization.

- **Training programs**: An incident response team is made up of different people who have skills and knowledge in areas such as threat intelligence, digital evidence management research, threat hunting, and malware analysis.

To maintain an adequate level of knowledge and skills among team members, it is important to develop a continuous training program where different levels of learning are considered for participants in different areas.

Process

Incident response processes are particularly important to avoid confusion, minimize damage, and reduce response time.

Incident handling criteria must be defined in different circumstances and stages of the life cycle of the resolution to incidents, for example:

- Categorization of the type, level of criticality, and impact of the incident
- Criteria notifying the different areas of the company

- Criteria for informing law enforcement or regulators

- Standards for the management of digital evidence

Reporting and establishing record-keeping protocols are some key procedures that must be performed for proper incident management.

The OODA methodology for incident response

Observe, Orient, Decide, Act (OODA) is a methodology to use the available information and its context to make decisions in incident response. One way to apply it is by getting information from different sources such as logs, alerts, and threat intelligence and elaborating different hypotheses to take action, as shown in the following figure:

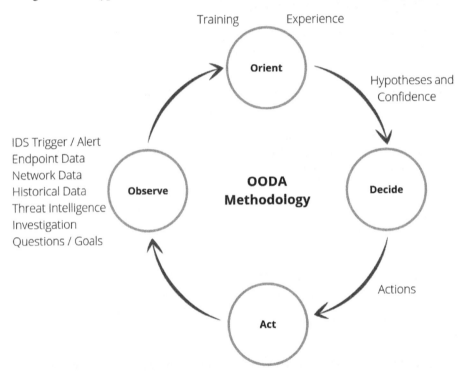

Figure 8.12 – The OODA methodology

The different elements of OODA methodology are discussed as follows:

- **Observe**: Collect information from multiple sources to identify anomalous behaviors to initiate an investigation.

- **Orient**: Using methodologies and frameworks, identify possible attack patterns or hypotheses about what possible paths the attacker could follow.

- **Decide**: Based on the evidence and indicators obtained, the information collected from different sources of threat intelligence, and your observations, define the best course of action to follow.

- **Act**: Apply the necessary measures to contain, remediate, and recover.

This methodology is particularly useful to identify the best way to quickly respond to a security breach.

Technology

The technology behind incident response is based on the systems used by security analysts to carry out their investigation, response, and management tasks. Incident response requires an infrastructure, hardware, and software that support the activities that are required in the event of a security breach.

It should be considered that sometimes the normal infrastructure of the organization could be affected, and alternative mechanisms should be used to be able to follow the procedures defined in the incident response plan.

These tools should include the following, for example:

- Incident response management software

- A threat intelligence platform

- An incident response toolkit

- Computers with software for investigation

- Independent network segments for connecting incident response and investigation team devices

- Basic network equipment and cables

- Sanitized storage drives

- Secure voice, messaging, and email communication tools

- Encryption software to protect the information

It is also particularly important that the infrastructure of the organization is configured to facilitate the collection of information that can be valuable. An example is to have a centralized log collection system, or tools that allow the rapid deployment of data collection agents from devices in the network that allows the execution of scripts, and also Yara and Sigma rules, which we will see in detail in *Chapter 13, Creating and Deploying Detection Rules*.

Aligning the incident response plan, the business continuity plan, and the disaster recovery plan

A cybersecurity incident could impact several aspects of the organization; in many cases, one of the most significant is the interruption in the continuity of business operations.

When this happens, a common mistake in organizations is prioritizing the continuity of the business operations over the incident response procedures. This does not necessarily have to be so; incident response, business continuity, and disaster recovery are processes that can and should be aligned. One of the goals of incident response plans is to help ensure that business operations can continue and that the business will continue to the recovery stage.

But let's review from a simplified point of view the differences between these plans and how they are integrated.

Incident response plans

The incident response plan defines the actions to be taken in a security breach and how to identify, analyze, contain, and eradicate threats. From there, take the lessons learned to improve the organization's security capabilities.

There are several aspects to consider when creating an incident response plan:

- Have a clear idea of the business mission, its key processes, and the related risks and threats to the business.

- Have the support of senior members of the organization to facilitate decision making and activities to be carried out.

- The basis of the plan must be realistic, with well-defined tasks and responsibilities, not just a compliance document.

- It must be an "active" document updatable considering the dynamic changes of the organization and the environment.

- The plan must be constantly tested to assess its efficiency and feasibility.

Now that we understand the aspects to consider while creating an incident response plan, next, we will look at the key roles to create an incident response team.

Incident response teams

According to NIST, a key component to responding efficiently to a cybersecurity incident is the incident response team. There are key roles that are performed in the team:

- **An incident response manager**: Responsible for coordinating activities if an incident occurs.

- **Incident handlers**: Responsible for carrying out the activities during the incident.

- **Company stakeholders**: These can be a combination of board members, cybersecurity staff, IT staff, the **Chief Information Security Officer (CISO)**, and public relations.

- **Other stakeholders**: These can be the board of external advisors, the legal team, or external service providers.

Additionally, you need to define the best model to distribute your teams according to the characteristics of your organization, as you will see next.

Incident response team models

Based on the requirements of the organization, teams can be organized into three different models:

- **Centralized**: In this model, all responsibility for incident management belongs to a single department.

- **Distributed**: There are several incident response teams spread across different locations, working independently.

- **Coordinated**: A main incident response team coordinates and works with other incident response teams.

Some considerations when defining the creation of these teams are the following:

- Will the team be made up of full-time employees or be outsourced?

- Is the high availability of services required (24/7)?

- Is there a budget specifically allocated for this?

Currently, any business depends on its technological infrastructure to operate. For that reason, and regardless of the size of the organization, companies need to develop an incident response capacity and plan to deal with cyberattacks.

Business continuity plan

Business continuity (**BC**) is an integral part of good cybersecurity practices and corporate governance. It has gained relevance due to the increase of risks and threats for organizations in the business and technological environments.

A **Business Continuity Plan** (**BCP**) is designed to ensure that the business continues to operate after an incident; this does not mean that the company should continue working at 100%, but that at least those processes and assets that are indispensable and critical for the organization must be kept in operation.

A BCM framework

According to the **European Union Agency for Cybersecurity** (**ENISA**), to implement a successful **Business Continuity Management** (**BCM**) plan, you need to explicitly know the critical business process and define the project's scope, objectives, and deliverables to align it to the business objectives.

Responsibility for management falls on the Business Continuity Management team, and the number of members and the specific roles will depend on the size and type of the organization.

Additionally, for the governance of the business continuity process, a **Business Continuity Steering Committee** (**BCSC**) must be set up, which, unlike the Business Continuity Management team, acts at the time that it is required to ensure business continuity and ensure that plans are kept updated, reviewed, and tested.

NIST 800-34 (Contingency Planning Guide for Federal Information Systems) recommends that the BCSC should be overseen by a senior manager such as the **Chief Information Officer (CIO)**.

Business Impact Analysis (BIA)

A key part of the process of planning a business continuity plan is the **Business Impact Analysis (BIA)**. This analysis helps to measure the impact and losses caused by a cybersecurity incident.

Along with the BIA, the risk assessment information should be considered to determine the likelihood of a disruption in business processes. In this way, it will be possible to define the best strategy to ensure business continuity.

The BIA is also an essential part of disaster recovery (DR) and incident management (IM) plans.

Disaster recovery plans

A disaster recovery plan helps to ensure that the business can return to its normal operating state before a security incident occurs. A recovery plan must consider process and procedure development to ensure the restoration of systems and assets affected in an incident.

Depending on the incident, the outcome of the threat hunting activities and the investigation will help ensure no residual risks or threats that prevent a return to normalcy.

The **NIST Special Publication 800-184 "Guide for Cybersecurity Event Recovery"** defines that recovering from a cybersecurity incident could require rebuilding a system and restoring backup information involving people, processes, and technology.

According to the **Cybersecurity Framework (CSF)**, **recovery** is a critical function for a complete defense. The recovery process involves two phases focused on tactical and strategic results.

The tactical recovery phase involves executing a recovery plan defined proactively before an incident occurs.

The second phase is more strategic and focuses on mitigating the incident's impact and reducing the likelihood of future incidents.

A critical component to recover after a cybersecurity incident is planning. Recovery planning must consider an in-depth analysis of the essential business areas and the dependency of processes and systems. Also, it is crucial to explore different scenarios and how threats could impact the business.

Threat modeling is an integral part of scenario exploration as it does not consider risks superficially. Still, it helps to identify the capabilities and tools of adversaries in a more detailed way.

It is also essential to consider the legal, regulatory, and operational requirements to calculate the business impact and reduce recovery time.

Depending on the nature of the incident, the decision to initialize a recovery process may involve the recovery personnel, the incident response team, the CISO, or the business owners.

As you can see, there are points of convergence between incident response, business continuity, and disaster recovery. Therefore, these processes must be aligned to develop an effective response to cyberattacks, as shown in the following figure:

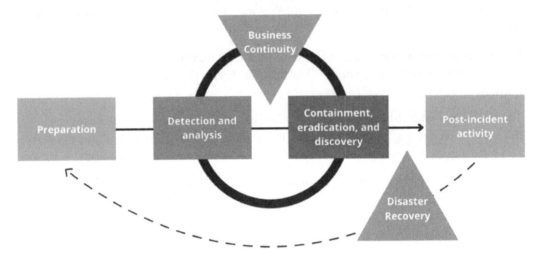

Figure 8.13 – Alignment between IR, BC, and DR

It is essential to establish coordinated actions between the different areas to implement the plans at specific moments of the incident to balance the priorities of the business continuity and the DFIR (Digital Forensics and Incident Response) investigation.

As you can see, the common goal of the **Incident Response (IR)**, **Business Continuity (BC)**, and **Disaster Recovery (DR)** plans is to reduce the impact on the business because of cybersecurity incidents.

For example, suppose that your **Security Operations Center (SOC)** detects a connection from a file server on the network to an IP identified as a **command and control** server (**C2**) related to a malicious campaign. This incident triggers the first response procedures.

As part of the IR procedures, you may need to initialize triage procedures to collect information from the compromised server and perform memory and hard drive acquisition procedures. Therefore, the operation of the server must be interrupted. If you do not have a secondary server, it probably also implies the interruption of the functions associated with that server.

This scenario should be considered in the development of the business continuity plan and for the definition of the **Recovery Time Objective (RTO)**; otherwise, there will be a conflict of interest between following incident response protocols and fulfilling the business continuity objectives.

Summary

In this chapter, you learned the importance of adopting a proactive posture for incident response and how these strategies can help you deal with different security breaches.

You learned about the correlation between people, processes, and technology to develop successful incident response programs and the importance of aligning business requirements with incident response procedures.

Finally, you learned about the relationship between incident response, business continuity, and disaster recovery plans and the importance of integrating them to respond more efficiently to cyberattacks.

In the next chapter, you will create an incident response policy, an incident response plan, and playbooks to respond to different categories of incidents.

Further reading

- NIST 800-61 Computer Security Incident Handling Guide: `https://nvlpubs.nist.gov/nistpubs/SpecialPublications/NIST.SP.800-61r2.pdf`

- Cyber incident response: Preparing for the inevitable: `https://www2.deloitte.com/content/dam/Deloitte/ca/Documents/risk/ca-en-deloitte-crisis-incident-response.pdf`

- Maslow's hierarchy of needs: `https://en.wikipedia.org/wiki/Maslow's_hierarchy_of_needs`

- Building an incident response program: creating the framework: `https://blog.malwarebytes.com/101/2018/03/building-an-incident-response-program-creating-the-framework/`

- Six steps for building a robust incident response function: `https://www.ibm.com/downloads/cas/QEBYPND1`

- Incident Response Process and Procedures: `https://cybersecurity.att.com/resource-center/ebook/insider-guide-to-incident-response/incident-response-process-and-procedures`

- How to Use OODA Loop in Your Incident Response Process in 2020: `https://www.cybertriage.com/2019/how-to-use-ooda-loop-in-your-incident-response-process/`

9
Creating Incident Response Plans and Playbooks

When a cybersecurity incident occurs, not all organizations are prepared to deal with it, especially small and medium-sized ones. For organizations, the creation of **incident response plans** (**IRPs**) and playbooks is essential because they describe how an organization is prepared when identifying a security breach.

Responding to cybersecurity incidents is not just about acquiring and implementing technology or following IR guides; you need to start from a baseline that considers the organization's level of maturity and aligns the IR program with the requirements and vision of the business.

A comprehensive IR program should include a policy, a plan, and playbooks of different incident types. You also need to align this program with other programs such as **business continuity** (**BC**) and **disaster recovery** (**DR**).

Establishing and correctly implementing these plans at the right time can make a difference in an organization's ability to recover from a security breach.

In this chapter, you will learn about the following topics:

- Creating IRPs
- Creating IR playbooks
- Testing IRPs and playbooks

Technical requirements

In case you haven't already, you need to download and install VMware Workstation Player from this link `https://www.vmware.com/products/workstation-player/workstation-player-evaluation.html`.

You'll also need to download the following from the book's official GitHub repository `https://github.com/PacktPublishing/Incident-Response-with-Threat-Intelligence`:

- Virtual machine:
  - IR-Laptop
- Lab file:
  - Chapter09

Creating IRPs

An IRP is a document that describes the procedures to follow in case of a security incident. The management area must support this document.

The IRP generally defines a route to follow when a security incident occurs. This plan must be consistent with existing organizational capacity, resources, and infrastructure.

The elements of an IRP are listed here:

- Mission
- Objectives and strategies
- Management approval
- The organization's position on IR
- Metrics to measure the capacity and efficiency of the plan

- Path to raise the maturity levels of the organization's IR capability

- Definition of alignment of the plan with the organization

This last point is crucial since one of the objectives of IR is to help in the BC process and the organization's operations.

This plan, as with any plan or policy, should be reviewed periodically (according to **National Institute of Standards and Technology (NIST)** recommendations, at least annually); this would allow procedures to be kept in place, considering that the circumstances of the environment and the threat landscape are highly dynamic and changing.

Another essential point to consider is that the affected organization needs to report incidents or interact with third parties outside the organization at any given time.

This communication may involve customers, providers of different services, regulatory or governmental entities, or even law enforcement, depending on the nature of the incident, as shown in the following screenshot:

Figure 9.1 – NIST model of communication with third parties

As you learned in *Chapter 2, Concepts of Digital Forensics and Incident Response*, these are the main steps for an IRP: *Prepare, Identify, Contain, Eradicate, Recover, and Learn.*

Different roles and responsibilities are defined, as follows:

- **Security operations center (SOC)**: This is the first line of defense, whereby staff are responsible for threat detection and triggering security alerts.

- **Incident manager**: Responsible for coordinating activities between stakeholders and determining the best plan of action.

- **Computer IR team**: They are responsible for following procedures and providing technical expertise.

These roles could be different depending on the size, characteristics, posture, and maturity level of the organization.

The structure of an IRP is fundamental as it should describe in general how to handle cybersecurity incidents.

To create an IRP, you must follow these steps:

1. Start the **IR-Laptop** VM using the following credentials:

   - **Username**: `investigator`

   - **Password**: `L34rn1ng!`

2. On the **IR-Laptop** VM, create a new folder under `C:\Users\Investigator\Desktop\Workspace\Labs\Chapter-9` called `IR_Plans_and_Playbooks`.

3. For this practice lab, we will use the template created by Sysnet. Just register and download the *Security Incident Response Plan* template from here: `https://sysnetgs.com/security-incident-response-plan-template/`.

   We will focus specifically on the following sections:
   - *Introduction*
   - *How to recognize a security incident*
   - *Roles and responsibilities*
   - *External contacts*
   - *Incident Response Plan Steps*
   - *Testing and Updates*

4. Review the content of the `CompanyInfo.pdf` file previously downloaded.

5. Open the `Security_Incident_Response_Plan_1.dotx` template and fill it with the appropriate information.

Upon completion, you will have created an IRP for the company. In the next section, you will learn how to create IR playbooks.

Creating IR playbooks

IR playbooks are detailed action plans that describe actions to be taken in specific security incidents. Unlike IRPs, these playbooks are more of the checklist type of actions for specific types of attacks such as phishing, information leaks, ransomware, **denial-of-service (DoS)** attacks, defacement of a website, and so on.

The components of an IR playbook could comprise the following:

- The condition that initiates an incident
- Workflow of steps to follow
- The incident completion status

There are several websites from where you can download IR playbook templates; these templates can be very useful, and you can use them as a basis to create your own playbooks.

Incident Playbook

Incident Playbook is a project created by the IR community to facilitate the creation of IR playbooks. You can view more details at this link: `https://github.com/austinsonger/Incident-Playbook`.

One interesting feature is that the playbooks seek to be aligned with the **MITRE Adversarial Tactics, Techniques, and Common Knowledge (ATT&CK)** framework, and the playbooks are classified by tactics.

This project is under development and considers the creation of catalogs for rare incidents, exercise scenarios, use of tools, process automation, and integrations with different platforms through **application programming interfaces (APIs)**.

An example of an IR playbook is playbook: `Phishing`, which you can find here: `https://github.com/austinsonger/Incident-Playbook/blob/main/Playbooks/MITRE-ATTACK/Initial%20Access/T1566-Phishing-(T1566.001-T1566.002-T1566.003).md`.

In this playbook, you will find a mapping to MITRE ATT&CK tactics and techniques/ sub-techniques, as shown in the following screenshot:

MITRE

Tactic	Technique ID	Technique Name	Sub-Technique Name	Platforms	Permissions Required
Initial Access	T1566	Phishing		Google Workspace, Linux, Office 365, SaaS, Windows, macOS	

Figure 9.2 – MITRE ATT&CK tactics and techniques mapped with the playbook

Additionally, you will find specific tasks to be performed in the different stages of IR (investigate, remediate, contain, eradicate).

The integration with Atomic Red Team for attack emulation is considered within its roadmap to test the playbooks.

Public Playbooks

Public Playbooks (`https://gitlab.com/syntax-ir/playbooks`) is a project that includes repositories of tasks and workflows and is based on the *NIST 800.61 r2* guide.

The playbooks are organized into categories such as **IRP-Malware** and **IRP-Ransom** and have references to products and tools.

To follow a playbook, proceed like so:

1. Select the category of the playbook—for example, IRP-Malware (`https://gitlab.com/syntax-ir/playbooks/-/tree/main/IRP-Malware`).
2. Click on a specific phase of the IR process. In this case, we will select **1. Preparation**, as shown in the following screenshot:

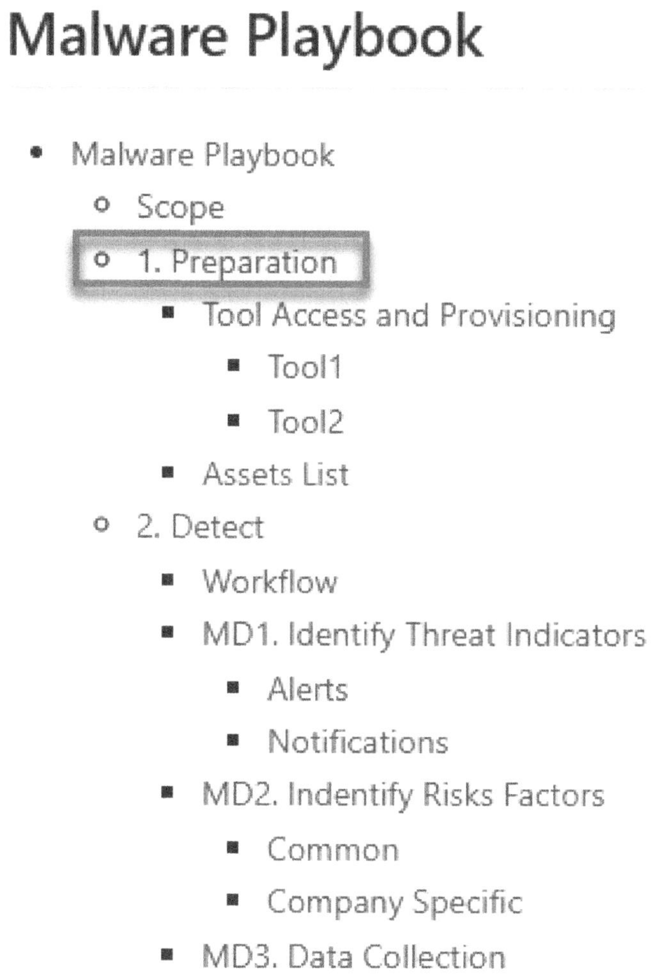

Malware Playbook

- Malware Playbook
  - Scope
  - 1. Preparation
    - Tool Access and Provisioning
      - Tool1
      - Tool2
    - Assets List
  - 2. Detect
    - Workflow
    - MD1. Identify Threat Indicators
      - Alerts
      - Notifications
    - MD2. Indentify Risks Factors
      - Common
      - Company Specific
    - MD3. Data Collection

Figure 9.3 – Selecting a phase or task of the IR process

3. Select **Expand** to see specific tasks of this process.

4. Scroll down to see the different stages of the playbook (**Preparation, Detect, Analyze**).

5. You will see the associated workflows—for example, in this case, the workflow to analyze malware, as shown in the following diagram:

Malware - Analyze

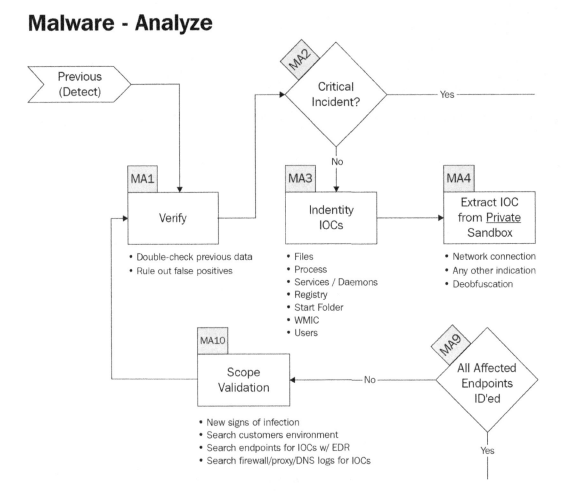

Figure 9.4 – Reviewing a playbook diagram

The advantage of these workflows is that you can download them directly from the container and customize them according to your own playbooks. Here's how to do this:

1. Open the Workflows section of the playbook.

2. Click on the Malware-Workflow.drawio file, as shown in the following screenshot:

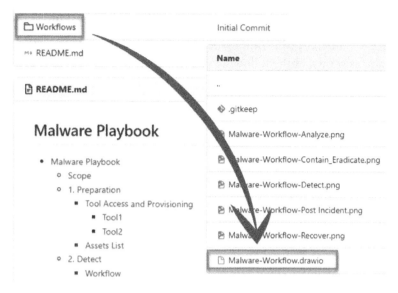

Figure 9.5 – Selecting a workflow diagram

3. Click on the download button, as shown in the following screenshot, and save the file in the `C:\Users\Investigator\Desktop\Workspace\Labs\Chapter-9\IR_Plans_and_Playbooks` path of your **IR-Laptop** VM:

Figure 9.6 – Downloading a workflow diagram

4. To edit the workflow template, open `draw.io` by clicking on the Windows taskbar shortcut, and then click on the **Open Existing Diagram** button, as shown in the following screenshot:

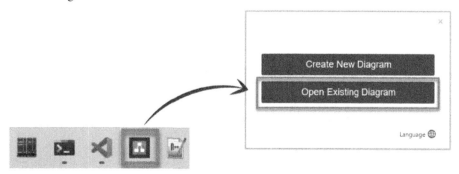

Figure 9.7 – Opening an existing diagram

5. Select the `Malware-Workflow.drawio` file and click the **Open** button.

You will see different workflows separated by tabs at the bottom of the `draw.io` program, as shown in the following screenshot:

Figure 9.8 – IR workflows' phases

This is also a project in development, so some playbooks may be incomplete or not have workflows assigned. The important thing is to collaborate with this type of project as much as possible to contribute to the community.

Ideally, these playbooks should be integrated into the organization's IR systems to automate the workflow and integrate tasks and assignments into the incident management system.

Now, we're going to create an IR playbook for an organization.

Scenario – An ounce of prevention is worth a pound of cure

On the dark web, one of the groups behind ransomware attacks publishes that they compromised an important insurance company. They claim they exfiltrated around 2 **terabytes** (**TB**) of information from different branches around the world. They threaten to publish this information if the company does not pay a ransom.

Shortly afterward, the company publicly confirms that they were victims of a ransomware attack and that several of their offices worldwide were affected, causing the interruption of some of their operations.

Internally, the company is working hard to ensure BC and reduce the impact. After the time limit elapses, the company decides not to pay the ransom and assumes the impact generated by this cybersecurity incident and information was made public.

You work at another insurance company, and the **board of directors** (**BOD**) is worried that this could happen to the company, so you are asked to start developing an IRP to respond to this kind of incident.

Creating IR playbooks

In this practice lab, we're going to create an integrated playbook from the *Ransomware Attack and Data Loss Incident Response* playbooks for the insurance company. These are the steps to follow:

1. First, create a new directory under `C:\Users\Investigator\Desktop\Workspace\Chapter-9` named `Playbooks`.

2. From *Public Playbooks* (`https://gitlab.com/syntax-ir/playbooks`), download the **IRP-Ransom** and **IRP-DataLoss** workflows in the same way you downloaded the previous workflow.

3. Open `draw.io` by clicking on the taskbar shortcut.

4. Click on the **Open Existing Diagram** button for every file.

5. Edit the workflows accordingly, integrating both into one.

6. Save your work.

As you learned, the development of IRPs and playbooks is an ongoing process and requires constant changes and validation in accordance with the environment and circumstances to ensure they are handy and functional.

Testing IRPs and playbooks

Once you have created an IRP and playbooks for different scenarios, it's time to validate them. The plans will always look spectacular on paper, but it is very important to check them to make sure they work, and it is best to test them before an actual incident happens.

Additionally, it is advisable to carry out periodic evaluations to identify possible gaps and make the corresponding adjustments; remember that threats evolve very quickly, and you probably need to adjust how to respond to new techniques or tools used by attackers.

I recommend you consider using *NIST Special Publication 800-84 Guide to Test, Training, and Exercise Programs for IT Plans and Capabilities* to create a formal testing plan. You can download it from here: `https://nvlpubs.nist.gov/nistpubs/Legacy/SP/nistspecialpublication800-84.pdf`.

This guide is structured into different phases, as follows:

*   *Establishing a Test, Training, and Exercise Program*

*   *Training Sessions*

*   *Tabletop Exercises*

- *Functional Exercises*
- *Tests*

Testing IRPs is critical; otherwise, there is a risk that they will not work correctly.

The results of these tests should lead to improved quality and effectiveness of the plans.

Simulation of attacks to measure response programs

Incident simulation exercises are an analogy of simulations that are carried out as part of preparations in case of natural disasters or fires and seek to measure the level of response of the organization to certain incidents.

The validation of plans must be performed at different levels by both executives and the IR team.

Types of security tests

There are several tools for simulating attacks under a Red Team or Purple Team approach, including **CALDERA** (https://www.mitre.org/research/technology-transfer/open-source-software/caldera%E2%84%A2) and **Atomic Red Team** (https://atomicredteam.io/). Within the security tests, the Purple Team exercises are the most integrated with different objectives, such as measuring detection and response capabilities.

Emulating behaviors with Atomic Red Team

To complete our labs, we are going to perform some atomic tests from the Atomic Red Team project (https://github.com/redcanaryco/atomic-red-team/wiki/Getting-Started).

Here's how to perform the tests:

1. Open a new **Windows Terminal console** on the **IR-Laptop** VM, right-clicking on the Windows Terminal icon and then clicking on Command Prompt, as shown in the following screenshot:

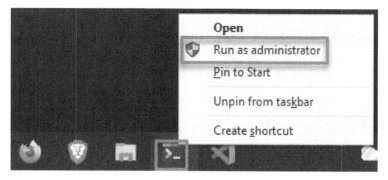

Figure 9.9 – Opening a new Windows Terminal console as administrator

2. This will open a **Windows Terminal/PowerShell** console, as this time we will work with a regular command console. Select the button with the down arrow to open a new tab with a **Command Prompt** console, as shown in the following screenshot:

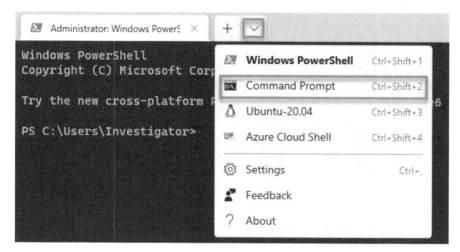

Figure 9.10 – Opening a new Command Prompt console

Both consoles are now open, and atomic tests can be run both in PowerShell and on the regular command line.

Conducting an atomic test

For this practice lab, we will use the `https://github.com/redcanaryco/atomic-red-team/blob/master/atomics/T1197/T1197.md` atomic test, which is mapped to the following MITRE ATT&CK tactic and technique:

- **Tactic: Defense Evasion**
- **Technique**: T1197 - BITS Jobs

Bitsadmin is a tool to create, download, and transfer jobs using the Windows **Background Intelligent Transfer Service (BITS)**. Bitsadmin is a legitimate tool that threat actors can use to download or transfer malicious files or even hide them using **Alternate Data Streams (ADS)**, so it is considered a **Living of the Land Binary (LoLBin)** tool.

There are four atomic tests related to emulating this behavior, as listed here:

- **Atomic Test #1 - Bitsadmin Download (cmd)**
- **Atomic Test #2 - Bitsadmin Download (PowerShell)**
- **Atomic Test #3 - Persist, Download, & Execute**
- **Atomic Test #4 - Bits download using desktopimgdownldr.exe (cmd)**

In this case, we will run the **Atomic Test #3 - Persist, Download, & Execute** atomic test. We'll proceed as follows:

1. First, we need to identify the inputs needed for the test. You can see these inputs in the following screenshot:

Name	Description	Type	Default Value
command_path	Path of command to execute	path	C:\Windows\system32\notepad.exe
bits_job_name	Name of BITS job	string	AtomicBITS
local_file	Local file path to save downloaded file	path	%temp%\bitsadmin3_flag.ps1
remote_file	Remote file to download	url	https://raw.githubusercontent.com/redcanaryco/atomic-red-team/master/atomics/T1197/T1197.md

Figure 9.11 – Inputs table for the atomic tests

2. To run the tests, simply replace the command-line parameter that corresponds to the inputs shown in *Figure 9.13*. Here's an example of how to do this:

```
bitsadmin.exe /setnotifycmdline #{bits_job_name}
#{command_path} NULL
```

3. The command would then be executed as follows:

```
bitsadmin.exe /setnotifycmdline AtomicBITS C:\Windows\
system32\notepad.exe NULL
```

4. In the Windows Command Prompt console, run the following commands by substituting the values defined in the inputs table:

```
bitsadmin.exe /create #{bits_job_name}
bitsadmin.exe /addfile #{bits_job_name} #{remote_file}
#{local_file}
bitsadmin.exe /setnotifycmdline #{bits_job_name}
#{command_path} NULL
bitsadmin.exe /resume #{bits_job_name}
timeout 5
bitsadmin.exe /complete #{bits_job_name}
```

5. To clean up the previous actions, run the following command:

```
del #{local_file} >nul 2>&1
```

6. These commands should be run as shown in the following screenshot:

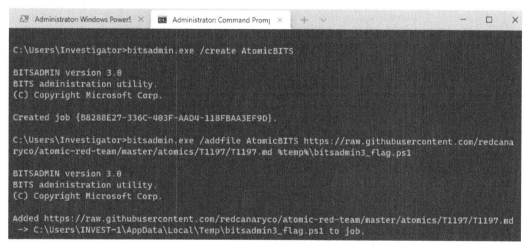

Figure 9.12 – Commands to run the atomic tests

This action should have generated an alert if it is not a regular activity of daily operations within the company's infrastructure. If no alert was triggered, it might mean there is a blind spot in detecting activity related to downloading tools or malicious programs from the internet.

On the other hand, we can use the information we gathered before and make it actionable.

If these exercises are performed on a regular basis, the organization's detection and response capacity will be substantially improved.

Testing an IRP using MITRE ATT&CK

Another way you can test your playbooks is by using MITRE ATT&CK to map simulated malicious activities according to specific attack scenarios. In this case, for example, we are going to simulate different techniques used by a threat actor in a ransomware attack. Follow these next steps:

1. On the **IR-Laptop** VM, open a web browser and navigate to the MITRE ATT&CK Navigator tool (`https://mitre-attack.github.io/attack-navigator/`).

2. Download the MITRE ATT&CK `ransomware.json` file (ransomware campaign) from the `Chapter-9` folder of the book's repository.

3. From the ATT&CK Navigator tool, select the **Open Existing Layer** link and then **Upload from local**, then select the `ransomware.json` file to upload the file from your **IR-Laptop** VM, as shown in the following screenshot:

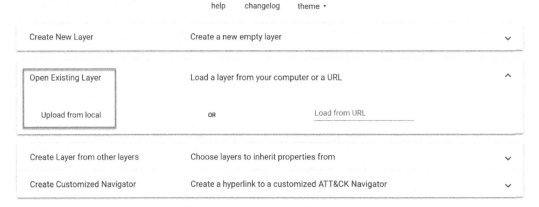

Figure 9.13 – Uploading a layer file to MITRE ATT&CK Navigator

> **Note**
> You can also access this map directly using the **Load from URL** option.

4. Identify different tactics and techniques described on the layer and look for atomic tests that can be performed using Atomic Red Team atomic tests from the *Windows Atomic Tests by ATT&CK Tactic & Technique* section (`https://github.com/redcanaryco/atomic-red-team/blob/master/atomics/Indexes/Indexes-Markdown/windows-index.md`).

5. Perform the tests on the **IR-Laptop** VM.

6. Identify and associate each atomic test with the *Ransomware Attack and Data Loss Incident Response* playbook you created earlier.

As a result of this lab, you were able to evaluate the *Ransomware Attack and Data Loss Incident Response* playbook you previously created, using the atomic test-based attack emulation exercises.

Summary

In this chapter, we learned how to assess an organization's IR capacity.

We also learned how to create an IRP considering the business's characteristics and develop playbooks with actions to respond to specific incidents.

Finally, we learned how to perform atomic tests that allow us to emulate attacks and thus identify threat detection blind spots and evaluate the effectiveness of IRPs.

In the next chapter, you will learn how to implement and use an **IR system** (**IRS**).

Further reading

To learn more on the topic, consult the following resources:

- *NIST Special Publication 800-61 Computer Security Incident Handling Guide* `https://nvlpubs.nist.gov/nistpubs/SpecialPublications/NIST.SP.800-61r2.pdf`

- *Cyber Security Incident Response Guide* `https://www.crest-approved.org/wp-content/uploads/CSIR-Procurement-Guide-1.pdf`

- *What is an Incident Response Plan and How to Create One* `https://www.varonis.com/blog/incident-response-plan/`

- *NIST Incident Response Plan: Building Your Own IR Process Based on NIST Guidelines* `https://www.cynet.com/incident-response/nist-incident-response/`

- *Incident Response Planning Guideline* https://security.berkeley.edu/incident-response-planning-guideline

- *How to build an incident response playbook* https://swimlane.com/blog/incident-response-playbook

- *Trial Before the Fire: How to Test Your Incident Response Plan to Ensure Consistency and Repeatability* https://www.cpomagazine.com/cyber-security/trial-before-the-fire-how-to-test-your-incident-response-plan-to-ensure-consistency-and-repeatability/

- *Best Practices for Testing Your Cyber Incident Response Plan* https://blog.rsisecurity.com/best-practices-for-testing-your-cyber-incident-response-plan/

- *Test your visibility into the top 10 ATT&CK techniques* https://redcanary.com/blog/top-atomic-red-team-tests/

10
Implementing an Incident Management System

An incident management system is a core component of the incident response process. Documentation and activity management allow the timely monitoring of each of the phases and facilitate decision making.

Fortunately, there are multiple incident management systems on the market, both open source and commercial, so you can make a diagnosis of the capabilities within the organization to then choose which is the best option.

TheHive is not just an incident ticketing system; this platform includes, among other things, case management capabilities, playbook integration, access to external intelligence sources through the tool known as **Cortex**, and support for MITRE ATT&CK, among other things.

In this chapter, you will learn how to use TheHive as an incident management system and we will cover the following topics:

- Understanding the TheHive architecture
- Setting up TheHive and creating cases
- Creating and managing cases
- Integrating intelligence with Cortex

Technical requirements

In case you haven't already, you need to download and install VMware Workstation Player from this link `https://www.vmware.com/products/workstation-player/workstation-player-evaluation.html`.

To access additional resources described in this chapter, you can visit the official GitHub repository of this book: `https://github.com/PacktPublishing/Incident-Response-with-Threat-Intelligence`.

You will need to download the Demo Virtual Machine with the latest versions of TheHive and Cortex by clicking on `https://marketing.strangebee.com/thehive-cortex-demo-virtual-machine` and completing the form with your information, as shown in the following screenshot:

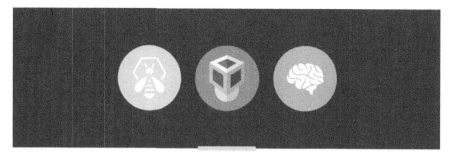

Figure 10.1 – Download of TheHive virtual machine

Once you've finished the registration, you will receive an email with the link to download the **virtual machine (VM)**.

> **Note**
> You can also download the VM used in this book from the book's VMs repository: `https://github.com/PacktPublishing/Incident-Response-with-Threat-Intelligence.`

To start using this virtual pre-installed version of TheHive, you need to import the downloaded `.ova` file using VMware Workstation Player by following these steps:

1. Click on the **Open Virtual Machine** option.

2. Click on the **Browse** button, name it `IR-TheHive`, and define the path where you want to import the VM.

3.　Click the **Import** button.

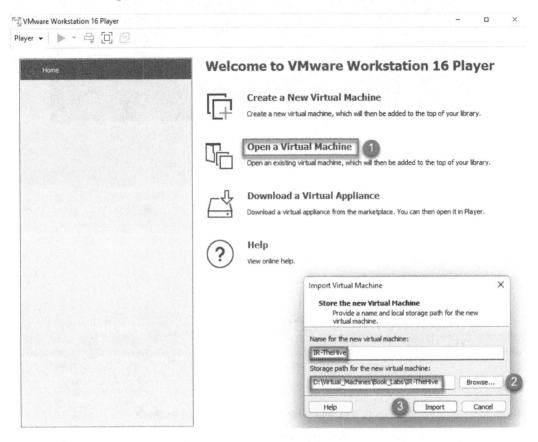

Figure 10.2 – Importing the .ova file

You might receive the following warning dialog box. If that's the case, just click the **Retry** button to continue with the importation process, as you can see in the following figure:

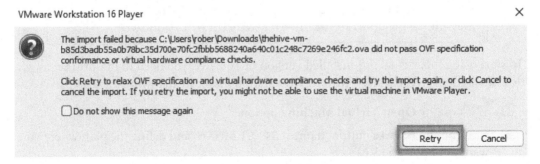

Figure 10.3 – Warning compatibility error message

> **Note**
>
> This warning appeared because the file does not comply with the OVF specification; however, this won't have an impact on the normal operation of the VM.

4. Once you finish the import process, start the VM and you will see the following message, which shows the IP address assigned to TheHive (it is configured to use a DHCP address, so you will see a different IP address in every case):

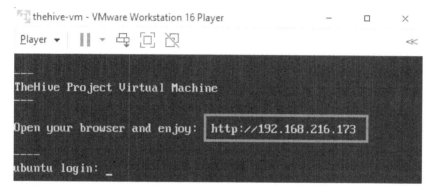

Figure 10.4 – TheHive VM initialized

You can connect to the TheHive dashboard from any browser to the IP address that appears on the virtual machine. You can configure different services and components of TheHive from the command line.

Now, let's review the architecture of TheHive and the functionalities of its components.

Understanding the TheHive architecture

TheHive is a scalable and modular incident management platform that can be installed in a standalone or a cluster distributed environment. Before the installation in a production environment, is very important to define the architecture according to the capacity needs of your organization.

For this module, we will use a preinstalled version of TheHive in a VM to focus specifically on the functionality and capacities of the product. You can consult the project's documentation for installation and configuration at the following link: https://docs.thehive-project.org/thehive/.

The incident management platform is composed of three components:

- **TheHive**: The incident and case management platform
- **Cortex**: An engine for observable analysis and response using threat intelligence
- **TheHive4**: A Python API client to expand the functionality to external sources

The architecture of TheHive and Cortex is developed as follows:

- AngularJS and Bootstrap for the frontend
- Scala, Akka, and Play on the backend
- Elasticsearch for the storage
- Python-based analyzers
- REST APIs for communication

The following figure shows the interaction between the different components of TheHive:

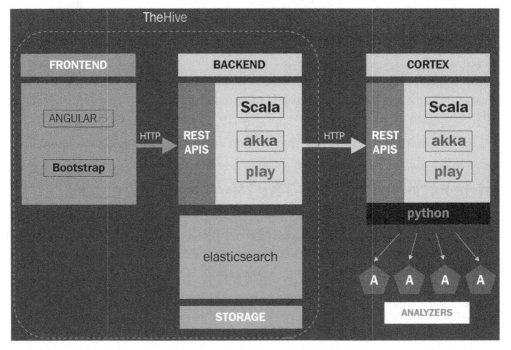

Figure 10.5 – TheHive architecture

The hardware requirements of TheHive and its components will depend, among other things, on the volume of data that is required to be processed. It is recommended to perform a diagnosis to consider the variables of each environment.

Setting up TheHive and creating cases

The first thing you should do before using TheHive is to customize the settings of the VM. To do this, provide the credentials that are configured by default using the following steps:

1. To connect to TheHive, you just need to navigate from your computer using a web browser to the same IP address assigned to your VM before. For instance, in this case, the IP assigned for me is `http://192.168.216.173/`.

   You will see the following interface where you can connect to the platform using the predefined user account and passwords and review the documentation about how to use TheHive virtual machine.

   Click on the link to open TheHive under the **Quick connect** section, as shown in the following screenshot:

Figure 10.6 – TheHive Project Virtual Machine main page

2. Use the default credentials to log in as administrator – in this case, `admin@thehive.local/secret` – and click the **Sign In** button, as shown in the following figure:

Figure 10.7 – TheHive login web page

The virtual machine comes with two organizations configured by default, **admin** and **demo**. The **admin** organization is prepared to configure the platform with special administrative privileges, while, on the other hand, the **demo** organization is preconfigured as an organization for testing purposes.

3. We are going to create a new organization, as shown in the following screenshot:

- On TheHive's main dashboard, click on the **New Organisation** button.

- On the opened dialog window, write the name and description of your organization. In this case, write the following parameters:

  - **Name**: `IR Labs`

  - **Description**: `Practice Lab Organisation`

  Click the **Save** button

Figure 10.8 – Creating a new organization

4. Once you create the new organization, it will appear on the bottom-left side of the **Organisations** panel. To configure the parameters for the new organization, click the **Configure** button, as shown in the following screenshot:

Figure 10.9 – Organization configuration

You can create the users that will operate the server and assign them a specific profile:

- **admin**: Can manage all the organization objects and users but can't create cases

- **analyst**: Can create and manage cases and the related objects as tasks, observables, and TTPs

- **read-only**: Can't create or modify objects and cases

5. To add a new user, click on the **Create New User** button. Fill in the following parameters:

- **Login**: investigator@gosecurity.ninja

- **Full Name**: Investigator

- **Profile**: analyst

Now, click the **Save user** button.

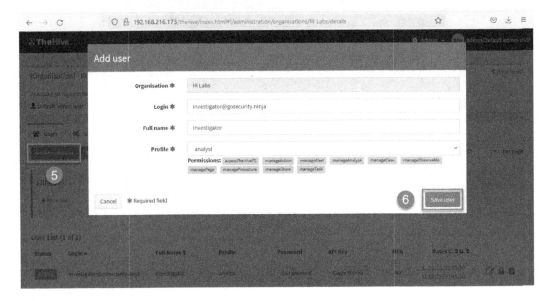

Figure 10.10 – Add user dialog box

Once you've created the new user, it will appear on the **Organization details** panel.

6. Change the password by clicking below the **Password** field, write the password L34rn1ng!, and click the green checkmark icon to save it (you can also assign an **API Key** if you want, following the same procedure).

User List (1 of 1)

Figure 10.11 – Creating a new password

There are more platform configurations that can be done here, but in this case, we will only make these changes for the time being.

7. To log out from the organization configuration panel, just click on the user profile button, at the upper right, and then click the **Logout** button, as shown in the following screenshot:

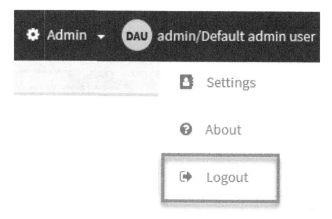

Figure 10.12 – Logging out of the organisation configuration panel

Now that we have created a new organization and added a new user, it's time to work with incident response cases.

Creating and managing cases

Incident response cases are the space where you can manage security incidents. Here, you can create cases in several ways:

- Manually
- Automatized
- Based on playbooks

In this part, we will cover the creation of new cases manually.

Log in to the main page of TheHive using the credentials of the new user created:

- Username: `investigator@gosecurity.ninja`
- Password: `L34rn1ng!`

When starting the session, you will see the main panel with the list of added cases. In this case, none will appear because you have just created the organization, as shown in the following screenshot:

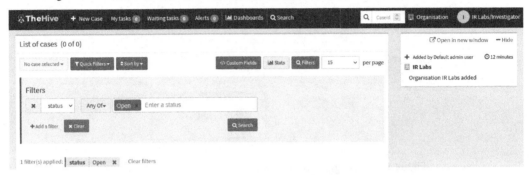

Figure 10.13 – List of cases on the main page

The scenario for our case is that the **Security Operation Center SOC** detected a new ransomware attack in one of the branches around the world. You will open a new case to start with the procedures related to this security incident.

To create a new case for this incident, follow these steps:

1. Click on the **+ New Case** button at the top left of the cases panel.

2. In the **Create a new case** window, fill in the fields using the following parameters under the **Case details** section:

    - **Title**: Ransomware Incident

    - **Severity**: High (**H**)

    - **TLP**: High (**RED**) – This parameter means **Traffic Light Protocol**, and indicates the restriction level to share information with others.

- **PAP**: High (**RED**) – This parameter means **Permissible Actions Protocol** and indicates to the analyst how to use IoCs in investigating the alert.

- **Tags**: **ransomware**, **malware**, **databreach**

- **Description**: Incident Response case related to a Ransomware attack and possible data breach.

3.   Click the + **Create case** button.

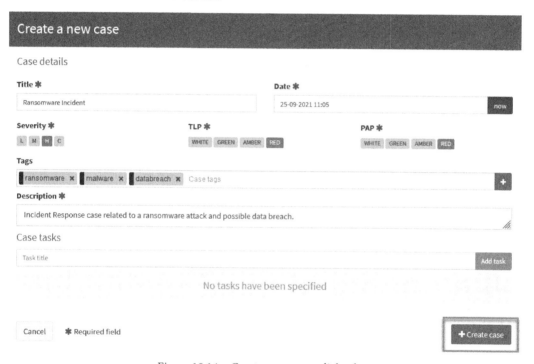

Figure 10.14 – Create a new case dialog box

You will see the details of the new case created, as shown in the following screenshot:

Figure 10.15 – General details of a case

Now that the case is created, the next step is to add the tasks or procedures based on the incident response plan or playbook related to ransomware incidents.

Adding and assigning tasks

In this case, we will add a task related to the process to do the triage and collect artifacts of the compromised systems:

1. In the **Tasks** section, click the **+Add Task** button, as shown in the following screenshot:

Figure 10.16 – Adding a new task

2. Under the **List of tasks** section, fill in the following parameters:

- **Group task**: Detection and Analysis
- **Task**: Triage and artifacts collection

Click the green checkmark button to save the task:

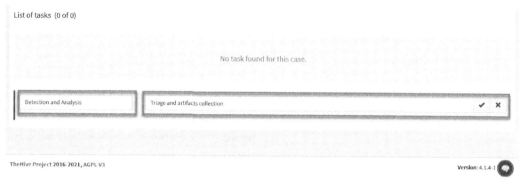

Figure 10.17 – Creating a new task

3. At the bottom of the page, you will see the new task created and you can assign it to who will be responsible for completing it. To do this, click on the button under the **Assignee** parameter and select **IR Labs/Investigator**, which corresponds to the organization and users you created, as shown in the following screenshot:

Figure 10.18 – Assigning tasks

You added a new task and assigned it to the user **Investigator**. This user will now be able to start working and documenting everything related to that activity.

To start working on this task, you need to do the following:

1. Navigate to the **Tasks** panel on the toolbar at the top.

2. Select the task to work on.

3. Click on the + **Add new task log** button.

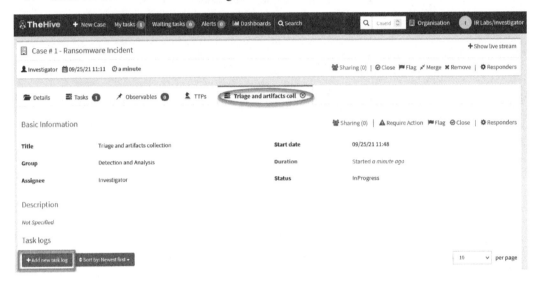

Figure 10.19 – Adding task logs

You will see the **Tasks logs** panel, where you can register the information related to this task.

4. Under the **Task logs section**, write the following details:

```
Collecting memory dumps and forensic artifacts from the
following computers:
```
```
HR-034-SP
```
```
AD-010-BA
```
```
RD-052-SP
```
```
MG-045-NY
```

5. Click the **Add log** button.

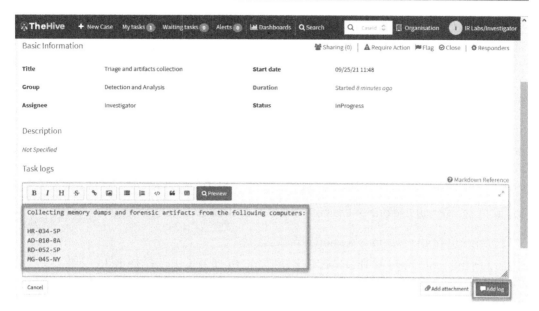

Figure 10.20 – Providing details regarding a task

You can add as many log entries as necessary and can add not just text; you can also add files and images when working on this task.

In the next part, you will learn how to create a case based on an incident response playbook.

Creating playbook case templates

TheHive allows you to create case templates based on incident response playbooks. In *Chapter 9*, *Creating Incident Response Plans and Playbooks*, we mentioned Austin Songer's project, `https://github.com/austinsonger/Incident-Playbook`, about creating incident response playbooks and how they can be mapped with the MITRE ATT&CK framework.

For our practical exercise, we will use the playbook related to ransomware incidents documented at `https://github.com/austinsonger/Incident-Playbook/blob/main/Playbooks/MITRE-ATTACK/Impact/T1486-Data-Encrypted-for-Impact-Ransomware.md`, assuming that the attack has already materialized, partially or totally.

> **Note**
> The best strategy is to identify and respond to attacks at an early stage, but in the same way, we must assume that in some cases, the attacker could evade our detection and protection systems. That's why it's important to create incident response playbooks for the different phases of an attack.

To create case templates based on incident response playbooks on TheHive, you must be signed in with **org-admin** privileges (you can see more details about roles and permissions here: `https://docs.thehive-project.org/thehive/user-guides/organisation-managers/organisations-users-sharing/`).

In this case, we will use one of the pre-configured users of TheHive virtual machine:

1. Log out of the previous session if necessary.
2. On the main page of TheHive, sign in using the following credentials:

   • **Login**: `thehive@thehive.local`
   • **Password**: `thehive1234`

   This is shown in the following figure:

Figure 10.21 – Signing in to TheHive

3. Click on the **Organisation** button.

4. Select the **Case Templates** tab.

5. Click on the **New template** button.

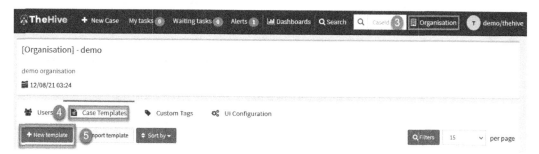

Figure 10.22 – Creating a new case template

6. In the **Create a new case** window, fill in the fields using the following parameters under the **Case Details** section:

- **Template name**: Ransomware Playbook

- **Display name**: Ransomware attack

- **Title prefix**: 001

- **Severity**: High (**H**)

- **TLP**: High (**RED**) – This parameter means Traffic Light Protocol, and indicates the restriction level to share information with others

- **PAP**: High (**RED**) – This parameter means Permissible Actions Protocol, and indicates to the analyst how to use IoCs in investigating the alert.

- **Tags**: **ransomware**, **malware**

- **Title prefix**: Playbook for Ransomware Attacks

Click on the **Save template** button. The complete information is shown in the following screenshot:

Figure 10.23 – Adding the details to a case template

Once we've created the template, we will add the tasks that we previously created in the ransomware incident response playbook.

7.   Select the **Tasks** tab and click on the **Add task** button, as shown in the following screenshot:

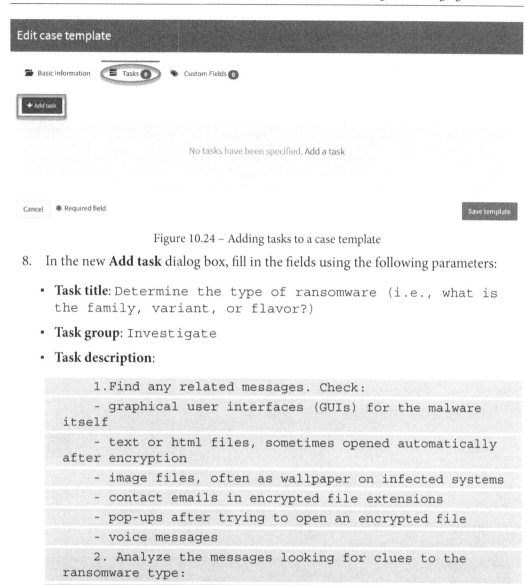

Figure 10.24 – Adding tasks to a case template

8. In the new **Add task** dialog box, fill in the fields using the following parameters:

- **Task title**: `Determine the type of ransomware (i.e., what is the family, variant, or flavor?)`

- **Task group**: `Investigate`

- **Task description**:

```
   1.Find any related messages. Check:

   - graphical user interfaces (GUIs) for the malware
itself

   - text or html files, sometimes opened automatically
after encryption

   - image files, often as wallpaper on infected systems

   - contact emails in encrypted file extensions

   - pop-ups after trying to open an encrypted file

   - voice messages

   2. Analyze the messages looking for clues to the
ransomware type:

   - ransomware name

   - language, structure, phrases, artwork

   - contact email
```

- **Assignee**: Click on the list and select the **thehive** user.

Click on the **Add task** button.

The complete information is shown in the following screenshot:

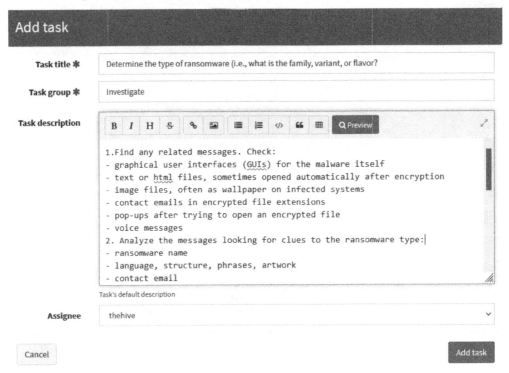

Figure 10.25 – Adding the task details

9. Once you've saved the new task, you will be returned to the **Edit case template** dialog box, and you will be able to observe the task you created, as you can see in the following screenshot:

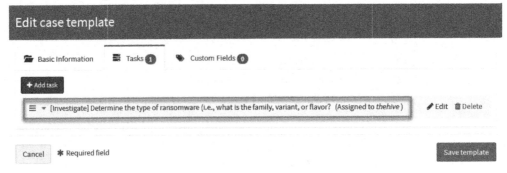

Figure 10.26 – Reviewing the added task

10. Add the rest of the tasks of the **Investigation** section from the **Playbook: Ransomware** `https://github.com/austinsonger/Incident-Playbook/blob/main/Playbooks/MITRE-ATTACK/Impact/T1486-Data-Encrypted-for-Impact-Ransomware.md`

    - *2. Determine the scope*

    - *3. Assess the impact*

    - *4. Find the infection vector*

11. Once you have finished adding the tasks that are defined in the playbook, click on the **Save template** button.

    Once we've created the case template based on the incident response playbook, we can use it when creating a new case.

    Let's use this template now by creating a new incident response case about a ransomware incident.

12. Click on the **New Case** button in the main menu, as shown in the following screenshot:

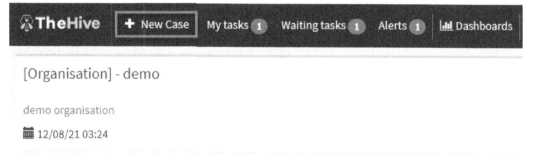

Figure 10.27 – Creating a new case

In the **Create new Case** dialog box, you will see the template recently created. If you do not see it, you can refresh the web page to clear the cache and load the new information.

13. Click on the **Ransomware attack** template under the **Select a template** section, as shown in the following figure:

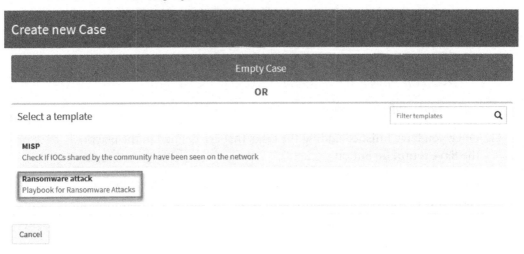

Figure 10.28 – Selecting a template to create the new case

In the **Create a new case** dialog box, you will see the information previously captured when you created the template, as well as the added tasks of the playbook. You can update or modify that information if necessary.

14. Fill in the **Title** field with the case name **Ransomware related security incident**, as shown in the following screenshot:

Figure 10.29 – Adding details to the new case template

15. Click on the **Create case** button.

16. Click on the **TheHive** main button and you will see the new case under **List of cases**, as shown in the following screenshot:

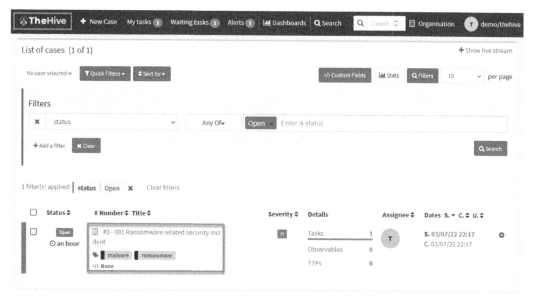

Figure 10.30 – Selecting the created case

You can now manage the case, selecting and assigning tasks to the incident responders and collaborators.

17. To start managing the case, click on the **001 Ransomware related security incident** case.

18. Click on the **Tasks** tab.

Under this tab, you will see the list of tasks based on the ransomware template created previously. Here, you can edit, add, or delete tasks according to the context of this case or assign the activities as appropriate, as shown in the following screenshot:

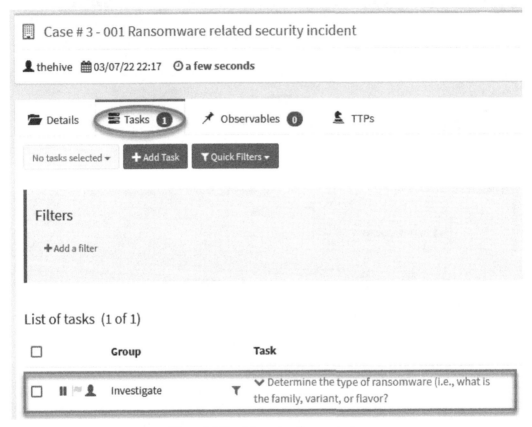

Figure 10.31 – Managing the case tasks

The best practice is to create incident response playbooks, as you learned to do in *Chapter 9, Creating Incident Response Plans and Playbooks*, and then integrate them into incident management platforms to act quickly and efficiently the moment they occur.

In the next part, you will learn how to add indicators of compromise related to a particular incident.

Adding observables

When you are working on an incident, it's very important to include information about **Indicators of Compromise (IoCs)** or **Indicators of Attack (IoAs)** as they are found. Take these steps to do this:

1. Navigate to the **Observables** panel.

2. Click the **+ Add observable(s)** button.

Figure 10.32 – Adding observables

This will open the **Create new observable(s) window**. Here you can add the details for any IoC found.

Fill in the fields with the following parameters:

*   **Type**: **hash**

*   **Value**: `561cffbaba71a6e8cc1cdceda990ead4`

*   **TLP**: **RED**

*   **Is IOC**: Checked

*   **Tags**: **malware**, **ransomware**, **hash**

*   **Description**: `Suspicious executable`

Click the + **Create observable(s)** button.

Figure 10.33 – Providing observables' details

3. The term *observable* is related to **IoC** or **IoA**. The idea here is to have a central repository where analysts can share intelligence and make it actionable.

   This is a powerful feature of TheHive because you can use Cortex running different analyzers. We are going to review this in more detail in the following section, where we will cover the functionality of Cortex.

   To get intelligence provided from Cortex, you just need to run the preconfigured analyzers. The analyzers are tools that connect to external sources of intelligence through APIs.

   Navigate to the **Observables** section.

4. Select the observable that you want to analyze – in this case, the hash that we added previously.

5. Click the **1 selected observable** button.

6. Click on the **Run analyzers** button, as shown in the following screenshot:

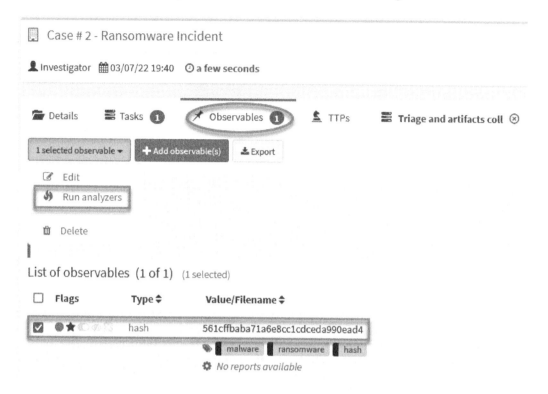

Figure 10.34 – Running analyzers for an observable

7. The **Analyzer observable(s)** window will open, and the external intelligence sources will be displayed. Depending on the observable, different sources of information may appear.

8. Select the sources from which you want to get intelligence.

9. Click the **Run selected analyzers** button.

10. In this case, you can select the following intelligence sources: **Maltiverse_ Report_1_0**, **TeamCymruMHR_1_0**, and **CIRCLHashlookup_1_0**, as shown in the following screenshot:

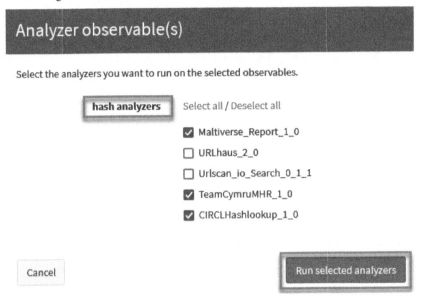

Figure 10.35 – Selecting specific analyzers

Now, wait a few moments for the analyzers to look for the information. The results will appear at the bottom of the observable in blue labels, as shown in the following screenshot:

Figure 10.36 – Results of running the analysis process

If no matches are found with those indicators, you can try with other intelligence sources.

If this indicator was seen before, you will view the context details and know if it is related to a campaign or known malicious actors. In this case, this hash is related to a malware sample, so we will get more details about this threat.

11. Click on the **Maltiverse:Report="n/a"** tag and you will see the details of the results of this analysis, as shown in the following screenshot:

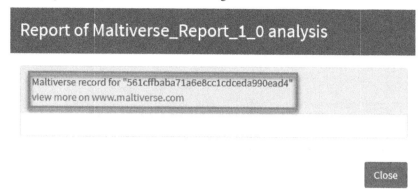

Figure 10.37 – Reviewing the analysis details

12. Copy the hash value to the clipboard and open a new tab on your web browser to navigate to the maltiverse web page: `https://www.maltiverse.com/`.

13. Paste the hash value of the malicious file into the **Search engine** textbox and then click on the **Search** button, as shown in the following screenshot:

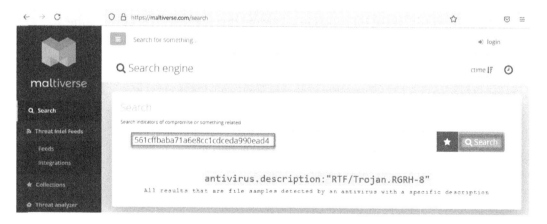

Figure 10.38 – Investigating an Indicator of Compromise (IoC)

On the **Search result** panel, you will see the name(s) of the file along with additional information, as shown in the following screenshot:

Search result

revil.exe,agent.exe
created **8 months ago** / modified **8 months ago**
Generic.Malware - Abuse.ch

md5: 561cffbaba71a6e8cc1cdceda990ead4

« ‹ 1 › »

Figure 10.39 – Reviewing the details of the results

14. Click on the name of the file(s).

You will see additional information regarding this malware, for instance, the number of antivirus detections, IDS alerts, processes, HTTP events, contacted hosts, and DNS requests. Scroll down the web page to see the antivirus positives, as shown in the following screenshot:

Antivirus positives

Antivirus	Threat
Elastic	malicious (high confidence)
MicroWorld-eScan	Gen:Variant.Graftor.952042
McAfee	Artemis!561CFFBABA71
Cylance	Unsafe
Cybereason	malicious.aba71a
Cyren	W32/Agent.DCD.gen!Eldorado
Symantec	Downloader
ESET-NOD32	Win32/Filecoder.Sodinokibi.N
Paloalto	generic.ml
Kaspersky	HEUR:Trojan-Ransom.Win32.Gen.gen
BitDefender	Gen:Variant.Graftor.952042
Avast	Win32:DangerousSig [Trj]
Ad-Aware	Gen:Variant.Graftor.952042
Sophos	Troj/Ransom-GIQ
TrendMicro	Ransom.Win32.SODINOKIBI.AUWUJDFJ
McAfee-GW-Edition	Artemis!Trojan
FireEye	Generic.mg.561cffbaba71a6e8
Emsisoft	Gen:Variant.Graftor.952042 (B)

Figure 10.40 – Reviewing the antivirus detections

As you can see, there are detections referencing the threat as belonging to the Sodinokibi Ransomware family. Additionally, you can also search other intelligence sources, such as VirusTotal (`https://www.virustotal.com/`) and VirusBay (`https://www.virusbay.io/`).

In a cybersecurity incident, you will find different IoCs, and in the same way as you did with the hash value, you can add observables and analyze them as URLs, IP addresses, filenames, or Windows Registry keys, among other things.

At this point, we have valuable information that will allow us to search for this IoC on other devices.

However, in a cybersecurity incident, the context is also very important. In *Chapter 6, Understanding the Cyber Kill Chain and the MITRE ATT&CK Framework*, you became familiar with the MITRE ATT&CK framework. In the next part, you will learn how to document potential malicious behaviors (TTPs) in TheHive.

Documenting MITRE ATT&CK TTPs in TheHive

Another useful feature included in this version of TheHive is the integration with MITRE ATT&CK and the capability to add TTPs.

When you identify an IoA, you can directly map it with its corresponding technique/sub technique.

To add a new TTP, follow these steps:

1. Navigate to the **TTPs** panel at the top of the case toolbar.
2. Click the + **Add TTP** button.

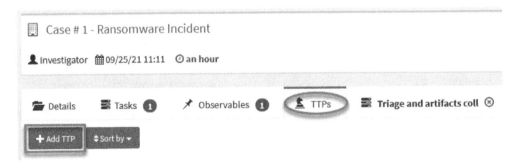

Figure 10.41 – Adding MITRE ATT&CK TTPs

3. In the **Add Tactic, Technique and Procedure** window, complete the fields with the following parameters:

    - **Tactic: Execution**
    - **Sub Technique: T1059.001 – Command and Scripting Interpreter: PowerShell**

    Click on the **Add TTP** button.

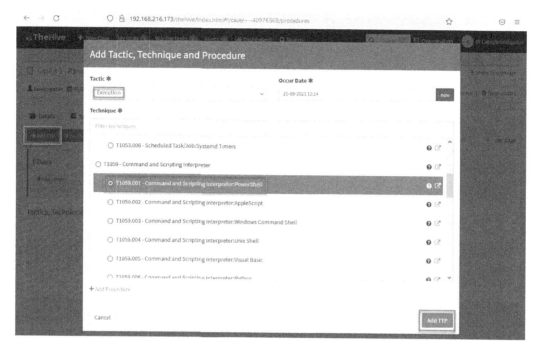

Figure 10.42 – Add Tactic, Technique and Procedure dialog box

At this point, you initiated a new security incident case and performed the following activities:

- You created a new case related to a security incident.

- You created a new task and assigned it to an analyst.

- You created a new entry for an observable and ran an analysis for intelligence information.

- You added a new TTP entry associated with the behavior of the attacker.

To view the dashboard with the key information about your cases, do the following:

1.   Click on the **TheHive** logo at the top left of the main panel.

2.   Click on the **Stats** button at the top right.

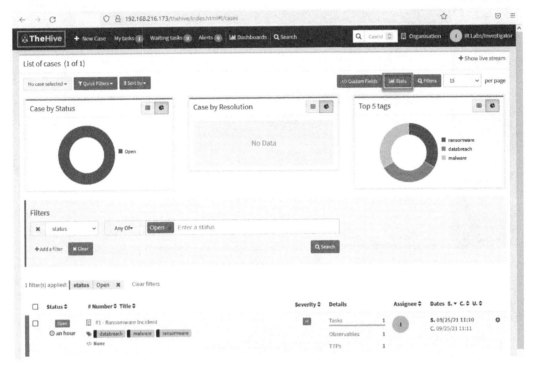

Figure 10.43 – TheHive case main dashboard

You will see information as shown in the preceding screenshot:

- **Case by Status**

- **Case by Resolution**

- Categories of cases by tag

- The list of cases with details

    You can customize this dashboard according to your preferences and needs if you log in as an organization administrator.

In the following section, you will learn in more detail how to configure the main functions of Cortex, the intelligence component of TheHive.

Integrating intelligence with Cortex

As was mentioned at the beginning of the chapter, Cortex is a powerful engine to analyze observables and get intelligence from external sources.

The integration of TheHive and Cortex allows you to get threat intelligence information from different sources without having to change to different platforms. As you learned in the previous part, you only need to register an observable and select the analyzers where the information will be searched.

Also, you can integrate Cortex with other threat intelligence platforms such as the **Malware Information Sharing Project** (**MISP**). The following diagram shows the way this integration can be done:

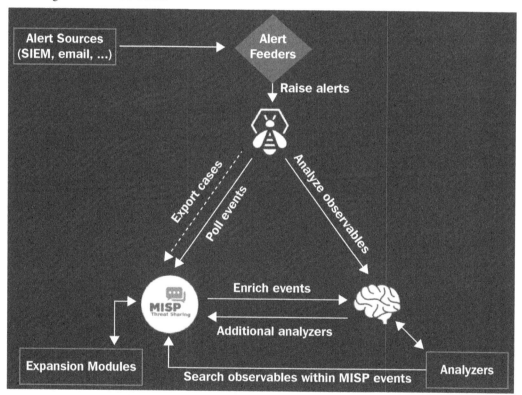

Figure 10.44 – TheHive integration with Cortex and MISP

It is also possible to initiate cases in an automated way by receiving alerts from different sources such as SIEMs and emails. This feature will be seen in the next chapter.

Configuring the analyzers

One of the features that you can configure in Cortex is the analyzers. The steps to configure analyzers are as follows:

1. Log in to the Cortex portal using the default `orgadmin` credentials, `thehive/thehive1234`, provided with the VM, as shown in the following screenshot:

Figure 10.45 – Cortex login page

2. On the main panel, you will see **Jobs History**, which shows the most recent analysis processed from TheHive or directly here and the results of those processes, as shown in the following screenshot:

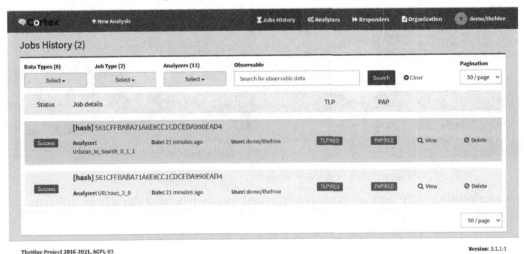

Figure 10.46 – Cortex Jobs History main page

Here, you can filter the analysis by **Data Types**, **Job Type**, and **Analyzers**, search by **Observable**, and delete a specific job.

3. Now, we will review the configuration of the analyzers included with Cortex. Click on the **Analyzers** button on the toolbar at the top of the main panel. You will see the list of analyzers enabled for this organization, as shown in the following screenshot:

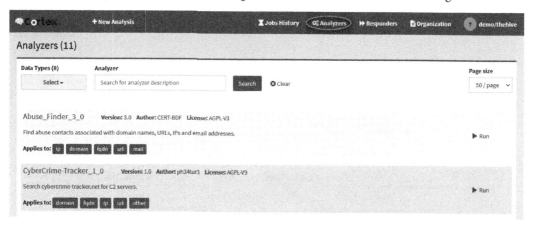

Figure 10.47 – Cortext-enabled Analyzers panel

4. If you want to enable or disable analyzers, you need to log off and then log on again by using the following administrator credentials: `admin/thehive1234`.

5. On the toolbar, select the **Organization** button.

6. Select the **Analyzers panel**.

Under the **Analyzer** section, you will see the list of analyzers, and on the right, the option to enable or disable them.

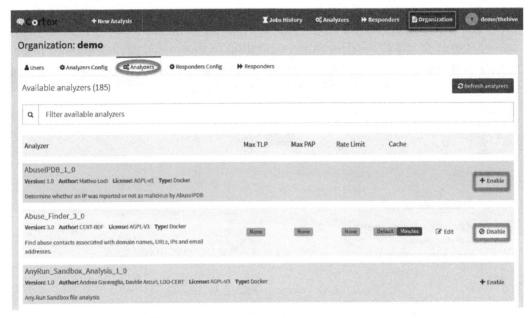

Figure 10.48 – Cortex Analyzers configuration panel

It's important to mention that some analyzers will require an API key, so before you can enable them, you will need to provide the required information.

> **Note**
> You can integrate additional analyzers such as VirusTotal, DomainTools, or many others into TheHive. Read the documentation in this Cortex GitHub repository: `https://github.com/TheHive-Project/ CortexDocs`.

Summary

In this chapter, you learned the importance of an incident response platform as a core component of incident response capabilities.

Also, you learned to set up an instance of the TheHive incident management platform and how to generate new cases, create and assign tasks to analysts, collect observables, and obtain external intelligence through Cortex.

At the time of writing this chapter, an important change had been announced for version 5 of TheHive's licensing model. The new version will no longer be under the AGPL v3 license (this does not apply to the Cortex intelligence tool), but there will be a Free Community version that will keep the main incident management capabilities. Version 4.4-1 will be supported until December 31, 2022.

As I mentioned earlier, and as part of my commitment to keeping the content current and up to date with the tools, I will include the changes applicable to the new version of this incident management platform within the additional material of this chapter available on GitHub.

In the next chapter, you will learn how to integrate multiple technologies to automatize incident response procedures.

Further reading

- TheHive project documentation: `https://docs.thehive-project.org/thehive/`

- TheHive turns 5 and adopts a model shaped for the future: `https://medium.com/strangebee-announcements/thehive-turns-5-and-adopts-a-model-shaped-for-the-future-95f908719c31`

- TheHive, Cortex, and MISP: How They All Fit Together: `https://blog.thehive-project.org/2017/06/19/thehive-cortex-and-misp-how-they-all-fit-together/`

- Incident Playbook: `https://github.com/austinsonger/Incident-Playbook`

- Cortex documentation: `https://github.com/TheHive-Project/CortexDocs`

11
Integrating SOAR Capabilities into Incident Response

In the previous chapter, we learned how to implement an **incident response** (**IR**) platform and integrate intelligence capacities. In this chapter, we are going to integrate **Security Orchestration, Automation, and Response** (**SOAR**) to improve the efficiency of the IR process.

To do this, we are going to use **Security Onion**, an open source and free platform to perform security monitoring, IR, and threat hunting, and we are going to implement additional orchestration tools to improve the investigation capabilities.

In this chapter, you will learn about the following:

- Understanding the principles and capabilities of SOAR
- A SOAR use case – identifying malicious communications
- Escalating incidents from detection
- Automating the IR and investigation processes

Technical requirements

In case you haven't already, you need to download and install VMware Workstation Player from this link `https://www.vmware.com/products/workstation-player/workstation-player-evaluation.html`.

You'll also need to download the following from the book's official GitHub repository `https://github.com/PacktPublishing/Incident-Response-with-Threat-Intelligence`:

- Virtual machines:
  - IR-Laptop
  - IR-SOAR
- Lab files:
  - Chapter11

Understanding the principles and capabilities of SOAR

The term *Security Orchestration, Automation, and Response* refers to the integration of multiple technologies and processes to exchange and centralize information in an automated way.

In security incidents, everything must flow, and every member of the team must perform the activities related to their role in a coordinated way with the other teams, using the appropriate tools and technologies, and following the previously defined procedures, all of them directed by a leader.

Benefits of SOAR-based IR

There are multiple benefits of implementing a SOAR-based IR model:

- Improves the organization's posture and capacity in the face of threats
- Allows you to integrate existing technologies within the organization

- Facilitates process automation and decision making

- Provides greater visibility and improves detection capabilities

- Reduces threat identification, containment, and elimination times

SOAR is particularly beneficial in environments that involve large-scale systems and that are performing manual processes. Without SOAR, this would be unmanageable. Automation and integration allow us to be efficient in this type of environment.

Implementing a SOAR model

Integrating SOAR capabilities in the organization is especially important to respond efficiently to cyberattacks. These are some of the characteristics of the SOAR model:

- **Security tools integration**: The different tools connect to each other using **Application Programming Interfaces (APIs)**, which are a collection of functions that allow interaction with other applications or services.

- **Centralization of various sources of information**: You will need to collect information from diverse sources including **Security Information and Event Management (SIEM)** device logs and threat intelligence platforms.

- **Alerting systems**: Alert systems can be configured to open IR cases in an automated manner if they meet certain predefined conditions.

- **Process automatization**: The capacity to create automatic workflows at distinct stages of the incident management life cycle.

- **IR playbooks**: One of the advantages of systems developed around a SOAR approach is that you can integrate playbooks; in this way, IR processes can be digitized and automated.

- **An incident management system**: IR teams need a centralized platform to manage and share information, assign tasks, document findings, report issues, obtain and generate intelligence, and make decisions.

In the next section, we are going to explore a use case to implement SOAR as part of the IR processes.

A SOAR use case – identifying malicious communications

Suppose that a monitoring system detects abnormal network behavior and tags the IP address or domain as suspicious and sends it to another system for verification in a database of malicious **indicators of compromise (IoCs)**.

If this indicator is confirmed to be malicious, the **Security Operation Center (SOC)** operator opens a new case for a cybersecurity incident and notifies the IR team. The incident responder can then open a new case using the playbook related to this incident and start assigning tasks to the IR team.

If the IR system has integration with a threat intelligence system, you can search for additional information containing the details of a potential campaign, threat actors, affected industries, and related IoCs, as shown in the following figure:

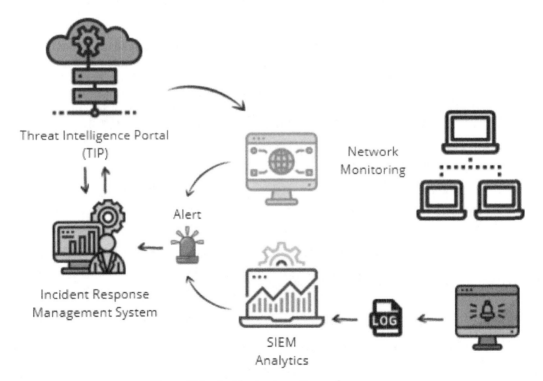

Figure 11.1 – Incident automation and response

Once you have intelligence information and malicious indicators, you can begin with the investigation of the incident, focusing on identifying the compromised devices and the containment of any malicious activity.

Preparing for the detection lab

Before we start with the practical exercises in this chapter, we will need to prepare the work environment. We are going to use **Security Onion**, which is a platform that integrates security tools for monitoring and threat hunting with centralized log management (`https://securityonionsolutions.com/software/`):

1. Start the IR-Laptop virtual machine and sign in using the following credentials:

    *   **Username**: `investigator`

    *   **Password**: `L34rn1ng!`

2. Start the IR-SOAR virtual machine as shown in the following screenshot. You do not need to sign in here for now:

Figure 11.2 – Starting the IR-SOAR virtual machine

The IR-SOAR virtual machine is a preconfigured server with the open source platform Security Onion that integrates multiple tools such as **Elasticsearch, Logstash, and Kibana (ELK)**, Suricata, Zeek, Wazuh, CyberChef, and the MITRE ATT&CK Navigator, and helps to facilitate the security orchestration processes.

Initial configuration of the IR-SOAR virtual machine

Once you start both the virtual machines, you will need to allow the IR-Laptop to connect to the management console. To do this, we are going to connect to the IR-SOAR virtual machine using a **Secure Shell (SSH)** connection:

1. Open an administrator terminal console by right-clicking on the Windows Terminal icon. Next, click on **Run as administrator**, as shown in the following screenshot:

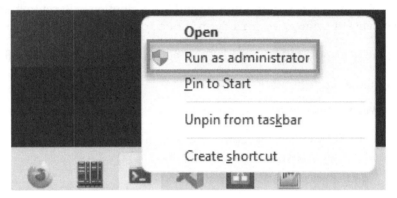

Figure 11.3 – Opening Windows Terminal as administrator

> **Note**
> We are opening Windows Terminal as *administrator* because we could require elevated privileges to perform some exercises later.

2. Open a new Windows Terminal/**Windows Subsystem for Linux (WSL)** tab by clicking on the down arrow button at the top, which will then display a drop-down menu. Select **Ubuntu** from this menu, as shown in the following screenshot:

Figure 11.4 – Opening a new WSL tab in Windows Terminal

3. From here, we are going to connect using SSH from the IR-Laptop (IP address 192.168.8.150) to the IR-SOAR server (IP address 192.168.8.5), providing the following parameters:

    ```
    ssh analyst@192.168.8.5
    ```

4. Accept the certificate of authenticity of the server.

    The previous steps are shown in the following screenshot:

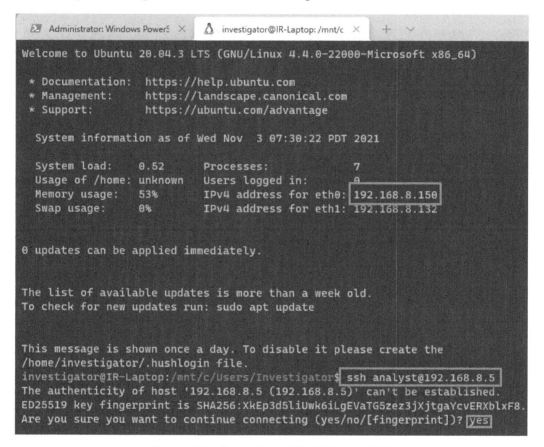

Figure 11.5 – Connecting to IR-SOAR using SSH

5. Enter the password `P4cktIRBook!`.

6. It is important to be sure that all the services and tools are up before starting. To check this, review the status of the containers by entering the following command:

```
sudo so-status
```

7. Provide the analyst password `P4cktIRBook!`.

    You will see the status of the containers, as shown in the following screenshot:

Figure 11.6 – Verifying the status of the containers

Once all the containers' statuses are `OK` (this could take some time, so you can press the up arrow to keep checking), we then can connect to the Security Onion management console.

8. Open a web browser from the IR-Laptop and connect to the following address: `https://192.168.8.5`.

Important Note

You might get the following privacy errors:

Brave:

Your connection is not private:

- Click on **Advanced**.

- Next, select **Proceed to 192.168.8.5 (unsafe)**.

Firefox:

Warning: Potential Security Risk Ahead:

- Click on **Advanced**.

- Next, select **Accept the Risk and Continue**.

Microsoft Edge:

Your connection isn't private:

- Click on **Advanced**.

- Next, select **Continue to 192.168.8.5 (unsafe)**.

9. Provide the following analyst credentials:

    - **Username**: `analyst@gosecurity.ninja`

    - **Password**: `L34rn1ng!`

    This is shown in the following screenshot:

Figure 11.7 – Log in to Security Onion

We already have everything we need to start working with Security Onion. As we did in the previous chapters, we will also use open source tools to perform the integration and orchestration process.

Security orchestration between TheHive and Velociraptor using n8n

Wes Lambert (Twitter handle @therealwlambert) is the principal engineer at **Security Onion Solutions LLC**, the company that developed Security Onion. He wrote the blog post *Zero Dollar Detection and Response Orchestration with n8n, Security Onion, TheHive, and Velociraptor* (which you can read at https://wlambertts.medium.com/zero-dollar-detection-and-response-orchestration-with-n8n-security-onion-thehive-and-10b5e685e2a1), where he describes how to integrate these tools to automate creating cases, from an alert in Security Onion to the beginning of an investigation using TheHive and Velociraptor.

In his GitHub repository (https://github.com/weslambert/SOARLab), Wes Lambert also shared the scripts and instructions on how to perform this integration, which we use as a basis for the configuration of the IR-SOAR server.

These are some of the Security Onion tools used for orchestration:

- **Alerts**: This console displays alerts generated by agents installed on endpoints, network traffic, or system logs.

- **Hunt**: This console is used to search for specific indicators using queries.

- **TheHive**: This is the incident management platform that we used in the previous chapter to create cases, document observables, and integrate with threat intelligence information (https://thehive-project.org/).

- **Velociraptor**: The tool for triage, investigation, and threat hunting that we used in *Chapter 4, Applying First Response Procedures* (https://github.com/Velocidex/velociraptor).

- **n8n**: This tool interconnects apps to create workflows using APIs (https://n8n.io/).

To use these tools from Security Onion, you just need to expand the main menu and click on the specific tool you want to use, as shown in the following screenshot:

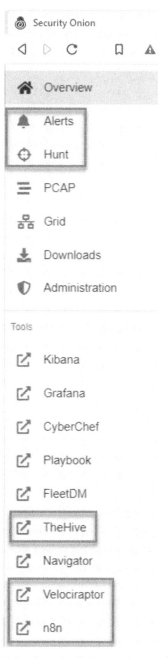

Figure 11.8 – Security Onion options and tools

To create the work environment, we will use the IR-Laptop virtual machine, sending the collected logs and information to the IR-SOAR virtual machine, as shown in the following figure:

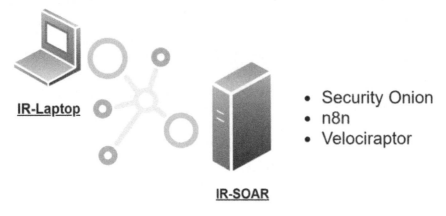

IR-Laptop

- Security Onion
- n8n
- Velociraptor

IR-SOAR

Figure 11.9 – Detection lab environment

Now that we are clear about our work scenario, we must install and configure the agents on the endpoints to collect the information.

Configuring the connection permissions for the client collection tools

Before you begin installing client-side collection tools, it is important to enable the connection permissions on the IR-SOAR server using the following steps:

1. Open the Windows Terminal/WSL console and run the following command:

    ```
    sudo so-allow
    ```

2. Type the following parameters:

    ```
    Please enter your selection:
    b
    Enter a single ip address or range to allow
    192.168.8.150
    ```

This will open port 5044 to receive logs from the endpoints in Logstash, as shown in the following screenshot:

```
[analyst@ir-soar ~]$ sudo so-allow
[sudo] password for analyst:
This program allows you to add a firewall rule to allow connections from a new IP address.

Choose the role for the IP or Range you would like to add

[a] - Analyst - ports 80/tcp and 443/tcp
[b] - Logstash Beat - port 5044/tcp
[e] - Elasticsearch REST API - port 9200/tcp
[f] - Strelka frontend - port 57314/tcp
[o] - Osquery endpoint - port 8090/tcp
[s] - Syslog device - 514/tcp/udp
[w] - Wazuh agent - port 1514/tcp/udp
[p] - Wazuh API - port 55000/tcp
[r] - Wazuh registration service - 1515/tcp

Please enter your selection:
b
Enter a single ip address or range to allow (example: 10.10.10.10 or 10.10.0.0/16):
192.168.8.150
```

Figure 11.10 – Configuring the connection rules

3. Repeat the same process using the w and r role options using the same IP address as the IR-Laptop.

With this configuration, we will be enabling connection permissions for the following roles:

- Logstash Beat
- Wazuh agent
- Wazuh registration service

Once we finish configuring the access permissions of the ports and services that we require to allow connectivity from the devices, we will then work on the installation and configuration of the agents that will send the information to the Security Onion server.

Client collection tools

To get the information needed to detect potentially malicious behavior on our computer, we must install agents that monitor the activity and send logs to the monitoring system. To collect this information, we will use the following tools:

- **Sysmon**: This is a Windows tool that works as a service and driver to monitor and register system activity and send it to the Windows event log.

- **Winlogbeat**: This is a tool for shipping logs and, in our case, Windows event logs to Elasticsearch.

- **Wazuh agent**: The Wazuh agent is a detection and monitoring tool that combines technologies based on signatures and anomalies detection.

- **Velociraptor client**: This is a **Velociraptor Query Language** (**VQL**) engine tool that executes queries to collect information from devices to perform high-level forensic analysis.

To install these tools on the IR-Laptop virtual machine, just follow the steps in the next subsection.

Installing and configuring Sysmon

Sysmon is a powerful tool that enriches monitoring and information collection capabilities to conventional Windows logs, such as filesystem changes, process creation, and network connections. Sysmon is a part of the Windows Sysinternals utilities for Windows troubleshooting and management.

To install Sysmon, follow these steps:

1. In Windows Terminal/PowerShell, change to the C:\Program Files directory:

   ```
   cd 'C:\Program Files\'
   ```

2. Download Sysmon by running the following command:

   ```
   wget -O Sysmon.zip https://download.sysinternals.com/
   files/Sysmon.zip
   ```

3. Unzip the Sysmon.zip file by running the following command:

   ```
   Expand-Archive -Path Sysmon.Zip -DestinationPath .\Sysmon
   ```

4. Switch to the created Sysmon directory.

   To improve the quality of the information we will collect, we need a configuration file. In this case, we will download the configuration file created by Olaf Hartong (Twitter handle @olafhartong).

5. Download the configuration file by running the following command:

   ```
   wget -O sysmonconfig.xml https://raw.githubusercontent.
   com/olafhartong/sysmon-modular/master/sysmonconfig.xml
   ```

6. To install Sysmon using the configuration file, run this command:

   ```
   .\Sysmon64.exe -accepteula -i .\sysmonconfig.xml
   ```

You will see the previous installation steps in the following screenshot:

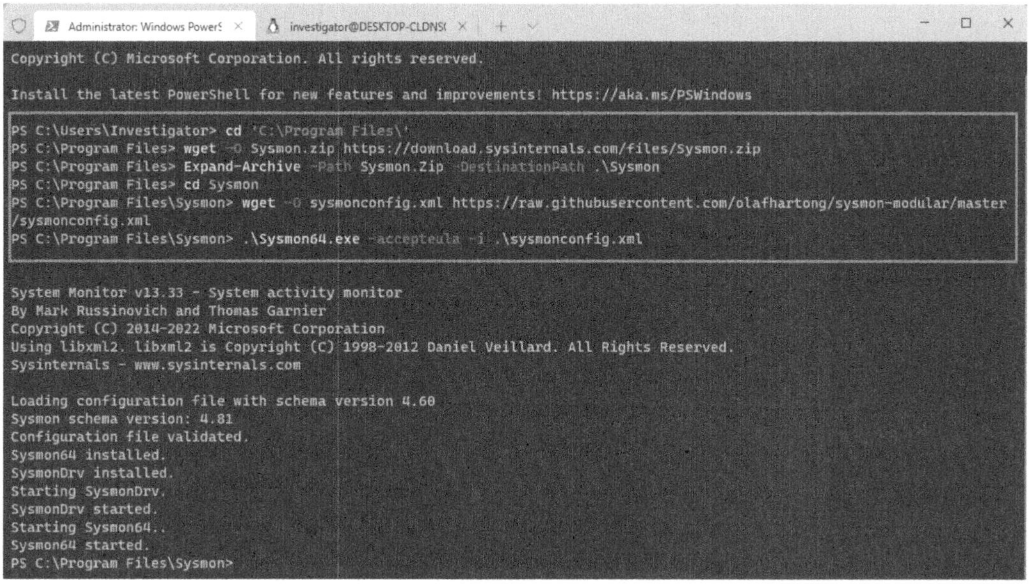

Figure 11.11 – Installing Sysmon

> **Note**
>
> We specified the `-accepteula` parameter to automatically accept the **end user license agreement (EULA)** on Sysmon installation; otherwise, you will be interactively prompted to accept it.

Once the installation is finished, Sysmon will begin logging system events and store them in the following Windows log repository: `Microsoft-Windows-Sysmon/Operational`.

Now, let's install the agents that will send the logs to Security Onion.

Installing and configuring Winlogbeat

Winlogbeat is a tool that can be installed as a Windows service and uses filters to send Windows event logs to Elasticsearch or Logstash using APIs. To install Winlogbeat, follow these steps:

1. On the IR-Laptop VM, open the web browser, navigate to the left panel of Security Onion, and click on the *hamburger* menu button.

2. Click on the **Downloads** button.

3. Finally, click on the **Winlogbeat** link to download the installer of the Winlogbeat agent, and save it to the `Downloads` folder.

The previous steps are shown in the following screenshot:

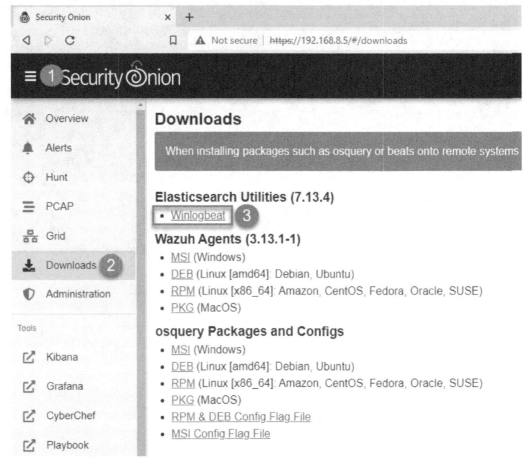

Figure 11.12 – Downloading Winlogbeat 7.13.4

> **Important Note**
> It is recommended to do it this way so that you can install a Winlogbeat agent compatible with this Security Onion version.

4. Double-click on the downloaded `winlogbeat-oss-7.13.4-windows-x86_64.msi` file, accept the license agreement, and click on the **Install** button, as shown in the following screenshot:

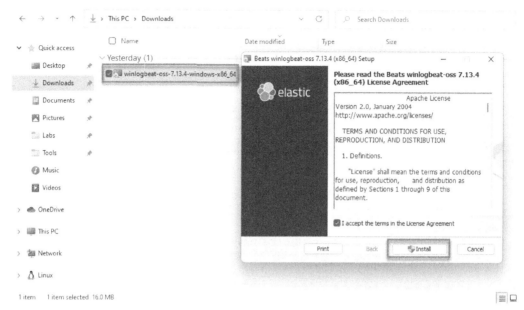

Figure 11.13 – Downloading the Winlogbeat agent

5. When the installation is finished, click on the **Finish** button, as shown in the following screenshot:

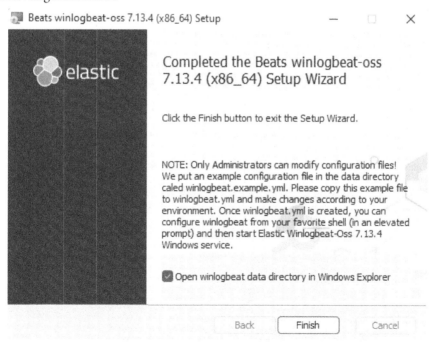

Figure 11.14 – Finishing the installation of the Winlogbeat agent

6. Open the Windows Terminal/PowerShell console, and switch to the `C:\` `ProgramData\Elastic\Beats\winlogbeat` directory:

```
cd C:\ProgramData\Elastic\Beats\winlogbeat
```

7. Download the `winlogbeat.yml` file from the `Chapter-11` folder in the GitHub repository of this book and save it to the `C:\Users\Investigator\` `Workspace\Labs\Chapter-11` directory in your IR-Laptop VM.

8. Now, on the Windows Terminal/PowerShell console, copy the `winlogbeat.yml` file to the `winlogbeat` directory by running the following command:

```
cp C:\Users\Investigator\Workspace\Labs\Chapter-11\
winlogbeat.yml
```

9. To test the `winlogbeat.yml` file settings and verify that it is configured correctly, run the following command:

```
winlogbeat test config -c .\winlogbeat.yml -e
```

In the last line, you should see the message `Config OK`, which indicates that the configuration file has the correct syntax, as shown in the following screenshot:

```
2021-11-03T15:25:01.372-0700     INFO     instance/beat.go:309     Setup Beat: winlogbeat; Ver
sion: 7.13.4
2021-11-03T15:25:01.375-0700     INFO     [publisher]     pipeline/module.go:113  Beat name:
IR-Laptop
2021-11-03T15:25:01.376-0700     INFO     beater/winlogbeat.go:69 State will be read from and
persisted to C:\Program Files\winlogbeat\data\.winlogbeat.yml
Config OK
PS C:\Program Files\winlogbeat>
```

Figure 11.15 – Verification of the configuration file

10. Finally, run the following command to start the Winlogbeat service:

```
Start-Service winlogbeat
```

Winlogbeat is now working and sending the Windows event logs, including the Sysmon logs, to Security Onion. Next, we will install the Wazuh agent in a similar way.

Installing and configuring the Wazuh agent

The Wazuh agent is a **host-based intrusion detection system** (**HIDS**) that will be monitoring the activity in the **operating system** (**OS**) directories, Windows processes, and registry keys to identify any suspicious activity and report it to our monitoring server. The steps to install and configure Wazuh are as follows:

1. Open your web browser, navigate to the left panel of Security Onion, and click on the hamburger menu button.

2. Click on the **Downloads** button.

3. Click on the **MSI (Windows)** link to download the installer of the Wazuh agent, and save it to the Downloads folder.

The previous steps are shown in the following screenshot:

Figure 11.16 – Downloading the Wazuh agent

Important Note

It is recommended to do it this way so that you can install a Wazuh agent compatible with this Security Onion version.

---

4. Double-click on the downloaded `wazuh-agent-3.13.1-1.msi` file, accept the license agreement, and click on the **Install** button, as shown in the following screenshot:

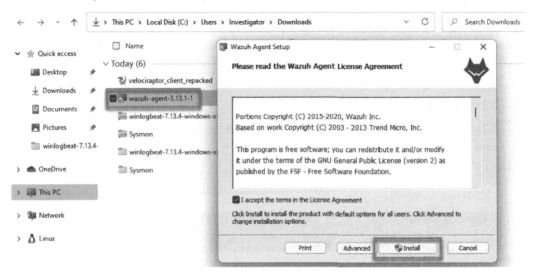

Figure 11.17 – Installation of the Wazuh agent

5. When the installation is finished, select the **Run Agent configuration interface** checkbox and click on the **Finish** button, as shown in the following screenshot:

Figure 11.18 – Running the Wazuh agent configuration interface

If you did not receive any error messages, the program was installed correctly, and now you only need to configure the connection parameters to Security Onion.

6. On Windows Terminal/PowerShell, change to the `C:\Program Files (x86)\`
   `ossec-agent` directory and run the following command to define the server to
   which the information collected by Wazuh should be sent:

```
.\agent-auth.exe -m 192.168.8.5
```

Once you have run the command, all connection procedures will appear on the
screen, as shown in the following screenshot:

```
PS C:\Program Files (x86)\ossec-agent> .\agent-auth.exe -m 192.168.8.5
2021/11/04 07:23:33 agent-auth: INFO: Started (pid: 8992).
2021/11/04 07:23:33 agent-auth: INFO: Starting enrollment process to server: 192.168.8.5
2021/11/04 07:23:33 agent-auth: INFO: Connected to 192.168.8.5:1515
2021/11/04 07:23:33 agent-auth: INFO: Registering agent to unverified manager.
2021/11/04 07:23:33 agent-auth: INFO: No authentication password provided.
2021/11/04 07:23:33 agent-auth: INFO: Using agent name as: IR-Laptop
2021/11/04 07:23:33 agent-auth: INFO: Request sent to manager
2021/11/04 07:23:33 agent-auth: INFO: Waiting for manager reply
2021/11/04 07:23:33 agent-auth: INFO: Received response with agent key
2021/11/04 07:23:33 agent-auth: INFO: Valid key created. Finished.
2021/11/04 07:23:33 agent-auth: INFO: Connection closed.
PS C:\Program Files (x86)\ossec-agent> |
```

Figure 11.19 – Enrollment of the Wazuh agent

Now, return to the dialog box of **Wazuh Agent Manager** and follow the next steps
to complete the connection process.

7. Write the IR-SOAR IP address in the **Manager IP** textbox: `192.168.8.5`.

8. Click on the **Save** button.

9. Click on the **Manage** menu, then click on the **Start** option.

10. Click on the **Refresh** button.

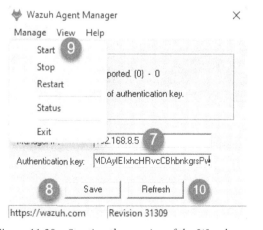

Figure 11.20 – Starting the service of the Wazuh agent

You will see the authentication key generated in the enrollment process, and the status of the agent will be shown as **Running**.

The Wazuh agent is now working and sending HIDS logs to Security Onion.

Installing and configuring the Velociraptor client

First, we will need to download the customized Velociraptor client to register the IR-Laptop VM on the server and be able to collect the forensic artifacts. To do this, we will need to copy the file from a restricted directory of the IR-SOAR server to the analyst's home directory and then download it to our VM by following these steps:

1. On the Windows Terminal/WSL, make sure that you are connected to the IR-SOAR server. Otherwise, connect through SSH as we did previously.

2. Elevate the user privileges to root by running the following command:

    ```
    sudo -i
    ```

3. Copy this file to the /home/analyst directory by running the following command:

    ```
    cp /opt/so/conf/velociraptor/clients/windows/
    velociraptor_client_repacked.exe /home/analyst/
    ```

4. Close the root session by running the following command:

    ```
    exit
    ```

    Following these steps, you were able to copy the installation file from a restricted directory by elevating privileges, as you can see in the next screenshot:

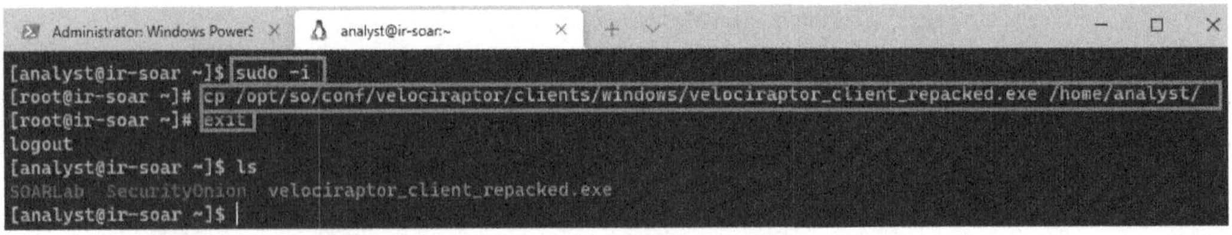

Figure 11.21 – Copying the Velociraptor client

5. Close the remote session by running the following command:

    ```
    exit
    ```

6. On the IR-Laptop virtual machine, copy the file from the server by running the following command:

```
scp analyst@192.168.8.5:/home/analyst/velociraptor_
client_repacked.exe /mnt/c/Users/Investigator/Downloads
```

Once you provide the P4cktIRBook! password, you will see the copying process, as shown in the following screenshot:

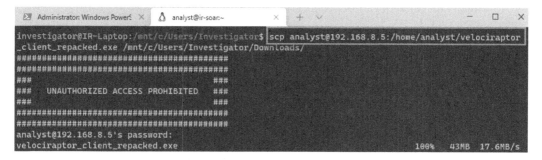

Figure 11.22 – Downloading the Velociraptor client from the server

7. To install the Velociraptor client, click on the Windows Terminal/PowerShell tab, then move to the C:\Users\Investigator\Downloads directory.

8. Run the following command:

```
.\velociraptor_client_repacked.exe service install -v
```

On the screen, you will see the process of installing Velociraptor and the initialization of the service, as shown in the following screenshot:

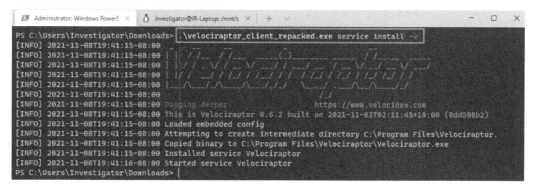

Figure 11.23 – Installing the Velociraptor client as a service

Now, the Velociraptor client will connect to the IR-SOAR server, and we can collect artifacts from the IR-Laptop.

To verify this, follow these steps:

1. From the **Security Onion** console, on the left menu, click on **Velociraptor**, and a new tab will open. Now, enter the following login credentials:

    *   **Username**: investigator

    *   **Password**: L34rn1ng!

    The details filled in can be seen in the following screenshot:

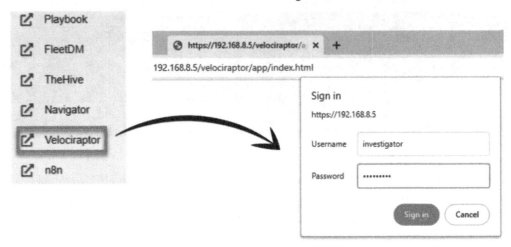

Figure 11.24 – Login credentials on the Velociraptor console

2. In the main dashboard, click the button on the right side of the search textbox and select **Show All**. The **client ID** of the IR-Laptop should appear, as you can see in the following screenshot:

Figure 11.25 – Verifying the Velociraptor client enrollment to the server

In the next section, we will create a security incident case from a detection alert generated in the monitoring SOC.

Escalating incidents from detection

An important feature when we are talking about SOAR is the capacity to escalate or automate processes between systems.

We can do this in several ways. We can either automate alerts to receive notifications under certain conditions and take some specific actions according to an IR playbook or we can trigger a new case from a SOC alert.

Emulating suspicious behavior

To emulate suspicious behavior, we are going to create a new Windows user to trigger an alert, and then we will escalate this alert to open an incident case.

First, let's generate a security event related to the creation of a local Windows user from the command line:

1. To create the new user, write the following command on the Windows Terminal/ PowerShell console:

```
New-LocalUSer -Name "PamB" -NoPassword
```

The new user is now created and enabled, as you can see in the following screenshot:

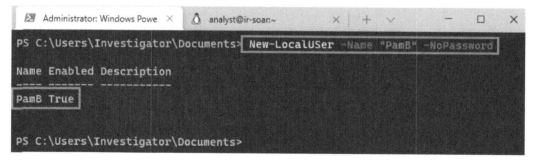

Figure 11.26 – Creation of new Windows user account

2. In your web browser, navigate to the **Alerts** section of the **Security Onion** console, as shown in the following screenshot:

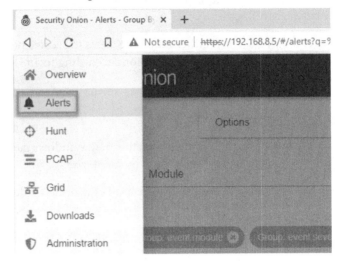

Figure 11.27 – Navigation to the Alerts dashboard in Security Onion

3. Set the filter period to 1 hour to see the events that were last generated. You will focus on alerts related to the creation of the new user, as shown in the following screenshot:

Figure 11.28 – Identifying the alerts generated

Although the creation of a user can be a regular activity, in this case, the user was not created following the normal procedures of the company and could be considered suspicious, so it should be investigated further.

To begin the review, and get more details about this event, do the following:

1. Right-click on the text of the **User account enabled or created** alert and select the **Drilldown** option, as shown in the following screenshot:

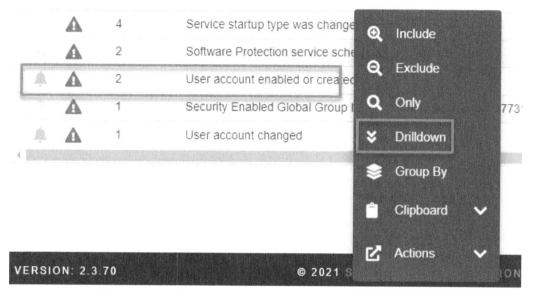

Figure 11.29 – Filtering information related to user account creation

You can now see the filtered information that shows only the two alerts generated by the agents installed on your computer; one of them generated by Wazuh and the other generated by Winlogbeat.

2.   Click on the left arrow button to display the details of the alert and review the details of the event. You will see the information related to the creation of the new user, as shown in the following screenshot:

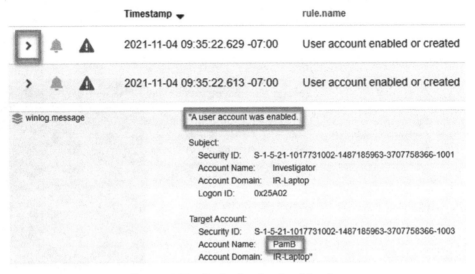

Figure 11.30 – Reviewing details of the alert

3.   Repeat the process with the other alert to compare them (Wazuh and Winlogbeat) and catch the similarities as well as the differences.

If we assume that this account is not registered as a change management process, it'll mean that this is a potentially malicious activity and could be considered a security incident.

4.   On the blue filter label, click on the **X** button to clean this filter, and make sure that the predefined **Group By Name, Module** query and the 1 hour time filter are set again, as shown in the following screenshot:

Figure 11.31 – Setting the alerts filter

With the application of this filter, you can see the alerts generated in the last hour.

Escalating an alert

To escalate this alert and create an IR case, follow these steps:

1. Click on the blue **Escalate** icon, as shown in the following screenshot:

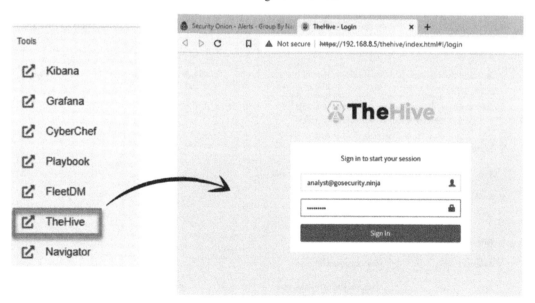

🔔 ⚠	2	User account enabled or created
Escalate	1	Security Enabled Global Group Member Added
🔔 ⚠	1	User account changed

Figure 11.32 – Escalating an alert to a case

2. On the left menu of Security Onion, click on the **TheHive** option to open a new tab that leads to the login page. To sign in, use the same credentials you used for Security Onion:

    - **Username**: analyst@gosecurity.ninja

    - **Password**: L34rn1ng

    The details can be seen in the following screenshot:

Figure 11.33 – Opening the TheHive management console

You will see the new **User account enabled or created** case generated automatically from the **Alerts** console in Security Onion:

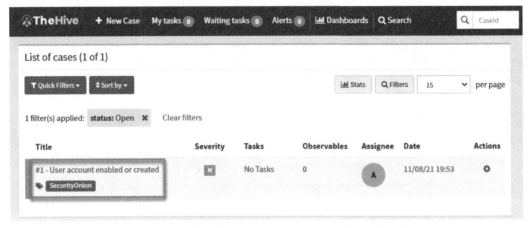

Figure 11.34 – Identifying the new case created from the alert

3. Click on the case to see the details and description of this incident, as shown in the following screenshot:

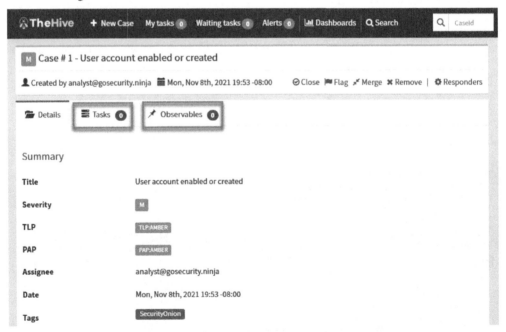

Figure 11.35 – Reviewing the details of the case

We can now use the IR playbook of this type, assigning new tasks and documenting new observables (IoCs) that we find in the systems.

In this case, we escalated an alert for the creation of an IR case manually, but we could also do it automatically by using tools such as **ElastAlert**, which you can find here: `https://elastalert.readthedocs.io/en/latest/`.

For the next practical scenario, we are going to automate some activities of IR and investigation.

Automating the IR and investigation processes

In this section, we are going to start an investigation from the generation of an alert and the creation of a case of an incident. First, we need to emulate an attack.

Emulating the attack

To emulate malicious behavior and generate the detection of this activity, we will use the following tools:

- **Certutil**: A Windows command-line utility that is regularly used to get certificate authority information and to configure certificate services. A threat actor can abuse this utility to download malicious programs from the internet and/or encode the content of these files to avoid detection.

- **ProcDump**: This tool is part of the Windows Sysinternals utility suite and is used to monitor applications and generate crash dumps to analyze and determine the causes of the failure. A threat actor can abuse this tool by creating a dump of processes such as **Local Security Authority Subsystem** (**LSASS**), from which Windows credentials can be extracted using tools such as Mimikatz.

To get started, follow these steps:

1. On the Windows Terminal/PowerShell, run the following command:

   ```
   certutil.exe -urlcache -split -f https://download.
   sysinternals.com/files/Procdump.zip
   ```

   You will receive an error message like the one in the following screenshot:

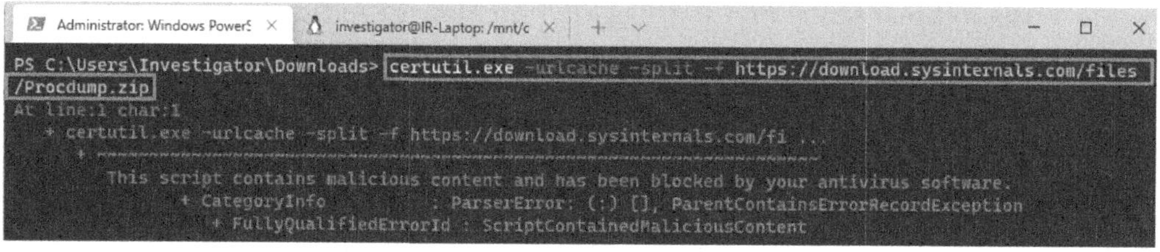

Figure 11.36 – Downloading a file from the internet using certutil.exe

This is because Windows Defender correctly detected that this is a potentially malicious activity. So, to execute the command successfully, we must temporarily disable the real-time detection option first.

2. Click on the show hidden icons button and then click on Windows Security:

Figure 11.37 – Opening the Windows Security console

3. On the **Windows Security** panel, click on **Virus & threat protection**:

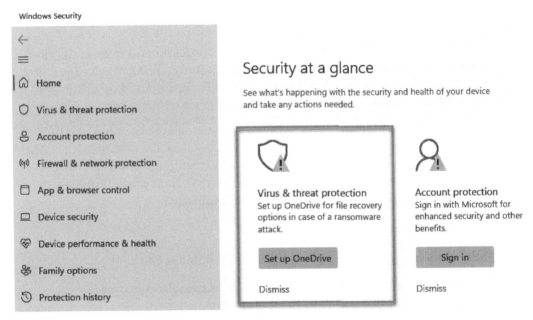

Figure 11.38 – Configuring Virus & threat protection

4. In **Virus & threat protection settings,** click on **Manage settings**:

⚙ Virus & threat protection settings

No action needed.

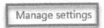

Figure 11.39 – Changing protection settings

5. Click to change the **Real-time protection** status to **Off**:

Real-time protection

Locates and stops malware from installing or running on your device. You can turn off this setting for a short time before it turns back on automatically.

Cloud-delivered protection

Provides increased and faster protection with access to the latest protection data in the cloud. Works best with Automatic sample submission turned on.

Figure 11.40 – Disabling Real-time protection

6. On the **User Account Control** dialog box, click on the **Yes** button:

Do you want to allow this app to make changes to your device?

 Windows Security

Verified publisher: Microsoft Windows

Show more details

Figure 11.41 – Authorizing changes in Windows Security configuration

Now that the real-time detection option is disabled, you can run the command again.

7. On the Windows Terminal/PowerShell, run the following command:

```
Certutil.exe -urlcache -split -f https://download.
sysinternals.com/files/Procdump.zip
```

8. Unzip the file by running the following command:

```
Expand-Archive -Path .\Procdump.zip
```

9. Change to the `Procdump` directory:

```
cd .\Procdump
```

10. Create a dump file from the LSASS process by running the following command:

```
.\procdump64.exe -accepteula -ma lsass.exe config.dmp
```

You can see an example of the execution of these commands in the following screenshot:

```
PS C:\Users\Investigator\Downloads> certutil.exe -urlcache -split -f https://download.sysinternals.com/files
/Procdump.zip
**** Online ****
  000000 ...
  0aa305
CertUtil: -URLCache command completed successfully.
PS C:\Users\Investigator\Downloads> Expand-Archive -Path .\Procdump.zip
PS C:\Users\Investigator\Downloads> cd .\Procdump\
PS C:\Users\Investigator\Downloads\Procdump> .\procdump64.exe -accepteula -ma lsass.exe config.dmp

ProcDump v10.11 - Sysinternals process dump utility
Copyright (C) 2009-2021 Mark Russinovich and Andrew Richards
Sysinternals - www.sysinternals.com

[20:16:39] Dump 1 initiated: C:\Users\Investigator\Downloads\Procdump\config.dmp
[20:16:39] Dump 1 writing: Estimated dump file size is 53 MB.
[20:16:39] Dump 1 complete: 53 MB written in 0.7 seconds
[20:16:40] Dump count reached.

PS C:\Users\Investigator\Downloads\Procdump>
```

Figure 11.42 – Downloading and executing ProcDump

We emulated a potential malicious activity that generated information that we can analyze to create an IR case and generate a hunt for these artifacts in different devices on the network.

Now, we are going to collect potential IoCs on the suspicious computer using Velociraptor.

Creating a hashes database

First, we must create a database of hashes in Velociraptor to facilitate the search process in an investigation. The steps are as follows:

1. Go to the Velociraptor console, and click on the **Client ID** button.

2. Click on the hamburger button (top left), then select **Collected Artifacts** on the menu.

3. Click on the + icon to create a new artifacts collection.

4. Select the **Generic.Forensic.LocalHashes.Glob** artifact.

   This will define the type of information you want to collect from the endpoint, as shown in the following screenshot:

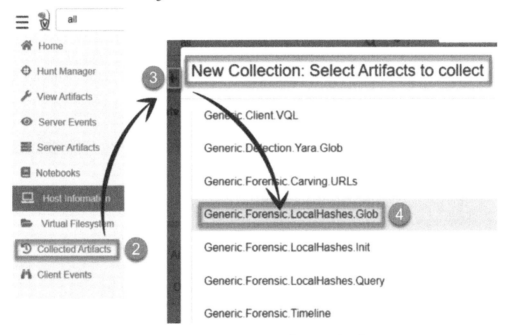

Figure 11.43 – Creating a new collection of artifacts

5. On **Configure Parameters**, click on **Generic.Forensic.LocalHashes.Glob** to change **HashGlob** to the `.zip` extension, as shown in the following screenshot:

New Collection: Configure Parameters

-	Artifact
-	Generic.Forensic.LocalHashes.Glob

HashGlob	C:/Users/**/*.zip
HashDb	hashdb.sqlite
SuppressOutput	☐ If this is set, the artifact does not return any rows to the server but will still update the local database.

Select Artifacts | Configure Parameters | Specify Resources | Review | Launch

Figure 11.44 – Configuring the parameters of the new collection

6. In the menu at the bottom, click the **Launch** button, as shown in the following screenshot:

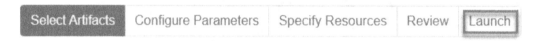

Figure 11.45 – Launching the new collection

This process will keep a client-side database of file hashes with `.zip` extensions. Now, let's add the hashes generated locally.

7. Click on the **Client Events** button.

8. Click on the **Update the client monitoring table** button.

9. Click on **Label group**, and select **All (2 artifacts)**, as shown in the following screenshot:

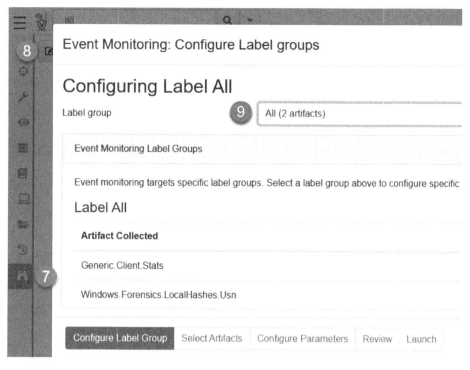

Figure 11.46 – Creating client event monitoring

10. Next, click on the **Select Artifacts** button.

11. Select the **Windows.Forensics.LocalHashes.Usn** artifact.

12. Click on the **Launch** button, as shown in the following screenshot:

Figure 11.47 – Configuring the artifacts for event monitoring

Finally, we are going to configure **Server Event Monitoring** to look for artifacts that meet specific criteria by adding a tag in TheHive.

13. Click on the **Server Events** button.

14. Click on the **Update the server monitoring table** button.

15. Make sure that the **Custom.Flows.Write** and **Custom.Server.Automation. Quarantine** artifacts are selected (colored in blue), otherwise, click on **Custom. Server.Automation.Quarantine** to select the artifact, as shown in the following screenshot:

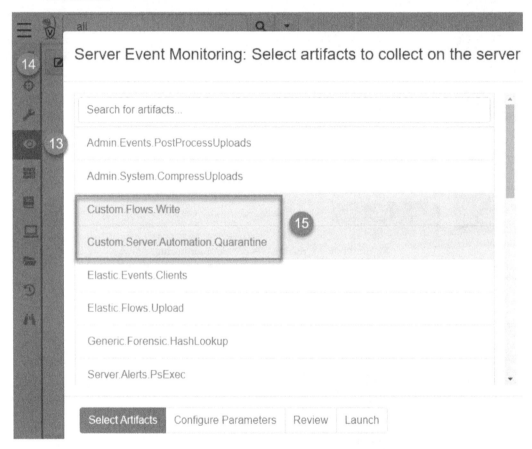

Figure 11.48 – Configuring Server Event Monitoring

16. Click on the **Launch** button.

17. With this configuration, it will create a hunt in Velociraptor to look for matches in the systems on the network for every *observable* of the cases created in TheHive that contain a filename or a hash.

Now, we are going to configure the connection parameters from Velociraptor to TheHive using the API key to interact between both systems.

Setting TheHive parameters in Velociraptor

To integrate these systems, it is necessary to configure some TheHive parameters within Velociraptor.

First, let's get the API key from the `analyst@gosecurity.ninja` user:

1. On your web browser, go to the **TheHive** console and click on the top-right **Admin** button, and then the **Users** button, as shown in the following screenshot:

Figure 11.49 – Accessing TheHive user configuration

2. On the **API key** section, click on the **Reveal** button and then click the copy key icon, as shown in the following screenshot:

Figure 11.50 – Getting the user API key

3. Go back to the **Velociraptor** dashboard.

4. Click on the **Velociraptor** icon on the top left.

5. Click on the **View Server Configuration** link, as shown in the following screenshot:

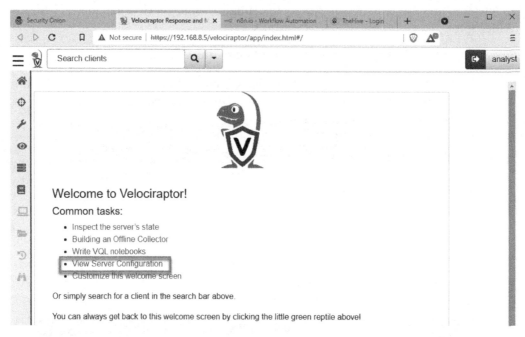

Figure 11.51 – Viewing the Velociraptor server configuration

6. In the **Server Metadata** section, add the values related to the TheHive server, as shown in the following screenshot:

Figure 11.52 – Adding TheHive parameters on Velociraptor

We are almost done! Now, we just need to create the workflow to automate the IR and investigation processes.

Creating workflows using n8n

This is the key component in the orchestration of TheHive and Velociraptor. Using n8n, we will create a workflow that will oversee the creation of observables on TheHive, containing filenames or hashes.

Depending on the content, n8n will send the instruction to Velociraptor to create a hunt that scans the devices in search of these IoCs automatically.

To create the workflow in n8n, follow these steps:

1. On the left menu of Security Onion, click on the **n8n** button to open a new tab on the web browser, as shown in the following screenshot:

Figure 11.53 – Opening the n8n console

We will use the workflow created by Wes Lambert for his *SOARlab* project. You can use any of the following methods to add this workflow:

- **Importing directly from the URL**: `https://gist.githubusercontent.com/weslambert/a8b43960fe3e5a3dd25468802743b074/raw/e552320367e25375a8d0f809e1c8ecca42de38da/n8n_thehive_velociraptor_workflow`.

- **Importing from file**: You can use the `n8n_thehive_velociraptor_workflow.json` configuration file, which you can download from the `Chapter-11` folder of the GitHub repository of this book.

In this case, we are going to import the workflow configuration from a file to do this.

2. On the left menu, click on the **Workflows** option and select **Import from File**, as shown in the following screenshot:

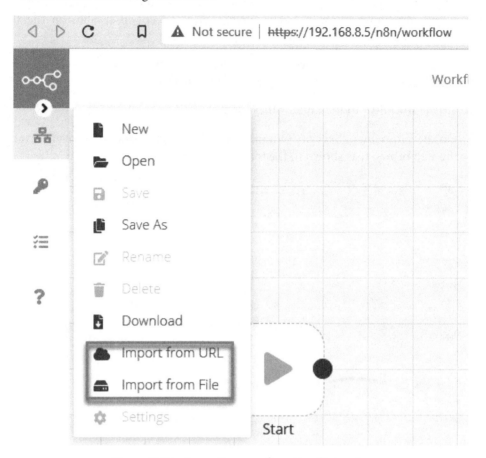

Figure 11.54 – Importing a configuration file to n8n

3. Move the workflow to the right of the green **Start** icon.

4. Click again on the **Workflows** button and then click on **Save As**.

5. In the dialog box, name your workflow as IR-SOAR and click on the **Save** button, as shown in the following screenshot:

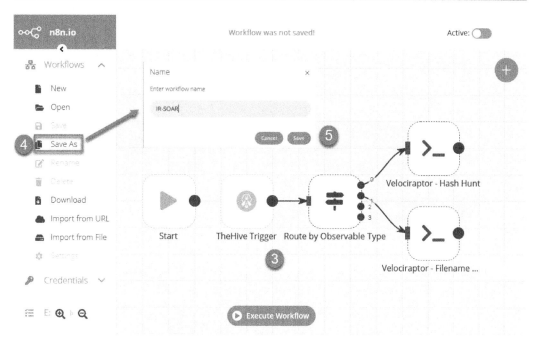

Figure 11.55 – Saving a workflow in n8n

With these simple steps, we added connectivity and automation between TheHive and Velociraptor, and now we have everything ready to create the attack emulation scenario.

To get started, we need to identify the previous activity on the monitoring server:

1. On your web browser, navigate to the **Security Onion** console.
2. Click on the hamburger button and then select the **Hunt** option:

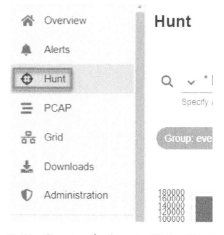

Figure 11.56 – Opening the Security Onion Hunt console

3.   Filter by **event.module:sysmon | groupby event.dataset**:

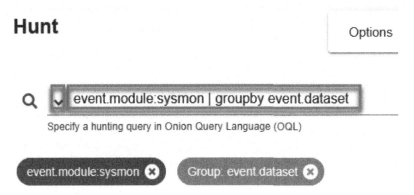

Figure 11.57 – Filtering the Sysmon events

Under **Group Metrics**, we will focus on the following `event.dataset` events, which may be more related to the event we have just generated:

Count ▼	event.dataset
211	registry_create_delete
75	file_create
68	image_loaded
67	registry_value_set
17	dns_query
5	process_access
3	process_creation
2	network_connection
1	process_terminated

Figure 11.58 – Identifying the events related to the malicious activity

4.   Filter the `dns_query` events by clicking on **event.dataset** and then clicking on the **Only** option:

Figure 11.59 – Filtering by the dns_query events

5. Find the `dns_query` generated by `certutil.exe`:

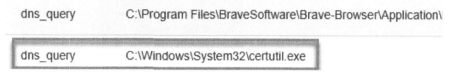

Figure 11.60 – Identifying certutil.exe malicious activity

6. Drilldown on the event to review the details:

Figure 11.61 – Reviewing the details of the certuil.exe DNS query

7. Reset this hunt by clicking on the **X** icon:

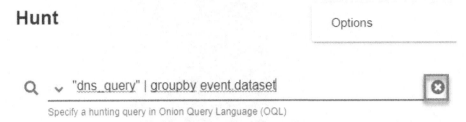

Figure 11.62 – Resetting dns_query

8. Filter again, but look for `process_creation` this time:

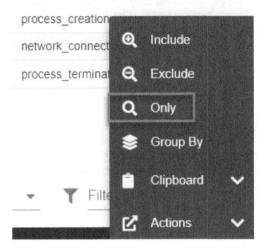

Figure 11.63 – Filtering by process_creation events

You will find two processes related to emulation activity, shown as follows:

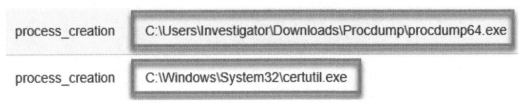

Figure 11.64 – Identifying the malicious processes

9. Drilldown on the events to review the details of these processes:

    - **Certutil**:

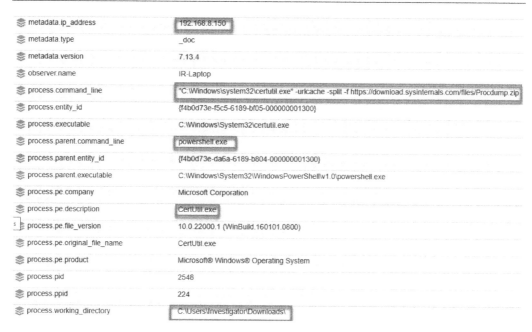

Figure 11.65 – CertUtil.exe process details

- **ProcDump**:

metadata.ip_address	192.168.8.150
metadata.type	_doc
metadata.version	7.13.4
observer.name	IR-Laptop
process.command_line	"C:\Users\Investigator\Downloads\Procdump\procdump64.exe" -accepteula -ma lsass.exe config.dmp
process.entity_id	{f4b0d73e-f626-6189-c805-000000001300}
process.executable	C:\Users\Investigator\Downloads\Procdump\procdump64.exe
process.parent.command_line	powershell.exe
process.parent.entity_id	{f4b0d73e-da6a-6189-b804-000000001300}
process.parent.executable	C:\Windows\System32\WindowsPowerShell\v1.0\powershell.exe
process.pe.company	Sysinternals - www.sysinternals.com
process.pe.description	Sysinternals process dump utility
process.pe.file_version	10.11
process.pe.original_file_name	procdump
process.pe.product	ProcDump
process.pid	4612
process.ppid	224
process.working_directory	C:\Users\Investigator\Downloads\Procdump\

Figure 11.66 – procdump64.exe process details

Now that we've identified the malicious activity, it is time to open a new IR case. In this case, we will do it in the same way as we did in the previous case:

1. Click on the escalate icon to create the new case in TheHive:

▼ ⚠	2021-11-08 20:16:38.872 -08:00
≋ @timestamp	2021-11-09T04:16:38.872Z
≋ @version	1
≋ agent.ephemeral_id	e9255dab-9f9f-4137-bf9e-17436e36af86
≋ agent.hostname	IR-Laptop
≋ agent.id	2f6c0b78-857b-461d-b34d-824474ac4e54
≋ agent.name	IR-Laptop
≋ agent.type	winlogbeat

Figure 11.67 – Escalating the event to an IR case on TheHive

2. Open the **TheHive** console, and you will see the new case created in the **List of cases** section:

Figure 11.68 – Reviewing the new event created from the SOC

3. Click on the case link to see the details of this incident, and then click on the **Observables** option to add an IoC:

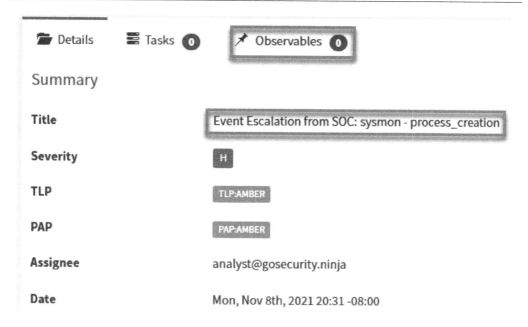

Figure 11.69 – Reviewing the details of the new event

We detected that someone downloaded the **ProcDump** tool from the internet and we are now interested in knowing whether there are more computers on the network that could have downloaded the same tool, which would mean that they are also compromised.

In this case, we are going to perform the hunt by hash, so we must first obtain this information by looking in the hash database that we generated with Velociraptor.

4. Go to the Velociraptor console, click on the **down arrow** and select **Show All**, as shown in the following screenshot:

Figure 11.70 – Showing the Velociraptor clients

5. Click on the **client ID**, and then click on the **Collected Artifacts** option, as shown in the following screenshot:

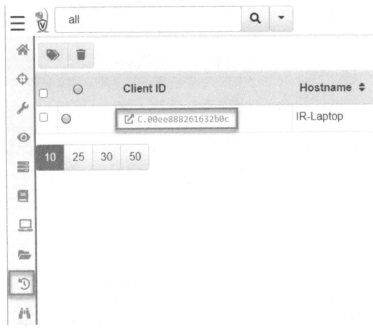

Figure 11.71 – Selecting the client ID

6. Select **Generic.Forensic.LocalHashes.Glob.** Click on the **Results** option, as shown in the following screenshot:

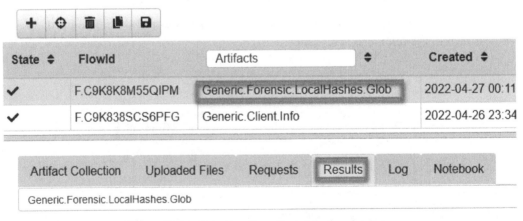

Figure 11.72 – Selecting the collected hashes database

7. Find the hash of the `Procdump.zip` file in the **Results** section, as shown in the following figure:

C:\Users\Investigator\Downloads\Procdump.zip   f0a99ed2f9e64ba438de802a1f1343ff

Figure 11.73 – Looking for the hash value of the Procdump.zip file

> **Note**
>
> The hash value of the `Procdump.zip` file will be different if you download a newer version of this file, so you must use the corresponding hash in that case.

8. Before creating the observable, let's go to the **n8n** tool console and then click on the **Execute Workflow** button. This will start the monitoring of new observables in TheHive:

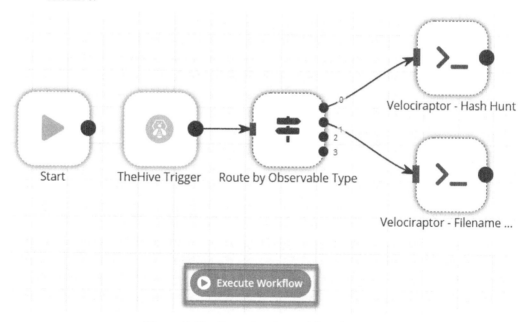

Figure 11.74 – Executing the workflow from n8n

9. Go back to the **TheHive** console to add the hash as a new observable by clicking on the **+ Add observable(s)** button:

Figure 11.75 – Adding a new observable

10. Create the new observable using the parameters described in the following figure (hash file of `Procdump.zip` – `f0a99ed2f9e64ba438de802a1f1343ff`):

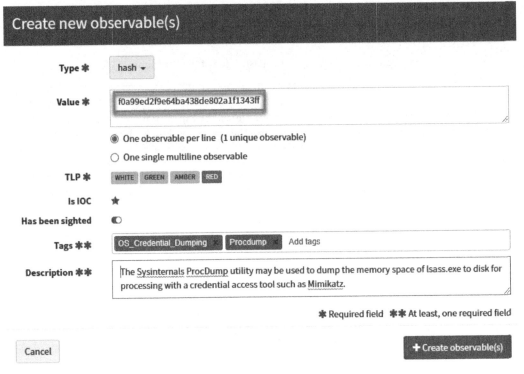

Figure 11.76 – Adding the parameters of the new observable

11. Once you have created the new observable, go to the Velociraptor console and click on the **Hunt** button. You will see the new hunt created by TheHive:

Figure 11.77 – Verifying the new hunt created by TheHive to look for the IoC

Now, Velociraptor will look for this IoC on the network to identify potentially compromised devices.

If necessary, you can also obtain the system files collected remotely; to do this, just scroll down to the **Results** section.

12. Click on the **Download** icon.

13. Click on the **Full Download** option.

14. Click on the link under **Available Downloads** and download the `.zip` file:

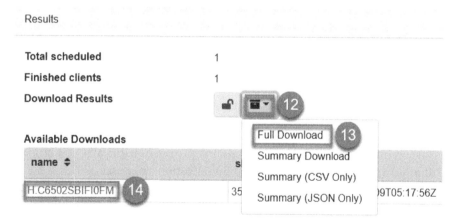

Figure 11.78 – Downloading the findings of the hunt

15. You can review the complete information by unzipping the file and looking for the different reports.

Another thing we can do as a part of the investigation is to go to the **Virtual Filesystem** section and access the system remotely to collect files to analyze them, as shown in the following screenshot:

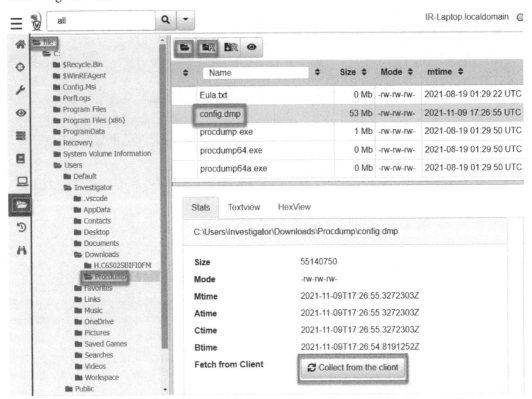

Figure 11.79 – Collecting files from the remote system using Virtual Filesystem

As you can see, integrating different solutions and processes using a SOAR model will help us to improve and speed up the IR and investigation processes.

Summary

In this chapter, you learned about the concept of integration and orchestration using different solutions known as SOAR, as well as the components needed to optimize and streamline IR processes.

You analyzed a use case of an IR of a suspicious communication from a device on the network to **command and control (C2)** on the internet.

You learned how to set up a SOAR environment, integrating the Security Onion (monitoring), TheHive (IR), n8n (workflows), and Velociraptor (artifacts collection, digital forensics, and investigation) open source tools.

You also learned how to escalate security incidents from alerts generated in a SOC and how to open a case from the IR platform to initiate the IR and investigation process.

In the next chapter, you will learn about detection engineering concepts and how to apply different analytics in IR to proactively uncover malicious behavior.

Further reading

- *Security Orchestration and Automation (SOAR) Playbook*: `https://www.rapid7.com/info/security-orchestration-and-automation-playbook/`

- *SOAR (security orchestration, automation, and response)*: `https://www.techtarget.com/searchsecurity/definition/SOAR`

- *Introducing Shuffle — an Open Source SOAR platform part 1*: `https://medium.com/shuffle-automation/introducing-shuffle-an-open-source-soar-platform-part-1-58a529de7d12`

- Awesome-SOAR list: `https://github.com/correlatedsecurity/Awesome-SOAR`

Section 4: Improving Threat Detection in Incident Response

Incident response is a demanding and changing practice. When there is a security breach, seconds count, and you must make quick decisions. At this point, the knowledge, experience, and skills of the incident response professional are critical. In this last part, you will learn the concepts of developing detection engineering and threat hunting to quickly identify any compromise or malicious behavior in order to contain the attack.

This section comprises the following chapters:

- *Chapter 12, Working with Analytics and Detection Engineering in Incident Response*
- *Chapter 13, Creating and Deploying Detection Rules*
- *Chapter 14, Hunting and Investigating Security Incidents*

12
Working with Analytics and Detection Engineering in Incident Response

So far in this book, you have learned about the fundamentals of incident response, the knowledge of the attacker's behaviors using threat intelligence, and the way that you can implement and use different tools to improve the capacity of your organization to respond to attacks.

However, in the critical moments when an incident occurs, it is essential to know what you need to look for and where to get relevant information.

There are multiple sources of information where you can get valuable data about malicious behaviors to define an identification and contention strategy. You can do this by implementing analytics and detection engineering in incident response.

In this chapter, we will cover the following topics:

- Configuring the detection lab
- Identifying and containing threats
- Implementing principles of detection engineering in incident response
- Using MITRE Cyber Analytics Repository (CAR), Invoke-AtomicRedTeam, and MITRE ATT&CK to test analytics

Technical requirements

In case you haven't already, you need to download and install VMware Workstation Player from this link `https://www.vmware.com/products/workstation-player/workstation-player-evaluation.html`.

You'll also need to download the following from the book's official GitHub repository `https://github.com/PacktPublishing/Incident-Response-with-Threat-Intelligence`:

- Virtual machines:
  - IR-Laptop
  - IR-Workstation
- Lab file:
  - `Chapter12`

Configuring the detection lab

Before we start the practical exercises in this chapter, we need to prepare our work environment.

To begin, start up the virtual machines that we will use throughout this chapter. To do this, start VMware Workstation Player. From there, do the following:

- Start the **IR-Laptop** virtual machine and sign in using the following credentials:

  - **Username**: `investigator`

  - **Password**: `L34rn1ng!`

- Start the **IR-Workstation** virtual machine and sign in using the following credentials:

  - **Username**: `investigator`

  - **Password**: `L34rn1ng!`

Once you have started both virtual machines, you can install and configure the tools that will be required to perform the practical lab exercises.

Implementing a threat hunting platform

In the previous chapter, you learned about some basic concepts for using the monitoring, detection, incident response, and orchestration Security Onion platform. As you learned, this platform contains valuable tools for active defense against threats.

In this chapter, you will learn how to install some of these tools individually on your **IR-Workstation** VM to create a threat hunting platform to work on the practical exercises provided in this chapter, as well as the next.

Installing ELK

ELK stands for the integration of three open source tools:

- **Elasticsearch**: Search engine and data analysis

- **Logstash**: A tool for ingesting, processing, and transforming data from multiple sources

- **Kibana**: The frontend that allows users to view the information that's been processed by Elasticsearch

These components of the Elastic stack work together to ingest, process, and display the information so that it can be managed and visualized, as shown in the following screenshot:

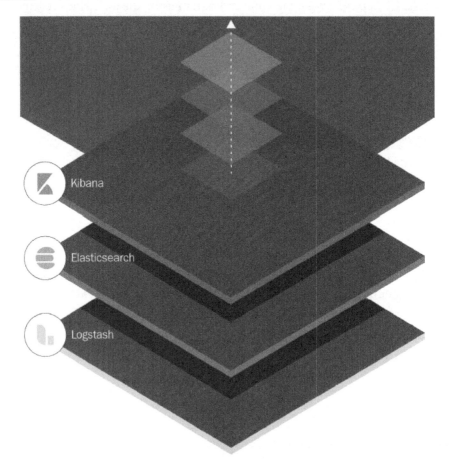

Figure 12.1 – ELK components

The first ELK component that we are going to install will be Elasticsearch. We will do so using the **Debian/Ubuntu** installation package.

Installing Elasticsearch

From your IR-Workstation VM, follow these steps:

1. Open a new Linux Terminal from the left toolbar or use the *Ctrl + Alt + T* shortcut.
2. Change to the Downloads directory:

```
cd Downloads
```

3. Execute the following command to download the Debian/Ubuntu installation file:

```
wget https://artifacts.elastic.co/downloads/
elasticsearch/elasticsearch-7.15.2-amd64.deb
```

This will result in the following output:

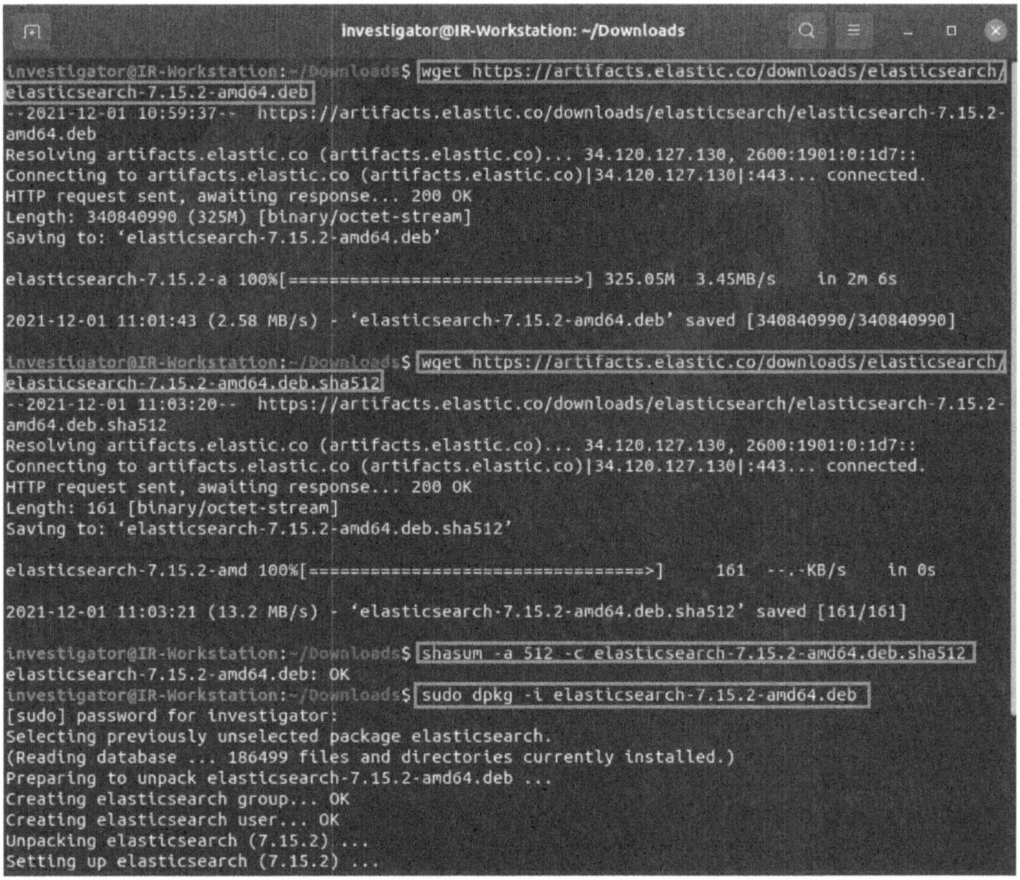

Figure 12.2 – Downloading the Elasticsearch installation package

4. Additionally, download the verification file to validate the integrity of the download by running the following command:

```
wget https://artifacts.elastic.co/downloads/
elasticsearch/elasticsearch-7.15.2-amd64.deb.sha512
```

5. To validate the checksum, run the following command:

```
shasum -a 512 -c elasticsearch-7.15.2-amd64.deb.sha512
```

6. Install Elasticsearch and provide your password if necessary:

```
sudo dpkg -i elasticsearch-7.15.2-amd64.deb
```

7. Now that we've installed the program, configure the Elasticsearch service so that it starts using **sysytemd** automatically by running the following commands:

```
sudo systemctl daemon-reload
sudo systemctl enable elasticsearch.service
```

To start the Elasticsearch service, run the following command:

```
sudo systemctl start elasticsearch.service
```

These commands can be seen in the following screenshot:

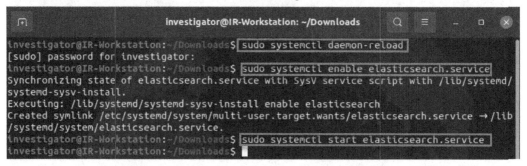

Figure 12.3 – Configuring and starting the Elasticsearch service

With that, you have installed and started the first component of ELK. Next, we are going to install and configure Logstash.

Installing Logstash

Installing Logstash is similar to what we did for Elasticsearch. Follow these steps:

1. Start by downloading the Debian/Ubuntu installation package by running the following command:

```
wget https://artifacts.elastic.co/downloads/logstash/
logstash-7.15.2-amd64.deb
```

2. To install Logstash, run the following command:

```
sudo dpkg -i logstash-7.15.2-amd64.deb
```

This will result in the following output:

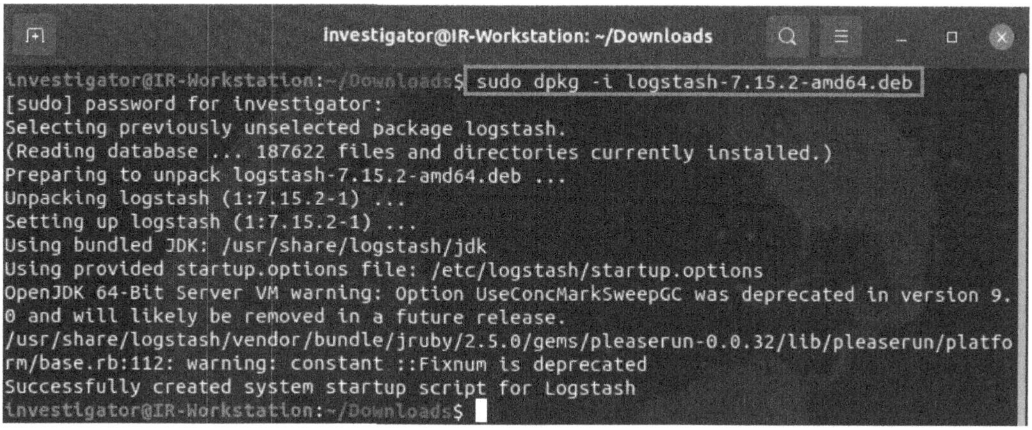

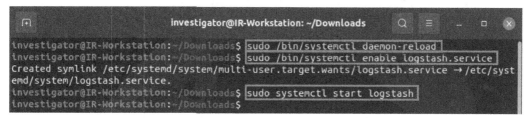

Figure 12.4 – Logstash installation

3. To configure the Logstash service so that it starts automatically, run the following commands:

```
sudo /bin/systemctl daemon-reload
sudo /bin/systemctl enable logstash.service
sudo systemctl start logstash
```

The preceding commands can be seen in action in the following screenshot:

Figure 12.5 – Configuring and starting Logstash

Now that you have started the Logstash service, let's install Kibana.

Installing Kibana

The last of the ELK components is **Kibana**, and the installation process is similar to what we saw for Elasticsearch and Logstash:

1. Download Kibana by running the following command:

```
wget https://artifacts.elastic.co/downloads/kibana/
kibana-7.15.2-amd64.deb
```

2. To install the Debian/Ubuntu package, run the following command:

```
sudo dpkg -i kibana-7.15.2-amd64.deb
```

3. To enable and start the service, run the following commands:

```
sudo /bin/systemctl daemon-reload
```

```
sudo /bin/systemctl enable kibana.service
```

In this case, we are going to configure Kibana to allow connections from the other devices on the network before starting the service.

4. First, use vim or nano to edit the configuration file and run the following command:

```
sudo vim /etc/kibana/kibana.yml
```

Change the server.host parameter to allow external connections and the elasticsearch.host parameter to define the URL for the Elasticsearch instance, as shown in the following screenshot:

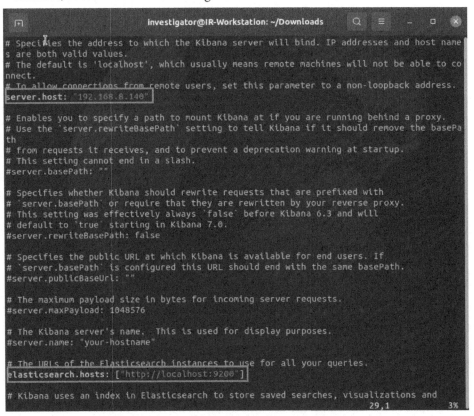

Figure 12.6 – Editing the Kibana configuration file

5. To start the Kibana service, run the following command:

```
sudo systemctl start kibana.service
```

6. Finally, open a web browser and navigate to `http://192.168.8.140:5601` from your IR-Workstation virtual machine.

    You will see a welcome message so that you can start using ELK, as shown in the following screenshot:

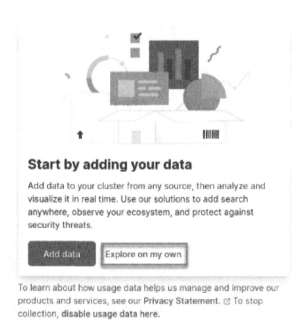

Figure 12.7 – The welcome page of ELK

7. Click on the **Explore on my own** button to enter the main ELK dashboard.

To start receiving information via ELK, we need to create a configuration file on Logstash that includes input, transformation, and output parameters.

Creating a Logstash configuration file

You can create a Logstash configuration file from scratch or you can use a preconfigured template. In this case, we are going to use a sample template:

1. On your Ubuntu Terminal, change to the `logstash` directory by running the following command:

    ```
    cd /etc/logstash
    ```

2. Using vim or nano, review the `logstash-sample.conf` file:

    ```
    sudo vim logstash-sample.config
    ```

    This will result in the following output:

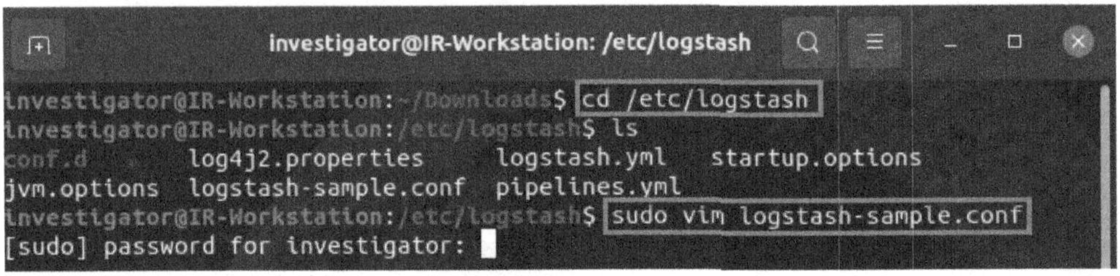

Figure 12.8 – Opening the Logstash configuration file

3. In this case, we are going to keep the default configuration for simplicity because we don't need to transform the input information. Additionally, we will use the Elasticsearch output parameters, as shown in the following screenshot:

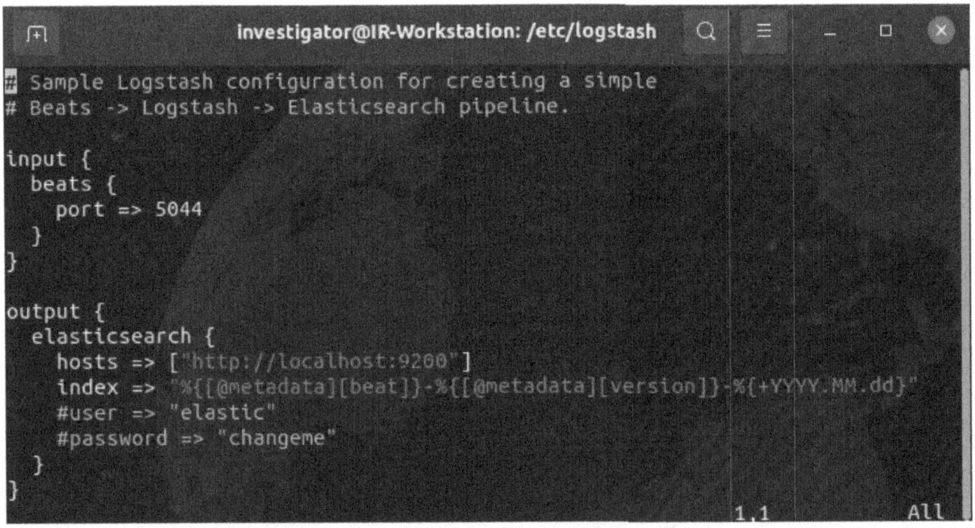

Figure 12.9 – Sample Logstash configuration file

4. Copy the `logstash-sample.conf` file to the `conf.d` directory and rename it `win.conf`, as shown in the following screenshot:

```
sudo cp logstash-sample.conf conf.d/win.conf
```

This will result in the following output:

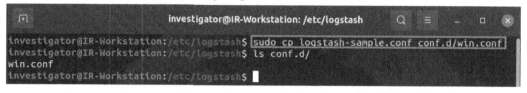

Figure 12.10 – Copying and renaming the Logstash configuration file

5. Restart the Logstash service to load the configuration file:

```
sudo systemctl restart logstash
```

Now, your ELK is ready to receive and process information from different devices to analyze on the platform.

Reconfiguring winglogbeat

In the previous chapter, you installed and configured `winlogbeat` to send the Windows logs to ELK on **Security Onion**.

To receive the logs from your IR-Laptop VM, you need to change the IP address in the `winlogbeat` configuration file so that the `output.logstash` parameter points it to the IR-Workstation VM. Follow these steps:

1. On your IR-Laptop VM, log in and open a `Windows Terminal/PowerShell` instance with administrator privileges.

2. Change to the `C:\Program Files\winlogbeat` directory.

3. Open the `winlogbeat.yml` file using Visual Studio Code.

4. Scroll down until you get to the `output.logstash:` section.

5. Change the `hosts:` parameter to `["192.168.8.140:5044"]`:

Figure 12.11 – The winlogbeat configuration file

6. Restart the `winlogbeat` service to load the changes by running the following command:

```
restart-Service winlogbeat
```

Your IR-Laptop VM will now send the Windows logs to the ELK instance on the IR-Workstation VM.

Creating an index in Kibana to visualize the information

The last part of configuring ELK consists of creating an index to define the way that Kibana will process and show the information on the dashboard. Follow these steps:

1. On the IR-Workstation VM, from the Kibana dashboard, click on the **Stack Management** link, as shown in the following screenshot:

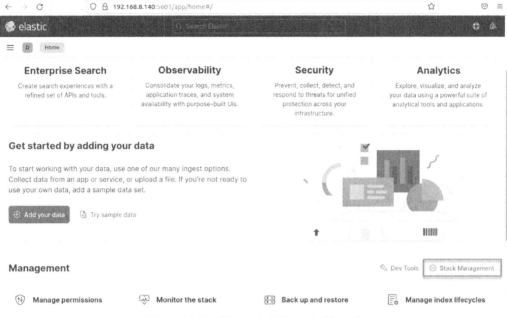

Figure 12.12 – The main Kibana dashboard

2. From the **Stack Management** dashboard, click the **Index Patterns** link.

3. Next, click on the **Create index pattern** button.

4. In the **Create index pattern** dialog box, in the **Name** textbox, write the following text:

```
winlogbeat*
```

5. In the **Timestamp** field, click on the menu and select the **@timestamp** value.

6. Click on the **Create index pattern** button, as shown in the following screenshot:

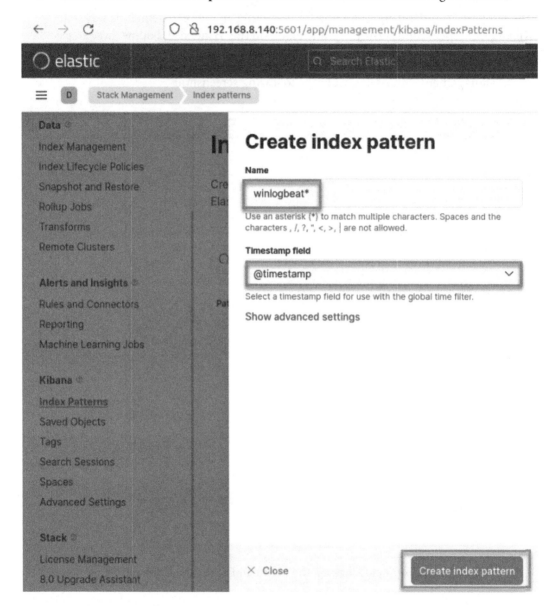

Figure 12.13 – The Create index pattern dialog box

Now that you've created an index, you can start visualizing the information in Kibana.

To open the **Discover** dashboard, follow these steps:

1. Click on the hamburger menu button at the top left of the dashboard. Click on the **Discover** link, as shown in the following screenshot:

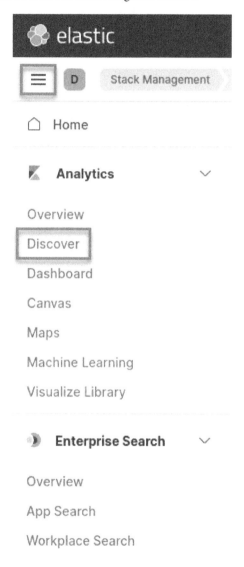

Figure 12.14 – Opening the Discover dashboard

2. On the **Discover** dashboard, you can see the log information you've received from the IR-Laptop VM, as shown in the following screenshot:

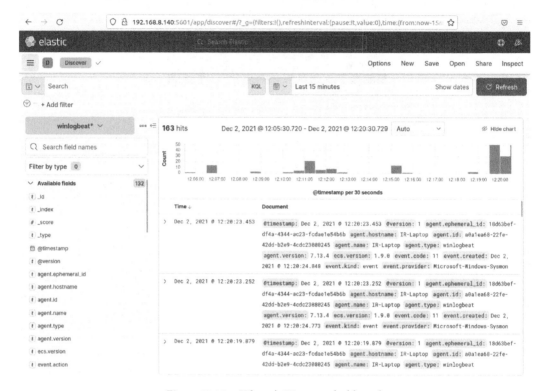

Figure 12.15 – Kibana's Discover dashboard

Congratulations – you finished installing and configuring the ELK stack on your IR-Workstation VM! Now, we are ready to learn about some concepts and strategies we can use to detect and contain threats.

Identifying and containing threats

As you learned in *Chapter 2*, *Concepts of Digital Forensics and Incident Response*, according to the SANS Incident Response process, phase 2 – identification, and phase 3 – containment, are essential to reduce the impact of a cyberattack, as shown in the following diagram:

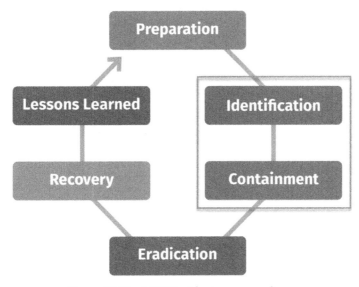

Figure 12.16 – SANS incident response phases

Incident response sometimes starts with the escalation of an alert or a user reporting the disruption of a service or the discovery of a data leak. Once a case has been created regarding an incident, the next step is to follow the playbooks associated with the incident.

The more information you have about the incident, the better you can understand the nature of the attack, especially if you use frameworks such as **MITRE ATT&CK** and you have reliable threat intelligence sources of information.

However, at this point, you just have information about the incident's symptoms, but not necessarily the root of the problem, which means that you may not know about the attack vector or the scope of the compromise.

Essentially, you can't move efficiently to the **containment** phase if you don't have enough information and context about the attack.

Hunting for threats in incident response

Between the detection phase and the containment phase, you need to be proactive, assertive, and efficient. Remember that sometimes, the attackers are on your network and every move can accelerate the attacker's actions if they discover that you are trying to catch them.

There are six steps that you can follow to dimension the level of compromise, look for malicious indicators, and use this information to limit the damage of the attack. These steps are shown in the following diagram:

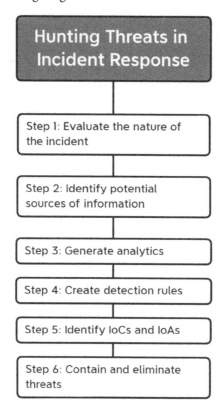

Figure 12.17 – Steps for hunting threats in incident response

Let's discuss these steps further:

1. **Step 1: Evaluate the nature of the incident**: To evaluate the nature of the attack, you need to analyze all the information that's available about the incident up to that point. By doing so, you can identify some **tactics, techniques, and procedures (TTPs)** that are used by the attackers.

2. **Step 2: Identify potential sources of information**: Once you understand the nature of the attack, you will need additional information to find malicious indicators of the attack, so it is very important to identify other potential sources that you can get this information from, such as logs from the systems, network traffic, and more.

3. **Step 3: Generate analytics**: When you identify the potential sources of information, you can model the way that you can detect malicious behaviors from these sources. This activity is known as detection engineering.

4. **Step 4: Create detection rules**: An efficient way to detect malicious behaviors, especially at a large scale, is by creating rules or regular expressions based on your previous analytics. For example, you can create **Yara**, **Sigma**, or **Zeek/Suricata** rules.

5. **Step 5: Identify IoCs and IoAs**: Once you have created your regular expression and rules, you can start searching for **Indicators of Compromise** (**IoCs**) and **Indicators of Attack** (**IoAs**) on the network using different tools.

6. **Step 6: Contain and eliminate threats**: Once you have identified threats on your network, you can apply the controls to contain and eliminate threats.

In the next section, you will learn some concepts surrounding detection engineering and how to use it to hunt threats in incident response.

Implementing principles of detection engineering in incident response

Detection engineering is the process of improving detection capabilities by using diverse sources of information to analyze potential threats, identify adversaries' tactics, techniques, and procedures, and incorporate analytics and detection rules to implement them in specific tools such as **Security Information and Event Management** (**SIEM**) or perform direct searches on devices.

This process should be technology-agnostic and focus on using existing analytics that have been created by other professionals or on the development of your analytics to detect malicious indicators.

To create good detection rules, you will need the following components:

- **Good threat intel**: As we learned in *Chapter 2, Concepts of Digital Forensics and Incident Response*, you can get this information from reports from security providers, or you can find them on the internet.

- **Plenty of sources of information**: There are multiple sources of information, including logs from operating systems, **Endpoint Detection and Response** (**EDR**), the cloud, network packages, and perimeter devices.

- **Quality information**: It's common to get a lot of false positives, so it is particularly important to depurate this information to have reliable data.

Detection engineering is a core activity for **security operations centers** (**SOCs**), and you can work together with the SOC in the **preparation** phase to develop analytics in case an incident occurs.

The goal is to reduce the detection time of malicious indicators by identifying potentially compromised devices in the incident and contain threats in time to limit their impact on the organization.

MITRE ATT&CK is a good resource for identifying data sources where you can find malicious indicators – you just need to look for the data components that contain valuable information for a particular technique/sub-technique in the detection section, as shown in the following screenshot:

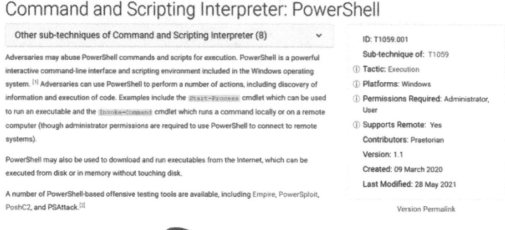

Figure 12.18 – The T1059.001 technique's detection data sources

Once you've mapped the data sources to this technique, you can review the information associated with the data components and create the analytics for detection.

In the next section, you will learn how to develop and test detection engineering so that you can use it in incident response.

Using MITRE CAR, Invoke-AtomicRedTeam, and testing analytics

So far, you have learned about the principles you can use to identify threats using data analytics and detection engineering. Sometimes, you will need to create analytics at the time of the incident response, but the idea is to do it proactively by creating a repository in advance to use when necessary.

Now, let's learn how to configure a laboratory to create and test analytics, as well as validate their efficiency.

Here, we will select a specific MITRE ATT&CK technique and from this technique, we will associate it with a MITRE **Cyber Analytics Repository** (**CAR**) analytic and create the implementation from the pseudocode.

Subsequently, we will emulate this technique using the `Invoke-AtomicRedTeam` tool to generate the IoA.

Once that activity has been recorded, we will use the analytics we created previously to detect this behavior through attack indicators, as shown in the preceding screenshot.

MITRE CAR

The MITRE CAR is a repository of analytics that was developed by MITRE based on the MITRE ATT&CK adversary model. The MITRE CAR knowledge base is defined by agnostic pseudocode representations and the implementations for specific detection technologies such as **Event Query Language** (**EQL**) and Splunk.

As described in the official MITRE CAR Portal, the analytics of CAR includes the following information:

- An explanation of the basis of the specific analytics
- Details about how these analytics can be implemented
- Mapping to ATT&CKS TTPs
- A pseudocode definition to implement in different technologies
- A unit test to trigger and validate the analytic

For example, you suspect that the attacker might be using PowerShell scripts to perform malicious activities. According to MITRE CAR, the analytical information to detect this behavior corresponds to CAR-2014-04-003. You can find details about this analytic at https://car.mitre.org/analytics/CAR-2014-04-003/, as shown in the following screenshot:

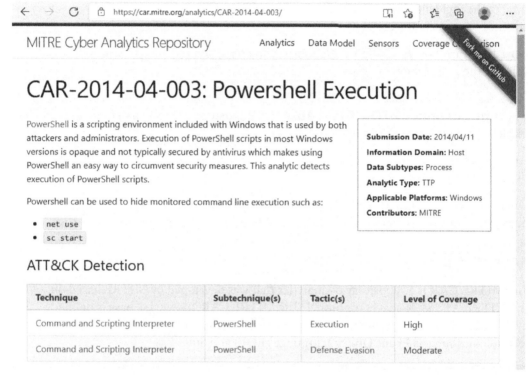

Figure 12.19 – The MITRE CAR analytic for PowerShell execution

In the **Implementations** section, you will find the pseudocode in a generic format that describes the components you need to look for.

```
process = search Process:Create
powershell = filter process where (exe == "powershell.exe" AND parent_exe != "explorer.exe" )
output powershell
```

Figure 12.20 – Pseudocode of the PowerShell execution

You can use this information to create your own rules or searches for specific technologies, such as **Eql** and **EQL native**.

```
process where subtype.create and
  (process_name == "powershell.exe" and parent_process_name != "explorer.exe")
```

Figure 12.21 – The Eql query to detect the PowerShell execution

Now, you can start hunting to find this pattern of behavior on computers and servers on the network.

There are other amazing projects that you should explore to create and use data analytics and develop detection engineering, such as **Threat Hunter Playbook,** `https://github.com/OTRF/ThreatHunter-Playbook`, and **Security-Datasets,** `https://github.com/OTRF/Security-Datasets`. Both projects were developed as part of the **Open Threat Research** community initiative, led by the brothers Roberto Rodriguez and Jose Luis Rodriguez (you can connect with them on Twitter at @ `Cyb3rPandaH` and @`Cyb3rWar0g`, respectively).

When you use data analytics and detection engineering in incident response, you will substantially improve the speed at which you identify malicious indicators and the capacity to contain the attack.

Installing Invoke-AtomicRedTeam

To finish configuring our detection lab, we need to install Red Canary's `Invoke-AtomicRedTeam` from `https://github.com/redcanaryco/invoke-atomicredteam`. To do this, follow these steps:

1. On your IR-Laptop VM, open a Windows terminal/PowerShell instance with administrator privileges.

2. Enable the execution permissions by running the following command:

    ```
    Set-ExecutionPolicy -ExecutionPolicy Unrestricted
    ```

3. Run the following command to download and install the **Execution Framework**:

    ```
    IEX (IWR 'https://raw.githubusercontent.com/redcanaryco/
    invoke-atomicredteam/master/install-atomicredteam.ps1'
    -UseBasicParsing)
    ```

4. Open Windows Defender and disable real-time protection.

5. Add the `C:\AtomicRedTeam` directory to Windows Defender Exclusions.

6. Now, run the following command to install the `Atomics` folder:

    ```
    Install-AtomicRedTeam -getAtomics
    ```

7. To start using the `Invoke-AtomicTest` function, you must import the module by running the following command:

    ```
    Import-Module "C:\AtomicRedTeam\invoke-atomicredteam\
    Invoke-AtomicRedTeam.psd1" -Force
    ```

You need to run this command every time you open a new PowerShell console. If you want to make this functionality always available, you need to add the import to your PowerShell profile, as described in the respective GitHub repository, by running the following commands:

```
Import-Module "C:\AtomicRedTeam\invoke-atomicredteam\Invoke-
AtomicRedTeam.psd1" -Force
$PSDefaultParameterValues = @{"Invoke-
AtomicTest:PathToAtomicsFolder"="C:\AtomicRedTeam\atomics"}
```

Now that you've installed Red Canary's `Invoke-AtomicRedTeam`, you can run your tests from a PowerShell console. You can find additional tests in the `Chapter-12` folder on GitHub.

Additionally, you can create tests using the Atomic GUI by running the following command:

```
Start-AtomicGUI
```

This will open the Atomic Test Creation interface on port `8487`, as shown in the following screenshot:

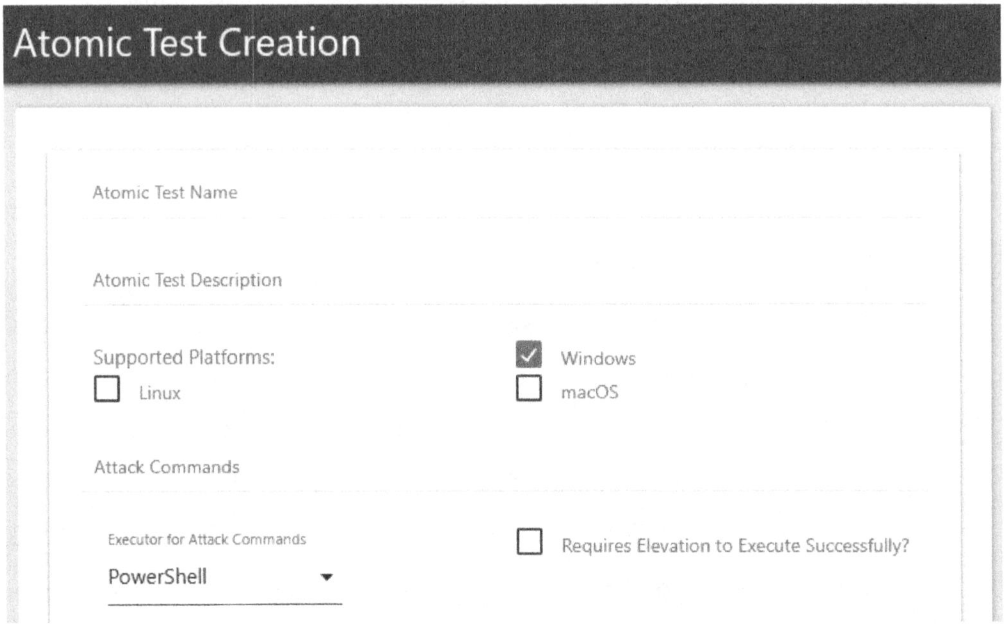

Figure 12.22 – Atomic Test Creation GUI

With the Atomic GUI, you can create tests for Windows, Linux, and macOS. You can find a short video demonstration about how to use this tool in this book's Code in Action section.

Testing detections and hunting

To start the test in our detection lab, we are going to select one of the MITRE ATT&CK techniques that's commonly used by attackers that we reviewed previously, known as `Command and Scripting Interpreter: PowerShell(T1059.001)` (`https://attack.mitre.org/techniques/T1059/001/`).

According to the **Red Canary 2021 Threat Detection Report** (`https://redcanary.com/threat-detection-report/`) and the **Kaspersky Cybercriminals' top LOLBins report** (`https://usa.kaspersky.com/blog/most-used-lolbins/25456/`), abusing Microsoft PowerShell, the legitimate software engine and scripting language, was the most common tool to be used in cyberattacks, so creating detection analytics for PowerShell-related activity will be very useful.

To start emulating this behavior using Red Canary's `Invoke-AtomicRedTeam`, follow these steps:

1. Via your Windows terminal/PowerShell console, change to the `AtomicRedTeam` directory:

    ```
    cd C:\AtomicRedTeam
    ```

2. Run the following command to see the list of tests that you can run for the **T1059.001** technique:

    ```
    Invoke-AtomicTest T1059.001 -ShowDetailsBrief
    ```

The output will be as follows:

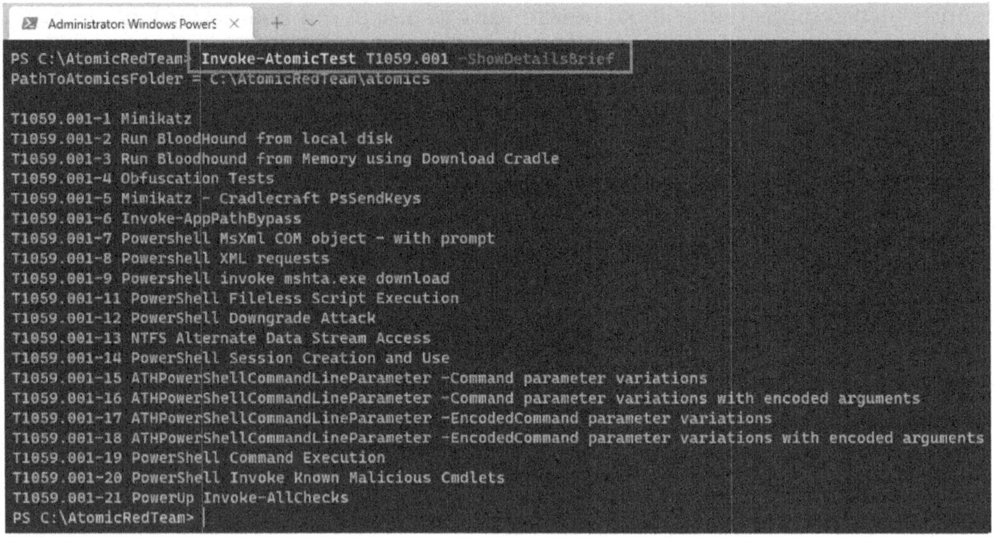

Figure 12.23 – List of tests related to the T1059.001 technique

3. You can get details of each test by running the following command:

```
Invoke-AtomicTest T1059.001 -ShowDetails
```

The output will be as follows:

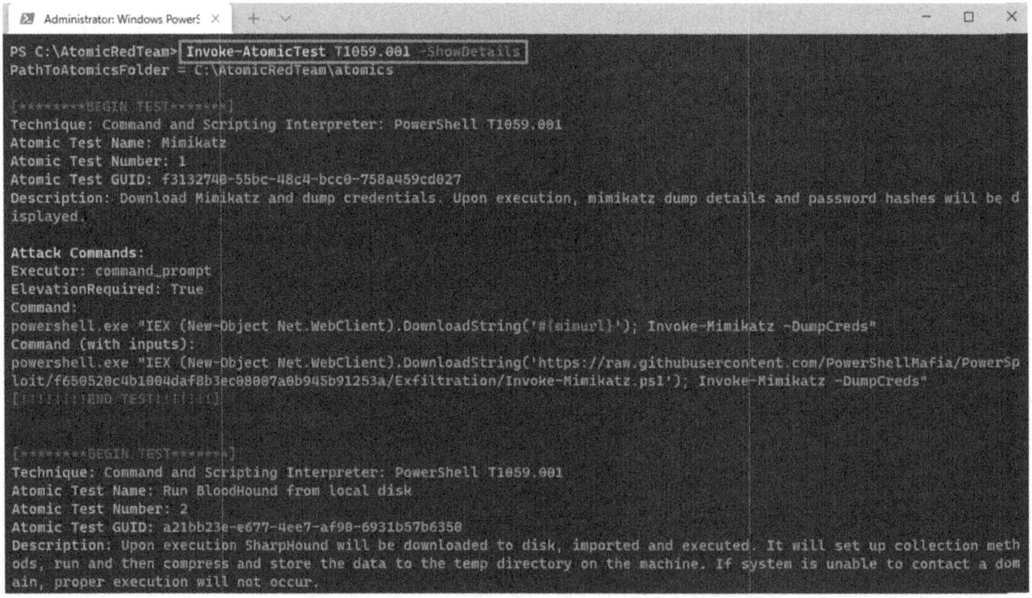

Figure 12.24 – Details of the T1059.001 tests

4. Sometimes, you need to configure or install additional tools to perform some of the tests, so it is recommended that you check the prerequisites before running a test. To do so, run the following command:

```
Invoke-AtomicTest T1059.001 -CheckPrereqs
```

You will see the following output:

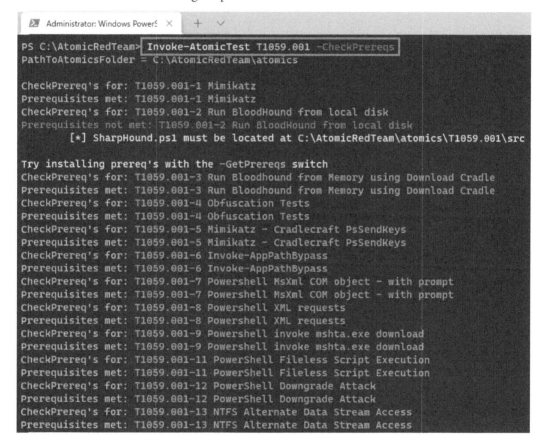

Figure 12.25 – Details of every T1059.001 test

5. In this case, we will focus on the **T1059.001-4 Obfuscation Tests** and **T1059.001-11 PowerShell Fileless Script Execution** tests.

To run the tests, execute the following command:

```
Invoke-AtomicTest T1059.001 -TestNumbers 4,11
```

You will be able to see the results of the tests, as shown in the following screenshot:

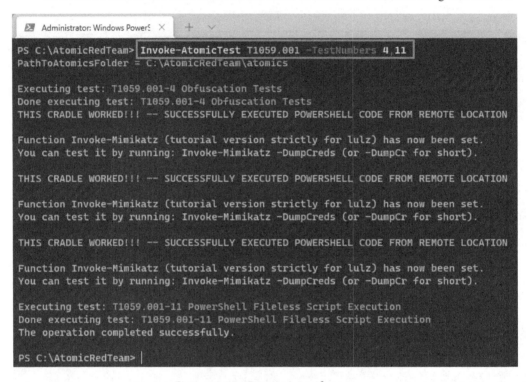

Figure 12.26 – Running specific tests

Now that you have run various tests on the technique to emulate this malicious behavior, let's create the analytics. According to MITRE ATT&CK, the data components we can use to detect this technique are as follows:

- Command execution
- Module load
- Process creation
- Script execution

With this information, we can identify the sources of information to detect any malicious PowerShell activity:

```
process = search Process:Create
powershell = filter process where (exe == "powershell.exe" AND parent_exe != "explorer.exe" )
output powershell
```

Figure 12.27 – Pseudocode of MITRE CAR CAR-2014-04-003

In this case, we will use Elasticsearch/Kibana as a hunting platform, so we are going to create the analytics to run it in **Kibana Query Language** (**KQL**). Assuming that we have installed Sysmon, we can create a query for detection using the information from the Sysmon documentation at `https://docs.microsoft.com/en-us/sysinternals/downloads/sysmon`, where the identifier for detecting process creation is **Event ID: 1**.

So, we could create the analytics using the following information:

- Process creation (Sysmon Event ID: 1)
- Command execution (`ParentCommandLine` and `ParentImage !=` `explorer`)

The result of our analytics would be as follows:

```
winlog.event_id : 1 and winlog.event_data.ParentCommandLine : *
Powershell.exe and not winlog.event_data.ParentImage :*explorer
```

Follow these steps to test the analytics:

1. Go to your IR-Workstation virtual machine and, in your previously opened web browser, navigate to **Kibana | Discover**.

2. On the **Kibana Search** window, paste the analytics and press the *Enter* key, as shown in the following screenshot:

> **Note**
> Don't forget to adjust the range of time according to the period when you ran the atomic test.

Figure 12.28 – Hunting for testing analytics

You will see the records that match the search criteria of your analytics.

3. Click the expand button to review the details of the identified events, as shown in the following screenshot:

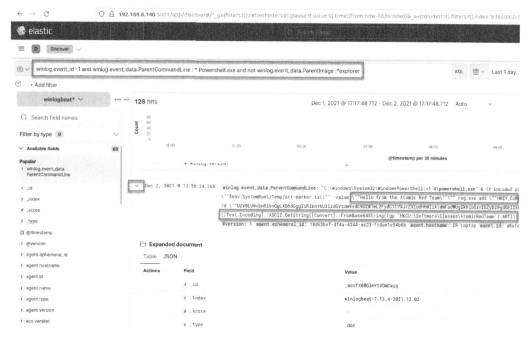

Figure 12.29 – Details about a specific event

4. Now, let's analyze each element of the detection and add it to a column to have all the components of the analytics in a single view.

Scroll down and click on the **Toggle column in table** button for the `winlog.event_id` field, as shown in the following screenshot:

winlog.event_data.User	IR-Laptop\Investigator
winlog.event_data.UtcTime	2021-12-02 21:39:16.610
winlog.event_id	1
winlog.process.pid	6,136
winlog.process.thread.id	3,612
winlog.provider_guid	{5770385f-c22a-43e0-bf4c-06f5698ffbd9}
winlog.provider_name	Microsoft-Windows-Sysmon
winlog.record_id	3,891

Figure 12.30 – Toggling the winlog.event_id column in the table

5. Scroll up and click on the **Toggle column in table** button for the `winlog.event_data.ParentCommandLine` field, as shown in the following screenshot:

Figure 12.31 – Toggling the winlog.event_data.ParentCommand Line column in the table

6. Scroll up and click on the **Toggle column in table** button for the `winlog.event_data.CommandLine` field, as shown in the following screenshot:

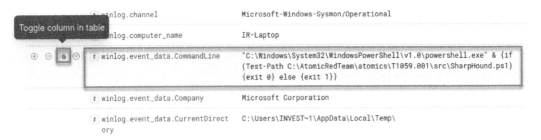

Figure 12.32 – Toggling the winlog.event_data.CommandLine column in the table

Now, you will see those filtered fields in column format, which will allow you to analyze and search for information, as shown in the following screenshot:

Figure 12.33 – Detected analytics fields for hunting for threats

Finally, review and identify the events related to the IoA that was generated when you ran the atomic tests using Red Canary's `Invoke-AtomicTest`.

As you can see, detection engineering and data analytics are very valuable when you need to identify possible malicious activity on your network in incident response.

Summary

In this chapter, you learned about the importance of detection engineering in incident response, how to create a detection lab by installing the ELK stack, and how to use the `Invoke-AtomicRedteam` framework to develop and test analytics.

You also learned how to find and contain threats efficiently using the MITRE CAR and MITRE ATT&CK frameworks.

In the next chapter, you will learn how to hunt threats by creating and using detection rules to find **Indicators of Compromise (IoCs)** and **Indicators of Attack (IoAs)**.

13

Creating and Deploying Detection Rules

In many security incidents, response times were long because threats were not detected early enough and adequately due to multiple factors. These include the improvement of the threat actor's ability to evade detection or the lack of detection of the monitoring tools because they did not have the configuration or information about that specific threat.

That is why it is so important to have a proactive approach in incident response, where it is assumed that, at some point, there will be security compromises that could not be detected by the **Security Operation Center (SOC)**.

One way to do this is through rules to hunt threats in a more specific way to have a clear idea about what and where you need to look for specific information, rather than very generically, as this would be the equivalent of looking for a needle in a haystack.

In this chapter, you will learn about the following:

- Introduction to detection rules
- Detecting malicious files using YARA rules
- Detecting malicious behavior using Sigma rules

Technical requirements

In case you haven't already, you need to download and install VMware Workstation Player from this link `https://www.vmware.com/products/workstation-player/workstation-player-evaluation.html`.

You'll also need to download the following from the book's official GitHub repository `https://github.com/PacktPublishing/Incident-Response-with-Threat-Intelligence`:

- Virtual machines:

  - IR-Laptop

  - IR-Workstation

- Lab file:

  - `Chapter13`

Configuring the detection lab

Before we start with the practical exercises of this chapter, we will need to prepare the work environment.

To begin, start up the virtual machines that we will use throughout the chapter. To do this, follow these steps:

1. Start **VMware Workstation Player**.

2. Start the **IR-Laptop** virtual machine and log in using the following credentials:

    - **Username**: `investigator`

    - **Password**: `L34rn1ng!`

3. Start the **IR-Workstation** virtual machine and log in using the following credentials:

    - **Username**: `investigator`

    - **Password**: `L34rn1ng!`

In the next part, we will start the **Elasticsearch, Logstash, and Kibana (ELK)** stack services on the IR-Workstation virtual machine.

Starting ELK stack services

As in the previous chapter, we will use the ELK stack to hunt for malicious behavior. If you didn't install it, follow the instructions described in *Chapter 12, Working with Analytics and Detection Engineering in Incident Response.*

If you started your virtual machine and the services are not initialized, run the following commands in a terminal of the IR-Workstation virtual machine:

1. Open a new terminal console using *Ctrl + Alt + T* or click on the **Terminal** button.

2. First, we will check the ELK services' statuses to verify whether they are already running:

    ```
    sudo systemctl status elasticsearch.service
    sudo systemctl status logstash.service
    sudo systemctl status kibana.service
    ```

3. If the services are not running, start them by running the following commands:

    ```
    sudo systemctl start elasticsearch.service
    sudo systemctl start logstash.service
    sudo systemctl start kibana.service
    ```

    This is shown in the following screenshot:

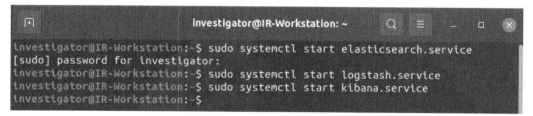

Figure 13.1 – Starting the ELK stack main services

Once we have our virtual machines ready, we will begin working on creating rules for threat hunting in incident response.

Introduction to detection rules

You learned in the previous chapter how to work with detection engineering to identify malicious behavior in incident response.

Sometimes, you can detect this behavior through monitoring, but other times, this will not be the case, and you must act proactively to identify this behavior. This will be a priority to contain threats.

Turning detection engineering into actionable security through detection rules is one of the most important skills to develop as an incident responder.

Detection rules are structured patterns of key information to search for specific indicators in the form of queries that you can run on different platforms such as ELK, Splunk, NetWitness, and CrowdStrike.

There are different kinds of rules; for example, there are rules to identify **Indicators of Compromise (IoCs)** or specific content as YARA rules, or rules to identify **Indicators of Attack (IoAs)** as Sigma rules. You will learn how to use both in this chapter.

Detection rules are mainly used for threat hunting, and these can be run centrally or directly on the devices that you want to investigate. You can also automate the process of hunting threats, or you can do it manually.

Detecting malicious files using YARA rules

YARA is a powerful tool developed by *Victor Manuel Alvarez* (Twitter handle @plusvic) from **VirusTotal**. With YARA, you can search files with specific content, and this is used by security professionals and malware researchers to identify and classify malicious files, but you can also use it to find any kind of content on a disk.

This tool is particularly helpful in incident response; for example, when you are in the triage process and you identify a file as potentially malicious, it will probably help you find that file on other devices across the network to size the compromise.

The creation of YARA rules is based on the identification of specific patterns of file contents, so you need to first get the suspicious file to analyze it and identify unique patterns that you could use to create the rule.

In the next subsection, you will learn the principal parts of the structure of a YARA rule.

Structure of a YARA rule

The structure of a YARA rule is quite simple, as is shown in the following figure:

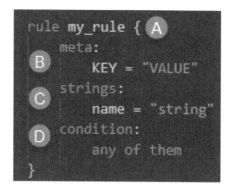

Figure 13.2 – Basic structure of a YARA rule

These are the main parts of a YARA rule:

- **The name of the rule** (**A**): In the name or identifier of the rule, you can describe the kind of content you are looking for.

- **The metadata section** (**B**): This section is designed to provide information about the rule. It is recommended that you include as much information as possible.

- **The strings section** (**C**): This is one of the key elements when you create a rule; you can specify multiple pieces of unique information that could be found in a particular file.

  According to the official documentation, there are three types of strings in YARA:

  - hexadecimal strings

  - text strings

  - regular expressions

  Text strings are case-sensitive by default, but you can use the `nocase` modifier at the end of the line to ignore the case.

  You can use the `wide` modifier to search 2-byte strings per character.

  If you don't define the `wide` modifier, the string will be ASCII by default.

- **The conditions section** (**D**): This is another key element of the rule; here, you can define the conditions that must be met for detection and reduce the possibility of false positives.

Not all the sections are mandatory, but the simplest YARA must include at least the name of the rule and a condition.

Creating YARA rules

There are several tools that you can use to create YARA rules. In fact, you can use any text editor, although it is recommended to use tools that support and recognize the specific syntax and the structure of a rule. In this way, it will be easier to create and debug the rules.

In this case, we are going to use **Visual Studio Code** (**VS Code**), since it has support for YARA by means of an extension queue you can download directly from the application. Other tools that can also support YARA are **Atom**, **Sublime** and **Far Manager**.

Installing the YARA extension on VS Code

To install the YARA extension, first, you need to open VS Code:

1. On the IR-Laptop virtual machine, click on the VS Code icon:

Figure 13.3 – Opening VS Code

2. Once VS Code is open, click on the extension button on the left-hand menu.

3. Write the word `yara` in the search extensions text box.

Once the YARA extension appears, click on the **Install** button. This will install the YARA extension, as shown in the following screenshot:

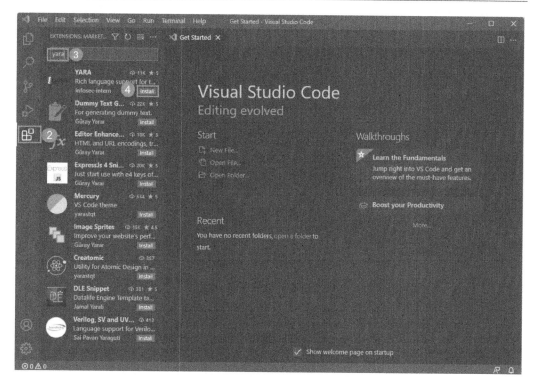

Figure 13.4 – Installing the YARA extension on VS Code

Once the installation is finished, you can review the details of how to use the extension and the included features. Now, you are ready to create and use your first YARA rule.

Analyzing and identifying patterns in files

An essential part of creating YARA rules is the identification of patterns in the files we want to search. There are several tools that can help us with this; in this case, we will use a tool known as **PeStudio**.

Downloading PeStudio

PeStudio is a tool to analyze files with a **portable executable** (PE) structure, for instance, Windows files with the .exe, .dll, and .bin extensions. You can find more details about the PE structure at https://docs.microsoft.com/en-us/windows/win32/debug/pe-format.

To download and install PeStudio, follow these steps:

1. Download the free version directly from `https://www.winitor.com/download`.

2. From the **Downloads** directory, right-click on the `pestudio.zip` file and select **Extract All...**.

3. Click on the **Browse...** button and navigate to the `C:\Users\Investigator\Workspace\Tools` directory.

4. Click on the **Extract** button.

The preceding steps are shown in the following screenshot:

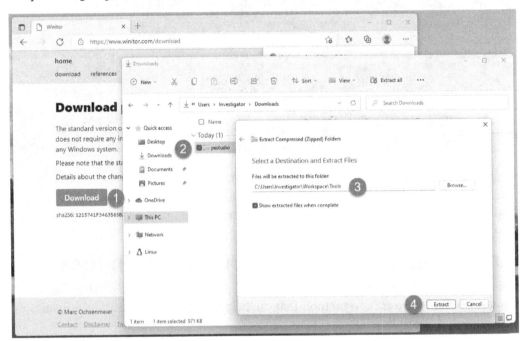

Figure 13.5 – Downloading and extracting PeStudio

This tool does not require installation, so once the folder is unzipped, it will be ready to use.

Using PeStudio

As mentioned previously, PeStudio will allow us to analyze the contents of a file that we could consider suspicious or malicious, and, in this way, we can create our YARA rule to search for that same file on other computers.

In *Chapter 11*, *Integrating SOAR Capabilities into Incident Response*, we downloaded the **ProcDump** tool from the **Windows Sysinternals** suite, which is used to dump processes from a computer and can be misused by malicious actors to obtain sensitive information such as passwords.

If at the identification stage in incident response, you found this program on one of the compromised computers and it was not an authorized tool for use on that computer, this could be an indicator that the threat actor used it as part of the attack.

We will use PeStudio to analyze this program. To do so, follow these steps:

1. Go to the `C:\Users\Investigator\Workspace\Tools\pestudio` directory and double-click on the `pestudio.exe` file. If a Microsoft Defender SmartScreen dialog box appears, simply click on **More info**, and then press the **Run anyway** button as this is a reliable tool, as shown in the following screenshot:

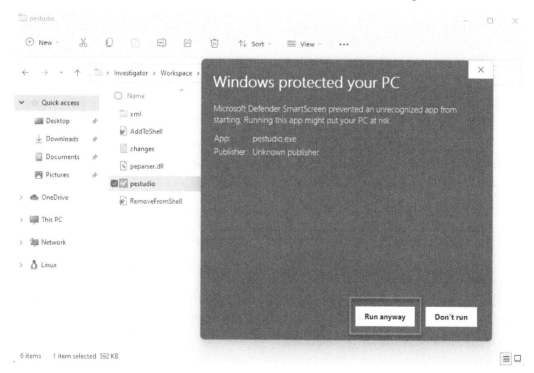

Figure 13.6 – Opening PeStudio

2. Once PeStudio is open, navigate to the `C:\Users\Investigator\`
    `Downloads\Procdump` directory and drag the `procdump64.exe` file to
    PeStudio, as shown in the following screenshot:

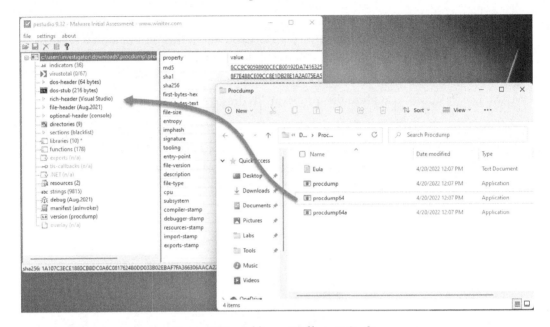

Figure 13.7 – Adding a PE file to PeStudio

PeStudio begins to classify the contents of the file according to its PE structure and
content so that it can be easily analyzed.

On the left side of the tool, you can see the different groups of information that are
identified in the file, and on the right side, its contents. For this example, we're going to
focus on the following:

- The number of suspicious indicators within the file

- The number of detections in **VirusTotal** (if any antivirus detects it as a malicious
  tool; in this case, it is not considered malicious by any antivirus)

- The sections of the file in a blacklist

- The strings contained in the file and from which we can choose those that can be
  used for detection

In this way, if you select the **0** (size) option, you will see the list of string values recognized
in the file, as you can see in the following screenshot:

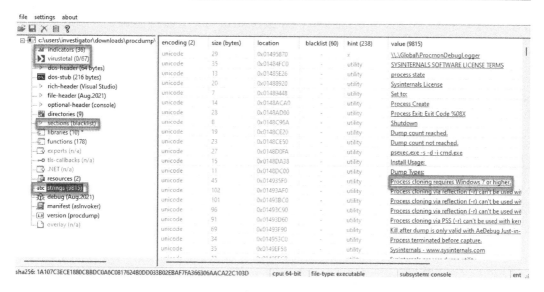

Figure 13.8 – Analyzing the content of a PE file

The challenge here is to identify the specific patterns that make this sample unique so that they can be used in search of this file.

For example, in the preceding screenshot, strings with messages appear that are unlikely to exist in other programs, so, they are good candidates to be used in our YARA rule.

On the other hand, if you move to the **sections (blacklist)** part, you will find highlighted in red the column that is in position 4 (in this case, the initial position is counted from 0) with a value in the name of **_RDATA**, as seen in the following screenshot:

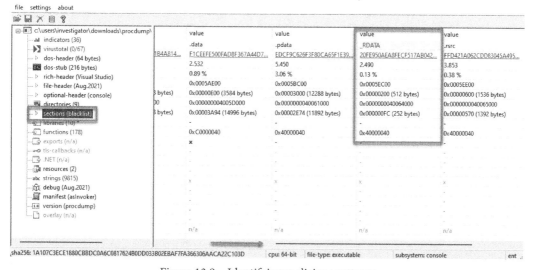

Figure 13.9 – Identifying malicious patterns

In this way, you can collect information for the construction of your rule.

Now, look for additional information that you consider unique in this file; it is important to mention that quantity does not necessarily mean quality.

Building a good rule does not always require many elements, but you must identify those that can be important.

Detecting potential threats using YARA rules

To start using YARA, you can download the most recent version from `https://github.com/VirusTotal/yara/releases`:

1. In this case, we will use YARA v4.2.0, which can be downloaded directly from here: `https://github.com/VirusTotal/yara/releases/download/v4.2.0/yara-v4.2.0-1885-win64.zip`.

2. Once you have downloaded the tool, unzip the `.zip` file into a new directory called `yara`, as shown in the `C:\Users\Investigator\Workspace\Tools\yara` path.

> **Note**
>
> You can add this directory to the environment variables of Windows to avoid explicitly specifying the path of YARA every time you execute a search using `yara`.

Once you have downloaded YARA, you are ready to create your first detection rule.

Open VS Code, click on the **File** menu, and select **New File**.

Now, click again on the **File** menu and select **Save As…**.

3. When the dialog box appears, change the save path to the `C:\Users\Investigator\Workspace\Labs\Chapter_13` directory.

4. On the **Save as type** option, change to `yara (*.yara;*.yar)`.

5. Name the file `procdump_tool.yara`.

6. Click on the **Save** button.

The preceding steps are shown in the following screenshot:

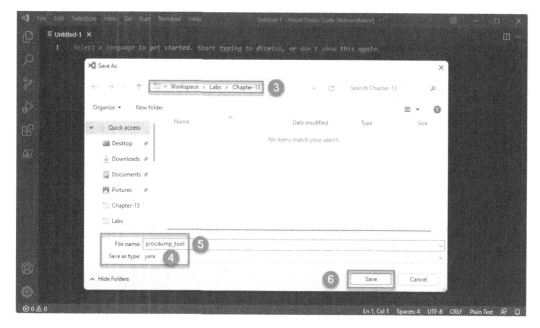

Figure 13.10 – Saving a YARA rule

When saving the file as a YARA type, VS Code will recognize the structure and syntax of the code, so that it can be debugged in a simpler way.

7. Type the word `rule` and press the *Tab* key. This way, VS Code will create the skeleton of a YARA rule, as shown in the following screenshot:

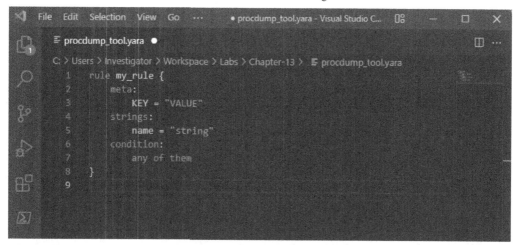

Figure 13.11 – Creating a skeleton of a YARA rule

Next, we can start creating the YARA rule providing the specific strings and conditions about what we want to detect.

There is no single way to create a YARA rule; the best rule is the one that works and is efficient. The best way to learn how to create rules is by practicing; your skills will be perfected as you gain experience in doing so.

To create the YARA rule, use the following information:

```
import "pe"
rule procdump_tool {
    meta:
        description = "Simple YARA rule to detect the presence
of Sysinternals Procdump"
        version = "1.0"
    strings:
        $s1 = "D:\\a\\1\\s\\x64\\Release\\ProcDump64.pdb" ascii
        $s2 = "Process cloning requires Windows 7 or higher."
wide ascii
        $s3 = "ProcDump Timed" wide ascii
    condition:
        (uint16(0)) == 0x5A4D and (filesize < 500000) and (2 of
($s*))
        and pe.sections[4].name=="_RDATA"
}
```

The rule to detect ProcDump in a device must look as in the following screenshot:

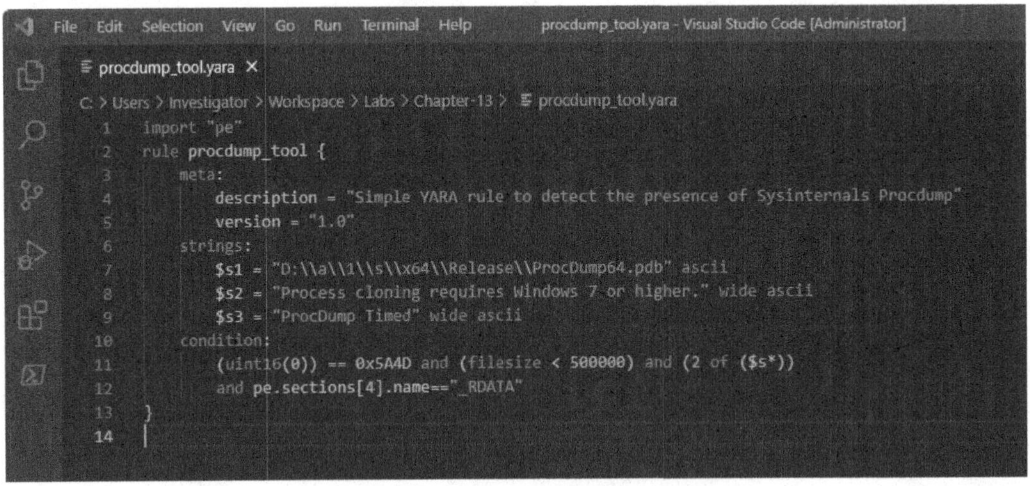

Figure 13.12 – Creating a YARA rule

The following are the elements of the rule explained in detail:

- `import "pe"`: As we will use information from one of the sections of the PE structure of the file, it will be necessary to define the import of the PE library in the first line.

- `rule procdump_tool`: In the name of the rule, we are going to describe the name of the tool and that it belongs to the category of a whitelisted tool, so it could not be considered malicious.

- `meta`: In the metadata section, we will simply define a description of what is sought to detect with this rule, and a version number that will serve in case the rule is updated to detect new versions of this tool.

- `strings`: In the strings section, we will simply use some of the strings that we found in this file that we consider to be unique to this program, along with their properties (as described previously).

> **Note**
>
> It is important to mention that we need to add the escape character (\) when we define a path of a file or folder or when there are special characters, as is the case in the `$s1` and `$s2` string variables.

- `conditions`: This part is very important because you can specify the criteria for the files that match this rule. For this case, we will use the following conditions:

  - `uint16(0) == 0x5A4D` – This condition defines that those files with a PE format will be considered for a strings search and refers to the magic number of the first sector of a Windows binary file that must contain the `0x5A4D` value *(ASCII for "'M'' and "Z"; MZ are the initials of Mark Zbikowski, who was a developer/architect of the MS-DOS file system)*.

  - `filesize < 500000` – This condition, like the previous one, speeds up the search process since only those files that are less than the specified size are considered for processing and searching.

- `2 of ($s*)` – With this condition, we are establishing that at least two of the strings must be identified within the file for it to match the rule.

- `pe.sections[4].name=="_RDATA"` – This is where we are using `import "pe"` to define the condition that the name of the **_RDATA** section exists, which is not common in binary files.

We created a YARA rule that would help us detect the ProcDump tool, and now, we are ready to test it.

Testing the YARA rule

Now, to work more efficiently, we will use the terminal integrated into VS Code. In this way, we can test our rule while we interact with it:

1. In VS Code, go to the **Terminal** menu and select **New Terminal**, as shown in the following screenshot:

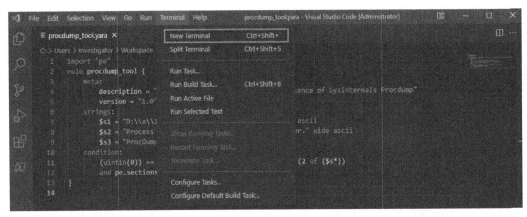

Figure 13.13 – Opening New Terminal in VS Code

This will open a **PowerShell** terminal at the bottom of VS Code (which is configured by default).

2. Let's open a **Command Prompt** terminal; simply click the **Launch Profile...** button and select **Command Prompt**, as shown in the following screenshot:

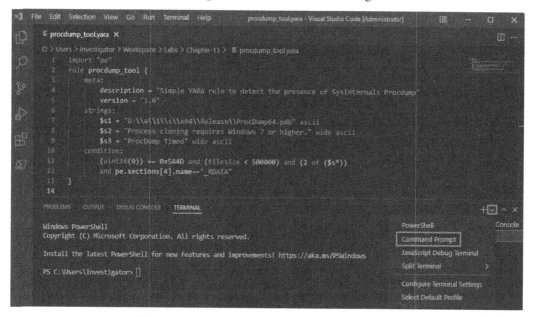

Figure 13.14 – Opening a Command Prompt console

Now, you have a Windows console window from where you can test your YARA rule and you can modify or debug it.

3. In the VS Code **Terminal** console, change to the directory where YARA is located:

```
cd C:\Users\Investigator\Workspace\Tools\yara
```

4. Type the following command:

```
yara64.exe -s "C:\Users\Investigator\Workspace\Labs\
Chapter-13\procdump_tool.yara" -r "C:\Users\Investigator\
Workspace\Tools"
```

In the preceding command, the following happens:

- The -s parameter instructs YARA to print the strings on the screen.

- The -r parameter instructs YARA to perform the search recursively from the indicated directory. Once you run the command, you can see that the rule designed to detect the procdump64.exe file matched the three strings and fits the criteria of the condition, as shown in the following screenshot:

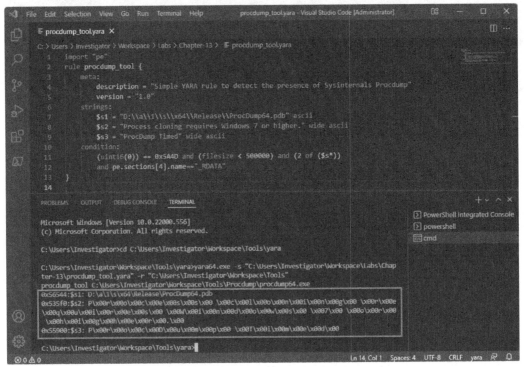

Figure 13.15 – Running a YARA rule

5. If you want to see the detection that matched the rule on the $s2 string, you can use a **CyberChef** recipe; just copy and paste the following text on the web browser:

```
https://gchq.github.io/CyberChef/#recipe=Unescape_
string()&input=UFx4MDByXHgwMG9ceDAwY1x4MDBlXHgwMHNceDAw-
c1x4MDAgXHgwMGNceDAwbFx4MDBvXHgwMG5ceDAwaVx4MDBuXHgwMGd-
ceDAwIFx4MDByXHgwMGVceDAwcVx4MDB1XHgwMGlceDAwc1x4MDBlXHg-
wMHNceDAwIFx4MDBXXHgwMGlceDAwb1x4MDBkXHgwMG9ceDAwd1x4MDB-
zXHgwMCBceDAwN1x4MDAgXHgwMG9ceDAwc1x4MDAgXHgwMGhceDAwaVx-
4MDBnXHgwMGhceDAwZVx4MDByXHgwMC5ceDAw
```

6. In the **Output** section of **CyberChef**, you will see the following string:

```
P.r.o.c.e.s.s. .c.l.o.n.i.n.g. .r.e.q.u.i.r.e.s.
.W.i.n.d.o.w.s. .7. .o.r. .h.i.g.h.e.r...
```

You will learn more about CyberChef in *Chapter 14, Hunting and Investigating Security Incidents.*

Modifying a YARA rule to improve detection

One way to test whether this rule does not generate false positives is to run it on different directories or computers, mainly performing searches against files of the operating system itself or known application files.

My colleagues from Kaspersky's **Global Research and Analysis Team** (**GreAT**) developed an open source tool that allows you to install and configure your own server to test your rules and improve the quality of detections. This project is called **Klara**, and you can download it from this repository: `https://github.com/KasperskyLab/klara`.

In this case, we designed a rule to focus on the detection of the `procdump64.exe` file specifically, but what happens to the other two files, `procdump.exe` and `procdump4a.exe`, which can also be used by a malicious actor? Why were they not detected?

We did not review the other two files to see whether they contained the same strings or conditions present in `procdump64.exe`.

When this scenario occurs, it is very important that our rule can also detect those variants of the program that could also represent a threat and not only specific versions. To do so, it is recommended to analyze all the files and discard those elements that may not be common to everyone, and perhaps include some other elements that we might have overlooked.

Take your time to analyze what you need to modify in your rule so that the other files can also be detected.

Again, there is no one-stop solution, and you might find different ways to do it. In this case, try different solutions, for instance, comment out the last condition and you will get a different result. In this example, you detected the other ProcDump files but not the first one, as is shown in the following screenshot:

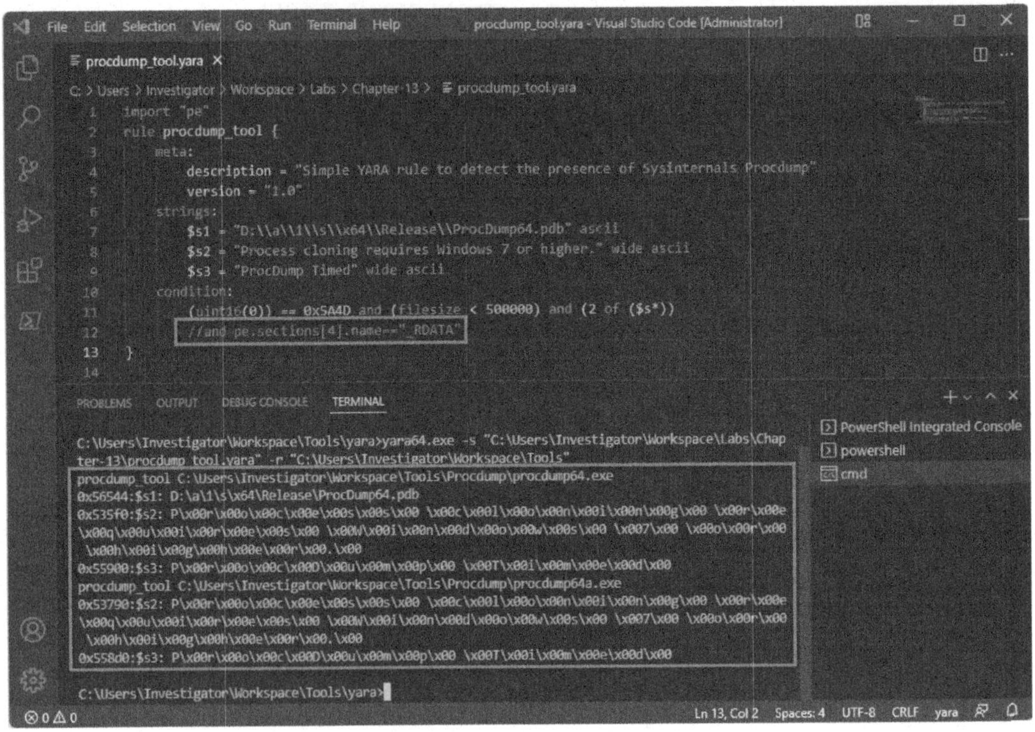

Figure 13.16 – Modifying the rule to detect related files

As you can see, if only the last condition is excluded (where the name of the _RDATA section is described), only the other versions of the program will be detected. This is because the _RDATA section doesn't exist in those files.

Now, it's your turn; try to find what you need to change on this rule to detect the three versions of the ProcDump tool by yourself.

As I mentioned before, YARA is an essential tool for incident response and there are many sources of information, courses, and repositories created by and for the community to make the detection process more efficient.

In the next section, we will learn about Sigma rules and how we can use them to identify malicious behavior.

Detecting malicious behavior using Sigma rules

One of the challenges for organizations is the standardization and integration of different security tools and the normalization of the formats that these tools use to process and store the information.

Sigma was created under the idea of developing generic rules in a structured format that can be transformed into specific query formats for different **Security Information and Event Management (SIEM)** systems. With Sigma, you can create rules under specific criteria of detection engineering, regardless of the platform you are using to hunt threats, as you can see in the following figure:

Figure 13.17 – The Sigma project

The advantage of this approach is that researchers can create universal rules shared with the community and used by everyone.

The main creators of the Sigma project are Florian Roth (Twitter handle `@cyb3rops`) and Thomas Patzke (Twitter handle `@blubbfiction`).

You can use Sigma along with other threat hunting tools such as YARA to detect threats in incident response.

The structure of Sigma rules is based on the YAML format, so it's very important to be familiar with this markup language. You can learn the basics of YAML here: `https://www.cloudbees.com/blog/yaml-tutorial-everything-you-need-get-started`.

Also, I recommend that you take a look at the Sigma specification wiki to learn about the structure of Sigma rules, at `https://github.com/SigmaHQ/sigma/wiki/Specification`.

Many targets support queries created by Sigma rules, such as Splunk, ELK, Azure Sentinel, ArcSight, QRadar, RSA NetWitness, and PowerShell.

Also, there are multiple projects and products that use Sigma, such as MISP, SOC Prime – Sigma Rule Editor, Uncoder.IO, THOR, and Joe Sandbox.

You can find more information on the GitHub of the project at `https://github.com/SigmaHQ/sigma`.

In the next part, you will learn how to get Sigma tools and create your own rules.

Cloning the repository

To have access to the Sigma project and the community Sigma rules, you can clone the repository to your IR-Laptop virtual machine:

1. Open a new **Windows Terminal/Windows Subsystem for Linux (WSL)** instance as administrator, as shown in the following screenshot:

Figure 13.18 – Opening a new WSL instance

2. Now, open a web browser and navigate to the Sigma GitHub project at `https://github.com/SigmaHQ/sigma`.

3. Click on the **Code** button and then on the *copy* button to send the clone URL to the clipboard, as shown in the following screenshot:

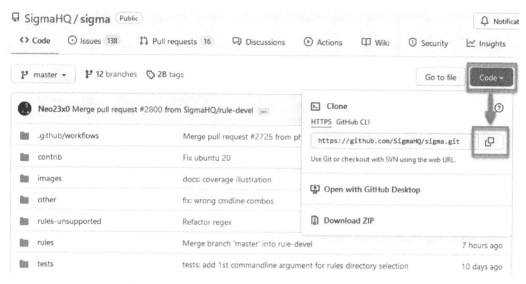

Figure 13.19 – Copying the Sigma GitHub project URL

4. To clone the repository, run the following command on the WSL terminal:

```
git clone https://github.com/SigmaHQ/sigma.git
```

This will clone the Sigma GitHub repository onto your IR-Laptop virtual machine, as shown in the following screenshot:

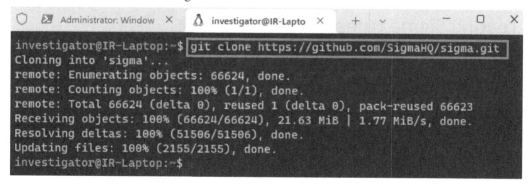

Figure 13.20 – Cloning the Sigma project

5. Now, change to the Sigma project directory and take a look at the content:

```
cd sigma
ls -l
```

You will see the different directories of the project, as shown in the following screenshot:

```
investigator@IR-Laptop:~$ cd sigma
investigator@IR-Laptop:~/sigma$ ls -l
total 108
-rw-r--r-- 1 investigator investigator  2735 Apr 20 14:34 BREAKING_CHANGES.md
-rw-r--r-- 1 investigator investigator  7380 Apr 20 14:34 CHANGELOG.md
-rw-r--r-- 1 investigator investigator   329 Apr 20 14:34 LICENSE
-rw-r--r-- 1 investigator investigator  1896 Apr 20 14:34 LICENSE.Detection.Rules.md
-rw-r--r-- 1 investigator investigator 15114 Apr 20 14:34 Makefile
-rw-r--r-- 1 investigator investigator   429 Apr 20 14:34 Pipfile
-rw-r--r-- 1 investigator investigator 43173 Apr 20 14:34 Pipfile.lock
-rw-r--r-- 1 investigator investigator 19134 Apr 20 14:34 README.md
-rw-r--r-- 1 investigator investigator    27 Apr 20 14:34 _config.yml
drwxr-xr-x 1 investigator investigator  4096 Apr 20 14:34 contrib
drwxr-xr-x 1 investigator investigator  4096 Apr 20 14:34 images
drwxr-xr-x 1 investigator investigator  4096 Apr 20 14:34 other
drwxr-xr-x 1 investigator investigator  4096 Apr 20 14:34 rules
drwxr-xr-x 1 investigator investigator  4096 Apr 20 14:34 rules-deprecated
drwxr-xr-x 1 investigator investigator  4096 Apr 20 14:34 rules-unsupported
-rw-r--r-- 1 investigator investigator  2105 Apr 20 14:34 sigma-schema.rx.yml
drwxr-xr-x 1 investigator investigator  4096 Apr 20 14:34 tests
drwxr-xr-x 1 investigator investigator  4096 Apr 20 14:34 tools
investigator@IR-Laptop:~/sigma$
```

Figure 13.21 – Reviewing the content of Sigma's GitHub project

In this case, we will use the content of the `tools` and `rules` folders to do the exercises.

Creating Sigma rules

You can convert rules into multiple query formats; in this case, we are going to run our queries in the IR-Laptop virtual machine looking for IoAs, so we will convert a Sigma rule into a PowerShell query.

In the previous section, we emulated malicious behavior; we used a **living-off-the-land** tool (`certutil.exe`) to download the `Procdump64.exe` tool (the command-line utility that creates crash dumps and is used sometimes by malicious actors).

After that, we ran ProcDump to dump the `lsass.exe` process and get the passwords from Windows.

This behavior generated multiple log entries on Windows-Sysmon. (If you didn't do this exercise or install Sysmon, you can follow the steps described in *Chapter 11, Integrating SOAR Capabilities into Incident Response.*)

In this case, we are going to create a Sigma rule to detect this behavior, but first, we will use the concepts of detection engineering that you learned about in *Chapter 12, Working with Analytics and Detection Engineering in Incident Response.*

Creating or analyzing detection engineering

Before creating a Sigma rule, we must first familiarize ourselves with the malicious behavior we want to detect and the possible sources of information to look for the IoA. We will start searching for this information in MITRE **Cyber Analytics Repository (CAR)**:

1. On your web browser, navigate to the **MITRE CAR** project in the **Analytics** section (`https://car.mitre.org/analytics/`).

2. Search for the analytics to detect the use of ProcDump on the system (you can use the *Ctrl + F* key shortcut and then write `procdump` in the search box). You will see **CAR-2019-07-002**, as shown in the following screenshot, which could be useful in this case:

| CAR-2019-07-002 | Lsass Process Dump via **Procdump** | July 29 2019 | • OS Credential Dumping |

Figure 13.22 – Analytics for the OS Credential Dumping behavior

3. Click on the **CAR-2019-07-002** link to go to the description and content of these analytics.

   Review the details of these analytics and go to the **Implementation** section; you will see the information you need to focus on for creating a detection rule. In this case, we are going to focus on a **process creation** where the name is `procdump*.exe` and the command line contains the `*lsass*` string, as shown in the following screenshot:

```
processes = search Process:Create
procdump_lsass = filter processes where (
   exe = "procdump*.exe"  and
   command_line = "*lsass*")
output procdump_lsass
```

Figure 13.23 – The ProcDump detection pseudocode

Now, using the previous information, we are going to create a very simple Sigma rule using VS Code.

4. Open VS Code.

5. Create a new file and save it as `proc_creation_win_procdump_lsass` in the `C:\Users\Investigator\Workspace\Labs\Chapter-13` path. Be sure that you select **YAML** in the **Save as type** field, as shown in the following screenshot:

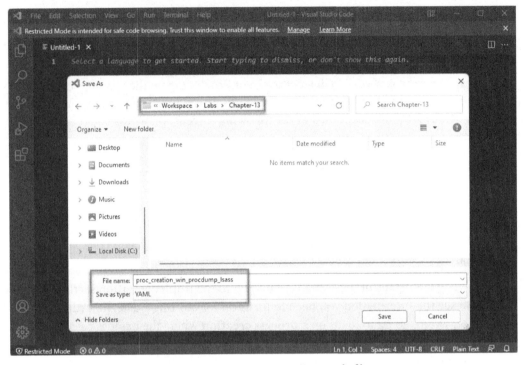

Figure 13.24 – Saving a new Sigma rule file

6. Review the Sigma specification wiki at `https://github.com/SigmaHQ/sigma/wiki/Specification` and create a Sigma rule based on the pseudocode of the `CAR-2019-07-002` analytics, focusing on the following attributes for detection:

   ▪ `EventID: 1` – This is the number of the Sysmon event ID for process creation.

   ▪ `'procdump*.exe'` – This looks for executable files for different versions of ProcDump.

   ▪ `'lsass'` – This looks for a string in a command-line execution called `"lsass"`.

> **Note**
>
> You can also download and use the `SigmaRuleTemplate.yml` file from the `Chapter-13` folder in the book's repository to create the Sigma rule.

Your rule should look like the following screenshot:

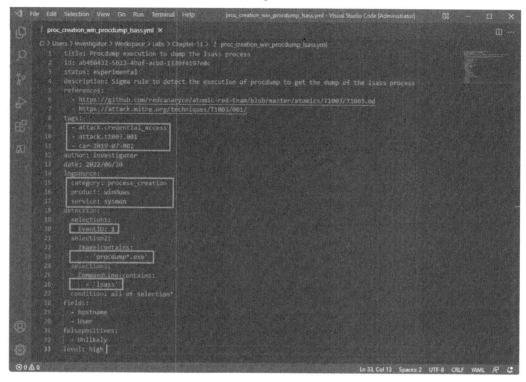

Figure 13.25 – Creating a Sigma rule

Something important that you should consider is that threat actors almost all the time will seek to evade detections, therefore, it is important to create rules that detect these evasion techniques. In this case, we are creating a rule that detects the execution of ProcDump in a simple and direct way to obtain the dump of the lsass.exe process.

For instance, an evasion technique could be to call the process ID of lsass.exe instead of the name of the process, and this will work combined with other techniques to avoid detection.

To learn more about creating Sigma rules, you can see the tutorial created by Florian Roth here: https://www.nextron-systems.com/2018/02/10/write-sigma-rules/.

Converting Sigma rules

As I mentioned at the beginning of this section, Sigma rules are designed to define a generic detection format that you can convert through the field mapping to specific searches to be used by multiple platforms, so we are going to need a converter to do this. We will use two Sigma rules converters:

- **Sigmac**: This is the current Sigma rules converter, but will be replaced by the Sigma CLI.

- **Sigma CLI**: This converter tool uses the `pySigma` library to convert generic rules into different search queries.

In the next part, we are going to learn how to install and use both tools.

Converting Sigma rules using Sigmac

Sigmac is the converter tool that uses the **Sigma library**; this library can be used to integrate with other projects and tools. To start using Sigmac, you will need to first install Python's **Preferred Installer Program** (**pip**) and then `sigmatools`:

1. First, update the sources of Ubuntu by running the following command in Windows Terminal/WSL:

   ```
   sudo apt update
   ```

2. To install `pip3`, run the following command:

   ```
   sudo apt install python3-pip
   ```

3. Now, install **Sigmac** by running the following command:

   ```
   sudo pip3 install sigmatools
   ```

4. To validate that everything is okay, and to review the help, run the following command:

```
sigmac -h
```

You will see examples of how to use this tool with the different parameters, as you can see in the following screenshot:

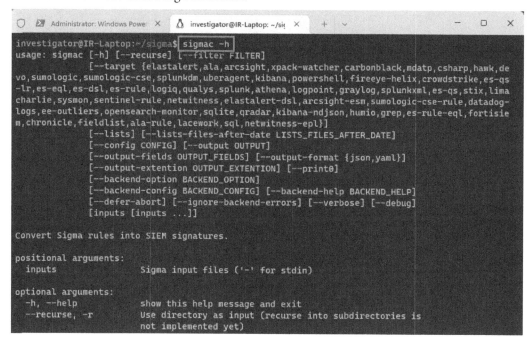

Figure 13.26 – Viewing the help of the Sigmac converter

Now that you have installed Sigmac, let's see how you can use it to convert rules for different targets.

5. Open a new terminal in VS Code.

6. On the VS Code menu, select **View** and then click on **Terminal**, as shown in the following screenshot:

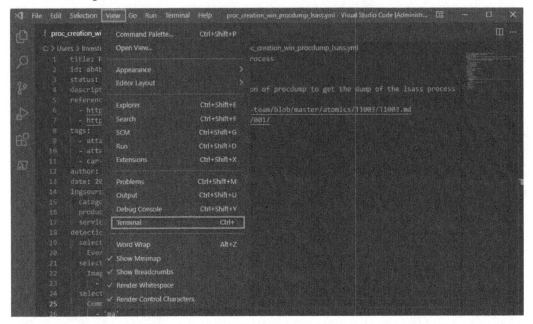

Figure 13.27 – Opening a VS Code terminal

At the bottom, you'll be able to see the built-in PowerShell console. In this case, we will need a WSL terminal, so we will have to add a new console.

7. Click on the **Launch Profile...** button and then click on **Ubuntu-20.04 (WSL)**, as shown in the following screenshot:

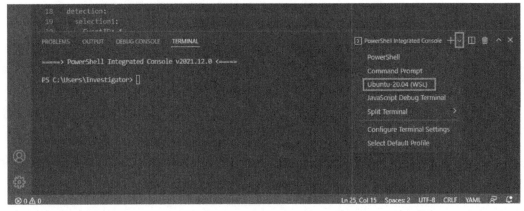

Figure 13.28 – Creating a new WSL terminal

You will see the new WSL console start working with the Sigmac converter.

8. Switch to the `sigma` directory:

```
cd /home/investigator/sigma
```

9. Run the `sigmac` command by providing the following parameters:

```
sigmac -t es-qs -c winlogbeat  /mnt/c/Users/Investigator/
Workspace/Labs/Chapter-13/proc_creation_win_procdump_
lsass.yml
```

In the preceding command, we performed the following actions:

- `-t es-qs` is the backend target where you will run the search query; in this case, an Elasticsearch query string.

- `-c winlogbeat` is the configuration source of the fields; in this case, Elastic's Winlogbeat.

- `.../Workspace/Labs/Chapter-13/proc_creation_win_procdump_ lsass.yml` is the path and the name of the Sigma rule.

You will see the converted Sigma rule as the output shown in the following screenshot:

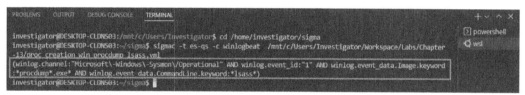

Figure 13.29 – Converting a Sigma rule into an Elasticsearch query

In the next part, you will run this query on Kibana.

Running the converted query on Kibana

To run the query created from the Sigma rule:

1. Open a web browser on the IR-Laptop and navigate to Kibana: `http://192.168.8.140:5601`.

> **Note**
>
> If you get the message **Kibana server is not ready yet** when accessing the Kibana website, you will need to review the status of the ELK stack services on the IR-Workstation virtual machine and, if necessary, start them.

2. Click on the hamburger menu button, and then select **Discover**, as shown in the following screenshot:

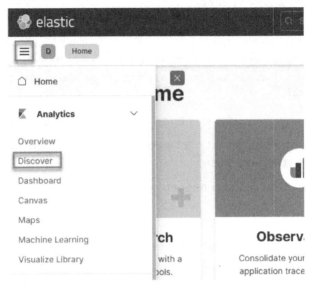

Figure 13.30 – Opening the Kibana Discover dashboard

3. In the **Show dates** section, be sure to cover the period where you dumped the `lsass.exe` process using ProcDump, as shown in the following screenshot:

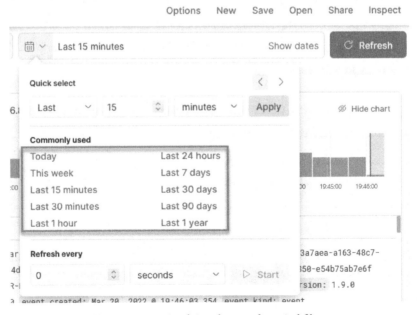

Figure 13.31 – Applying the search period filter

4. Copy the following query generated when you converted the Sigma rule:

```
(winlog.channel:"Microsoft\-Windows\-Sysmon\/Operational"
AND winlog.event_id:"1" AND winlog.event_data.
Image.keyword:*procdump*.exe* AND winlog.event_data.
CommandLine.keyword:*lsass*)
```

5. Paste the query in the search text box and click on the **Update** button to apply:

Figure 13.32 – Running an Elasticsearch query on Kibana

You will see the list of occurrences about the execution of ProcDump in the period defined.

6. Expand the event and scroll down to see more details about the fields that match our rule, as shown in the following screenshot:

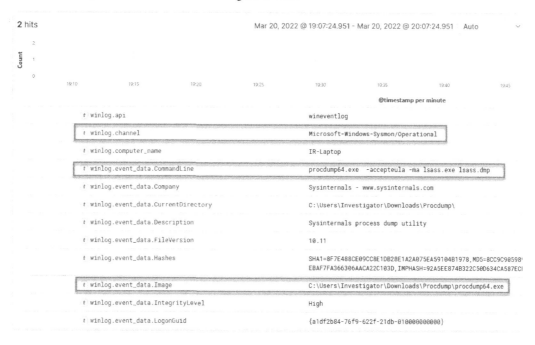

Figure 13.33 – Analyzing the detection patterns

Additionally, you can add more detection elements to the rule to make it more accurate; test it for yourself by applying the concepts learned and consulting the reference links.

In the next part, you will learn how to create Sigma rules using the Sigma CLI.

Converting Sigma rules using the Sigma CLI

For this part, we are going to convert Sigma rules into queries using the Sigma CLI.

1. First, we need to install the `pysigma` library by running the following command:

    ```
    sudo pip install pysigma==0.4.5
    ```

2. Install the **Sigma CLI** using `pip3` by running the following command on the WSL terminal of VS Code:

    ```
    sudo pip install sigma-cli==0.3.1
    ```

    This is shown in the following screenshot:

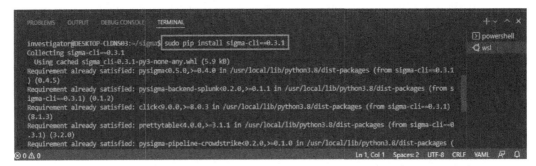

Figure 13.34 – Installing the Sigma CLI

> **Note**
>
> You can also install the most recent versions of `pysigma` and `sigma-cli` **by r**unning the following commands:
>
> ```
> sudo pip install pysigma
> sudo pip install sigma-cli
> ```

3. To see the help on the use of the tool, just run the following command:

    ```
    sigma convert --help
    ```

    Once the Sigma CLI is installed, we are going to convert Splunk queries from Sysmon and CrowdStrike **Falcon Data Replicator** (FDR) logs.

4. In VS Code, run the following command:

```
sigma convert -s -t splunk -p sysmon rules/windows/
process_creation -o splunk_queries.conf
```

In the preceding command, we performed the following actions:

- -s – This skips unsupported formats or rules that can't be processed by the backend.

- -t splunk – This is the target query format to be converted.

- -p sysmon – These are the pipelines' or rules' YAML files.

- rules/windows/process_creation – This is the path of the rules or the name of the rule file to be converted.

- -o splunk_queries.conf – This is the output file to save the queries.

You will see the conversion process, as shown in the following screenshot:

Figure 13.35 – Converting a Sigma rules collection to Splunk queries

5. Open the splunk_queries.conf file using vim by running the following command:

```
vim splunk_queries.conf
```

You will see the different Splunk queries converted from the rules files, as shown in the following screenshot:

Figure 13.36 – Viewing the Splunk queries

In the same way that you ran the query on Kibana, you can run any of these queries on Splunk.

As you can see, you can create generic Sigma rules from detection engineering, and then you can convert these rules into queries that can be run in different threat hunting platforms or SIEM solutions.

Using additional tools that use rules to scan for threats

Fortunately, the cybersecurity community is developing more tools that use rules to search for threat indicators. These are some of the most interesting and free tools:

- **THOR Lite** – This is a free multiplatform scanner (Windows, Linux, and macOS) that uses precompiled and encrypted signatures to detect different IoCs and supports different output formats (`https://www.nextron-systems.com/thor-lite/`).

- **Aurora** – This is a Sigma-based **endpoint detection and response** (**EDR**) agent; Aurora Lite is an alternative free version (`https://www.nextron-systems.com/2021/11/13/aurora-sigma-based-edr-agent-preview/`).

- **YaraMemoryScanner** – This is a script to scan the memory processes using YARA rules. The script is developed in PowerShell (`https://github.com/BinaryDefense/YaraMemoryScanner`).

- **yarGen** – This is a YARA rules generator tool developed in Python that creates rules from suspicious strings found in malicious files (`https://github.com/Neo23x0/yarGen`).

- **F-Secure Chainsaw** – This uses Sigma rules to search malicious behavior directly on the Windows XML EventLog EVTX log files (Windows and Linux).

- **Zircolite** – This also uses Sigma rules to search malicious behavior directly on EVTX files, but also audit, Sysmon for Linux, or JSONK/NDJSON logs. It is based on Python (`https://github.com/wagga40/Zircolite`).

- **Uncoder.io** – This is a universal web-based Sigma rule converter (`https://uncoder.io/`).

- **SIGMA UI** – This is an open source tool based on ELK that uses the Sigma converter tool (**sigmac**) (`https://github.com/socprime/SigmaUI`).

There are situations in enterprise environments where scalability is an important factor; for that reason, you should also consider tools that offer support for use cases where it is required to execute the rules on multiple devices on the network.

Summary

In this chapter, you learned about the importance of creating rules from detection engineering to detect IoCs, malicious tools, and malicious behavior.

You also learned the basic concepts about YARA and Sigma to create rules, and the different tools that can be used to improve the detection capabilities in incident response.

In the last chapter, you will have the opportunity to apply the knowledge learned in the different chapters of this book in practical scenarios of a simulated cybersecurity incident.

Further reading

- *Detecting the Unknown, A Guide to Threat Hunting*: `https://hodigital. blog.gov.uk/wp-content/uploads/sites/161/2020/03/ Detecting-the-Unknown-A-Guide-to-Threat-Hunting-v2.0.pdf`

- Official YARA documentation: `https://yara.readthedocs.io/en/ stable/`

- *Upping the APT hunting game: Learn the best YARA practices from Kaspersky*: `https://www.brighttalk.com/webcast/15591/388802`

- *SAS2018: Finding aliens, star weapons, and ponies with YARA*: `https://youtu. be/fbidgtOXvc0`

- *Using YARA to attribute malware*: `https://blog.malwarebytes.com/ threat-analysis/2013/10/using-yara-to-attribute-malware/`

- *ReversingLabs YARA Rules*: `https://github.com/reversinglabs/ reversinglabs-yara-rules`

- *Tool Analysis Result Sheet*: `https://jpcertcc.github.io/ ToolAnalysisResultSheet/`

- *Detecting Lateral Movement through Tracking Event Logs*: `https://www. jpcert.or.jp/english/pub/sr/20170612ac-ir_research_en.pdf`

- SOC Prime: *Sigma rules repository mirror and translations*: `https://sigma. socprime.com/`

14
Hunting and Investigating Security Incidents

This is the last chapter of the book; it has been an exciting journey and you have learned some new things. In this chapter, you can put into practice your knowledge by working on a practical case of a security incident.

Unlike the previous chapters, you will do most of the work, and you will be able to follow **incident response (IR)** procedures, organize activities in the **incident management (IM)** platform, and use different tools for hunting and investigation.

In this chapter, you will learn about the following topics:

- Responding to a data breach incident
- Opening a new IR case
- Investigating the security incident

Technical requirements

In case you haven't already, you need to download and install VMware Workstation Player from this link `https://www.vmware.com/products/workstation-player/workstation-player-evaluation.html`.

You'll also need to download the following from the book's official GitHub repository `https://github.com/PacktPublishing/Incident-Response-with-Threat-Intelligence`:

- Virtual machines:

  - IR-Laptop

  - SO-Platform

- Lab file:

  - `Chapter14`

Responding to a data breach incident

Michael Scott, the **chief executive officer** (**CEO**) of a global energy company, traveled to Asia a couple of months ago to attend one of the industry's most notable events.

Recently, confidential and strategic information from the company that was in the hands of very few people—including the CEO—began to circulate publicly.

This leak of information has impacted different areas of the business and has affected some negotiations that were taking place with different companies around the world.

Some of the published information was on the CEO's computer, and now, there are suspicions that his computer could have been hacked on the last trip.

You were assigned as the lead investigator of the case, so now, you need to do first response procedures and get the necessary information from the CEO's computer to start the investigation.

Analyzing the cybersecurity incident

According to this scenario, there are several elements that we need to consider. The initial point of our analysis is about the identification of places where information is stored, and which people have privileges to access that information.

In this case, within the circle of people who have that information in their possession is just the CEO, and there are suspicions that he may have been one of the targets of this security compromise.

On the basis of the circumstances and information we have, the first device to review is the CEO's computer, without ruling out that it may be necessary to review other devices.

As a first step, we must have a meeting with the CEO to get as many details as possible to allow us to have a clearer context and focus on the type of information we are looking to obtain.

Once we have the interview, we must request the CEO's computer to perform first-response procedures.

Selecting the best strategy

Considering the circumstances of the case, it would be very useful to perform procedures to obtain disk and memory forensic images from the CEO's computer. In this way, we would be able to review all the information and have evidence that the incident could have happened during the period between his trip abroad and the time when the information leak was discovered.

In addition, it would be very valuable to obtain specific artifacts of programs installed on the computer and the preprocessed information of timelines, executed applications, information about requests to domains or **Internet Protocol** (IP) addresses, and some other data that would allow us to speed up the investigation and enable us to use tools to obtain this information.

Preparing for the lab

In this case, we are simulating that we got these logs directly from the suspicious computer, so we are going to start the investigation from an alert generated in the **security operations center** (SOC).

Before we start with the practical exercises of this chapter, we will need to prepare the work environment. First, we are going to start the SO-Platform and IR-Laptop VMs.

> **Note**
>
> The SO-Platform VM has a pre-installed version 2.3.100 of Security Onion. This distribution already includes its IM module, **Cases**, and replaces TheHive to escalate alerts.

First, start the IR-Laptop VM and sign in using the following credentials:

- **Username**: Investigator
- **Password**: L34rn1ng!

After that, start the SO-Platform VM. You do not need to sign in here for now.

Once you start both VMs, go to IR-Laptop and proceed as follows:

1. Open a Terminal console with administrator privilege, by pressing *Shift* and right-clicking on the Windows Terminal icon, and then click on **Run as administrator**, as shown in the following screenshot:

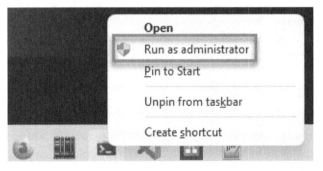

Figure 14.1 – Opening Windows Terminal as administrator

> **Note**
>
> We are opening Windows Terminal as an administrator because you may require elevated privileges to perform some exercises.

2. Open a new **Windows Subsystem for Linux (WSL)** Terminal by clicking on the down arrow button at the top to display a drop-down menu and select **Ubuntu-20.04**, as shown in the following screenshot:

Figure 14.2 – Opening a new Linux Terminal

3. As you used the IR-SOAR VM in *Chapter 11*, *Integrating SOAR Capabilities into Incident Response*, you will use the SO-Platform VM in this chapter, and both use the same IP address, you will need to flush the **Secure Shell** (**SSH**) keys first by running the following command:

```
ssh-keygen -f "/home/investigator/.ssh/known_hosts" -R
"192.168.8.5"
```

4. Switch to the /mnt/c/Users/Investigator/Workspace/Labs/Chapter-14 directory.

5. Connect by SSH from the IR-Laptop VM (IP address 192.168.8.150) to the SO-Platform VM (IP address 192.168.8.5), providing the following credentials:

    - **Username**: ssh analyst@192.168.8.5

    - **Password**: P4cktIRBook!

6. Once you are connected, create repositories where you are going to save the files related to some artifacts collected in the cybersecurity incident, as follows:

```
mkdir logfiles
mkdir pcapfiles
```

You can verify the created directories by running the `ls  -l` command, as shown in the following screenshot:

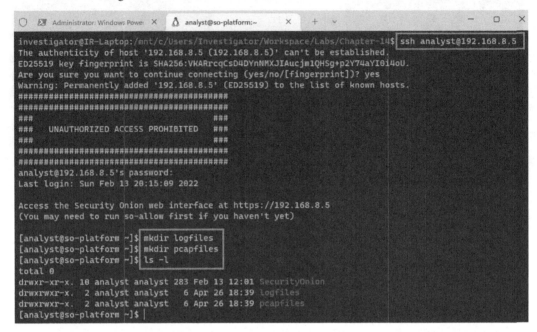

Figure 14.3 – Connecting to SO-Platform using SSH and creating evidence repositories

7. It is important to be sure that all services on Security Onion are up, so review the status by entering the `so-status` command providing the analyst password (`P4cktIRBook!`), as shown in the following screenshot:

Figure 14.4 – Validating the status of services

Once all the container statuses are showing a status of OK (this could take some time, so you can use the up arrow to keep checking the status of Security Onion services), we can now connect to the Security Onion management console.

8. Open a web browser and connect to the following address:
    https://192.168.8.5. Then, provide the analyst@gosecurity.ninja/
    L34rn1ng! credentials, as shown in the following screenshot:

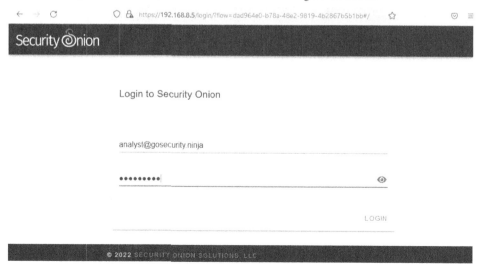

Figure 14.5 – Logging in to the Security Onion web interface

> **Note**
>
> You might get a privacy error, as follows:
>
> **Brave**: Your connection is not private. Click on **Advanced**. Next, proceed to 192.168.8.5 (unsafe).
>
> **Firefox**: Warning: Potential Security Risk Ahead. Click **Advanced**.... Next, click on **Accept the Risk** and **Continue.**
>
> **Microsoft Edge**: Your connection isn not private. Click on **Advanced**. Next, continue to 192.168.8.5 (unsafe).

At this point, you can start working with Security Onion to import system logs and network capture files.

Copying and importing evidence files

One of the features of Security Onion is the possibility to import system logs and network capture files for analysis from systems where you do not have **Security Information and Event Management** (**SIEM**) visibility or network monitoring. Here's how you can do this:

1. From the book's cloud repository, download the Chapter-14 folder.

2. Copy the content of this folder to your IR-Laptop VM and paste it under the C:\ Users\Investigator\Workspace\Labs\Chapter-14 directory.

3. Under the Chapter-14 directory, right-click on the AD-SRV_Logs.7z file.

4. Select **Show more options**.

5. Select the **7-Zip** option.

6. Finally, select **Extract Here**.

   Repeat the same process to extract the Corp-Laptop_Logs.7z and Network_ Captures.7z files.

   The process is illustrated in the following screenshot:

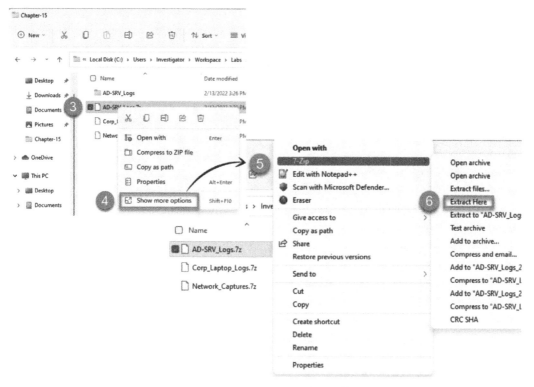

Figure 14.6 – Extracting evidence files

Now that we have extracted the needed files for the exercises, we will import these files into the SO-Platform VM.

7. On the Windows/WSL Terminal, log off your current connection from the SO-Platform VM by running the following command:

```
logout
```

8. Switch to the AD-SRV_logs directory:

```
cd AD-SRV_Logs
```

9. Verify the content of the directory by running the following command:

```
ls -l
```

10. Copy all files from the AD-SRV_Logs folder to the directories on the SO-Platform VM created previously:

```
scp -r AD-SRV_Logs analyst@192.168.8.5:/home/analyst/
logfiles/
```

This is shown in the following screenshot:

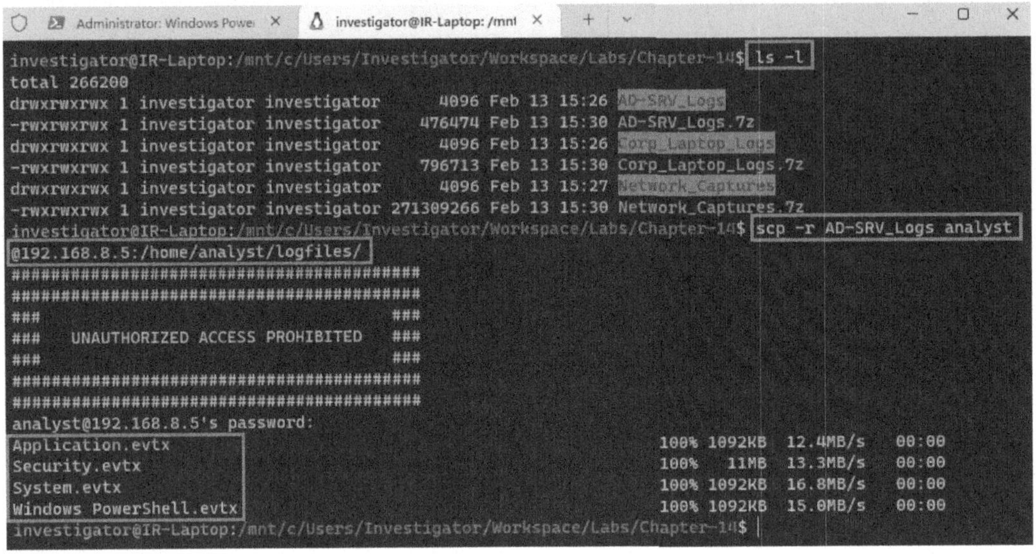

Figure 14.7 – Opening a new WSL Terminal

11. Repeat the same procedure to copy the `Corp_Laptop_Logs` directory, as follows:

```
scp -r Corp_Laptop_Logs analyst@192.168.8.5:/home/
analyst/logfiles/
```

12. Now, copy the network captures directory, as follows:

```
scp -r Network_Captures analyst@192.168.8.5:/home/
analyst/pcapfiles/
```

The last command can be seen in action in the following screenshot:

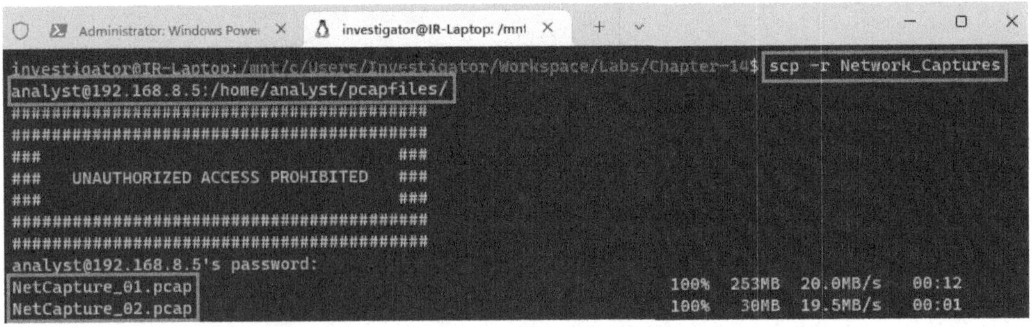

Figure 14.8 – Copying network traffic files

13. Once you finished the copying the files, log on again to the server using the usual credentials, as follows:

- **Username**: ssh analyst@192.168.8.5

- **Password**: P4cktIRBook!

Now that you have the files on the server, you can start importing them into Security Onion.

14. To import the network files into Security Onion, first switch to the pcapfiles/ Network-Captures directory by running the following command:

```
cd pcapfiles/Network_Captures/
```

15. Import the files by running the following command:

```
sudo so-import-pcap NetCapture_01.pcap NetCapture_02.pcap
```

The command and its output are shown in the following screenshot:

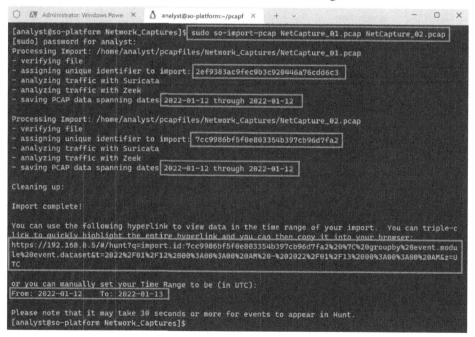

Figure 14.9 – Importing network traffic files

Once the process has been completed, you will see a **unique identifier** (**UID**) assigned to this import and a specific link to access directly information regarding the processed files. You can save this specific information in a text file for further revisions.

16. To start analyzing the content of these network packages, you can copy and paste the provided link on the navigation bar of your web browser. You will see the import ID and the filter applied, as shown in the following screenshot:

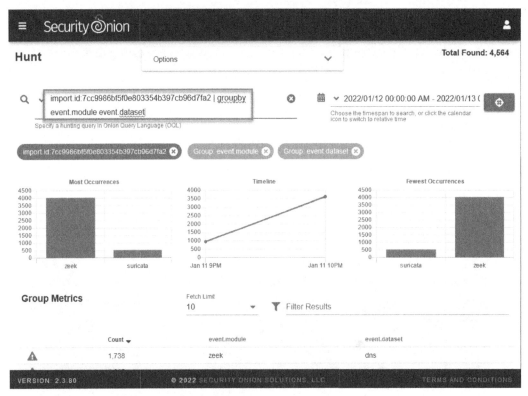

Figure 14.10 – Visualizing data generated from the import

This could be a good point to start an investigation because you can focus on this information directly.

17. To import the log files, repeat the same procedure, switching to the /home/ analyst/logfiles/AD-SRV_Logs directory and running the following command:

```
sudo so-import-evtx Application.evtx Security.evtx
System.evtx 'Windows PowerShell.evtx'
```

> **Note**
>
> Linux is a case-sensitive **operating system (OS)**; please ensure that you enter filenames, including directories, in the correct case.

18. Now, switch to the `/home/analyst/logfiles/Corp_Laptop_Logs` directory to import the log files from here, as follows:

```
sudo so-import-evtx Application.evtx Security.evtx
System.evtx Microsoft-Windows-Sysmon%4Operational.evtx
"Windows PowerShell.evtx"
```

As I mentioned before at the beginning of this chapter, the point at which we will start this IR case is from an alert generated in the SOC, so we will prepare our scenario to start the investigation.

Starting the investigation

After we have imported the logs and network files into our `SO-Platform` VM simulating the capture of traffic and log collection from the organization, we need to define a date range related to the incident. Here's how to do this:

1. On Security Onion, click on the **Alerts** panel.

2. To filter by date, click on the **Time Picker** functionality, just to the left of **Last** (clock with an arrowed circle), Next, click the date range section, then the custom range to be investigated, as follows:

    *   `January 10 to 14, 2022`
    *   `12:00:00 AM - 11:59:00 PM`

You will do the same for all hunting and investigation processes. The following screenshot provides an overview of the preceding steps:

Figure 14.11 – Filtering by date range

When you apply this filter, you will see several alerts with the severity level classified as **high** and other alerts with severity classified as **medium**; for now, we will focus on the following alerts:

		Count	rule.name	event.module	event.severity_label
🔔	⚠	527	ET POLICY SMB2 NT Create AndX Request For an Executable File	suricata	medium
🔔	⚠	12	ET MALWARE Possible Metasploit Payload Common Construct Bind_API (from server)	suricata	high
🔔	⚠	6	ET POLICY RDP connection confirm	suricata	low
🔔	⚠	4	ET POLICY Possible Kali Linux hostname in DHCP Request Packet	suricata	high
🔔	⚠	2	ET INFO Dotted Quad Host ZIP Request	suricata	medium
🔔	⚠	1	ET POLICY PE EXE or DLL Windows file download HTTP	suricata	high
🔔	⚠	1	ET INFO Python SimpleHTTP ServerBanner	suricata	low
🔔	⚠	1	ET INFO Executable Download from dotted-quad Host	suricata	high
🔔	⚠	1	ET HUNTING SUSPICIOUS Dotted Quad Host MZ Response	suricata	medium

Figure 14.12 – Prioritizing security alerts by their level of severity

The first alert that catches our attention is related to an apparent detection of possible malware related to a Metasploit payload.

3. To start investigating this alert, click on the detection rule name, expand the **Actions** option, and select **Hunt** (be sure to verify that the date range is established, as indicated in the previous section), as illustrated in the following screenshot:

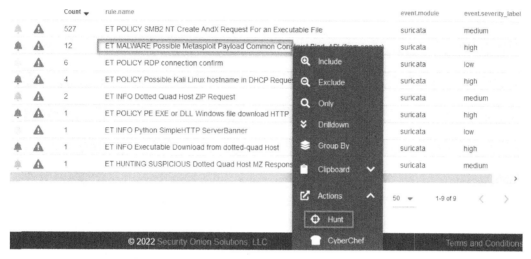

Figure 14.13 – Starting an investigation from an alert

You will see an **Events** list related to this alert, as illustrated in the following screenshot. You can take a different approach here; for instance, you can start looking for information by reviewing events by the most recent date or by the date closest to the start of the incident. In this case, we are interested in initiating an investigation by the date closest to the beginning of the incident:

Events

		Timestamp ▲	source.ip	source.port	destination.ip	destination.port	rule.name
>	⚠	2022-01-11 21:48:17.151 -08:00	172.16.245.128	9000	172.16.245.130	63782	ET MALWARE Possible
>	⚠	2022-01-11 22:51:04.831 -08:00	192.168.8.123	445	192.168.8.10	60098	ET MALWARE Possible
>	⚠	2022-01-11 22:51:23.800 -08:00	192.168.8.123	445	192.168.8.10	60099	ET MALWARE Possible
>	⚠	2022-01-11 22:51:25.240 -08:00	192.168.8.123	445	192.168.8.10	60100	ET MALWARE Possible
>	⚠	2022-01-11 22:51:38.804 -08:00	192.168.8.123	445	192.168.8.10	60098	ET MALWARE Possible

Figure 14.14 – Events view ordered by oldest events

When you identify and want to analyze a particular event, it is very useful to correlate with other activities carried out around that event. Security Onion takes several components of information such as IP addresses, among other things, to generate a single hash and thus correlate different pieces of information.

4. Scroll to the right side of the dashboard until you see the `network.community_id` column and click on the hash to display the contextual menu.

    Select **Actions** and then the **Correlate** option, as illustrated in the following screenshot:

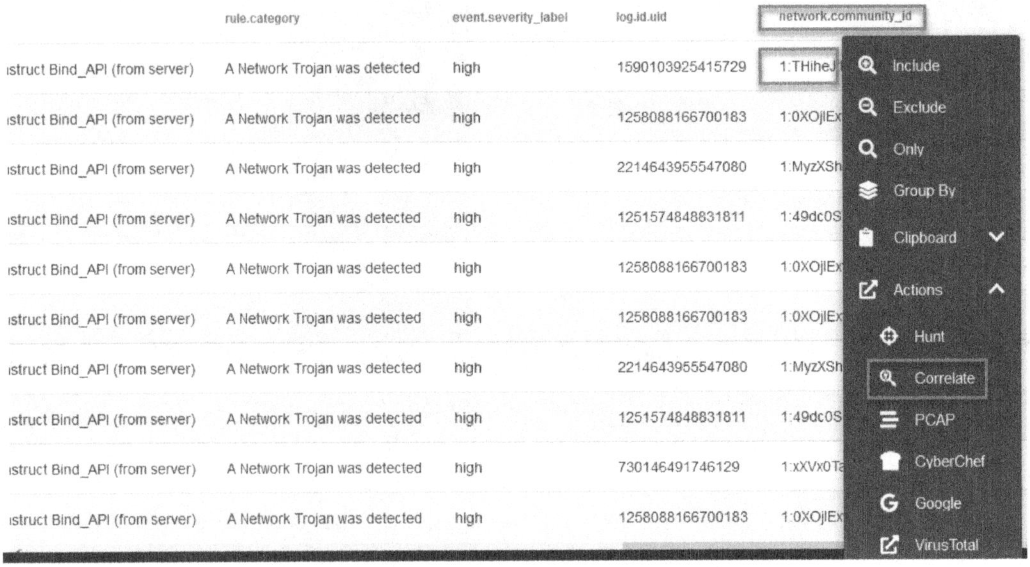

Figure 14.15 – Correlating information regarding an event

As a result, you will see a timeline of correlated events; in the first event, there is a connection from the victim's computer to port `9000`, and after that, interaction with a Python `SimpleHTTPServer` to download several files, and finally, a Metasploit payload, as shown in the following screenshot.

Timestamp ▲	source.ip	source.port	destination.ip	destination.port	rule.name
2022-01-11 21:48:17.024 -08:00	172.16.245.130	63782	172.16.245.128	9000	
2022-01-11 21:48:17.110 -08:00	172.16.245.130	63782	172.16.245.128	9000	
2022-01-11 21:48:17.147 -08:00	172.16.245.128	9000	172.16.245.130	63782	ET INFO Python SimpleHTTP ServerBanner
2022-01-11 21:48:17.147 -08:00	172.16.245.130	63782	172.16.245.128	9000	ET INFO Executable Download from dotted-quad Host
2022-01-11 21:48:17.148 -08:00	172.16.245.128	9000	172.16.245.130	63782	ET HUNTING SUSPICIOUS Dotted Quad Host MZ Response
2022-01-11 21:48:17.148 -08:00	172.16.245.128	9000	172.16.245.130	63782	ET POLICY PE EXE or DLL Windows file download HTTP
2022-01-11 21:48:17.151 -08:00	172.16.245.128	9000	172.16.245.130	63782	ET MALWARE Possible Metasploit Payload Common Construct

Figure 14.16 – Timeline of correlated events

5. We are going to investigate the initial connection to port `9000`.

    Click on the first event under the `destination.port` field, and then click on **Actions** and **PCAP** to view the network traffic, as shown in the following screenshot:

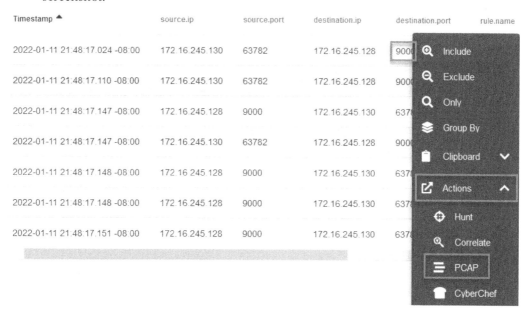

Figure 14.17 – Opening the packet capture (PCAP) of a specific event

You will see all the traffic between the victim's computer—`172.16.245.130`— and the potential attacker's computer—`172.16.245.128`.

6. Filter the view to see unwrapped packets from the encapsulation, clicking on the **Show all Packets** and **Include hexadecimal representation** buttons to deselect them, as shown in the following screenshot.

Figure 14.18 – Showing only unwrapped packets

Once you modify the view, you will see the contents of the packages clearly and identify some interesting elements, such as the following:

- A file called `TradeAPP_Windows.exe` was downloaded via `http` from a `172.16.245.128:900` address using a `GET` command.

- You can also see that the remote server is a `Python SimpleHTTP` server and the content of the traffic is an executable file.

These findings are indicated in the following screenshot:

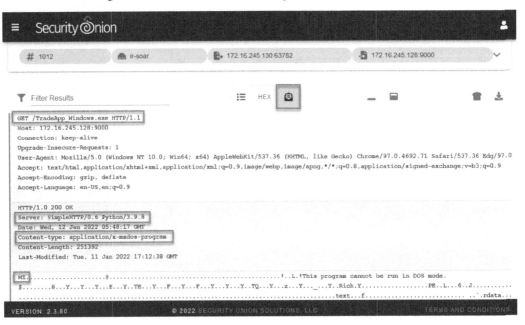

Figure 14.19 – Analyzing the content of the PCAP

As the server is within the same network segment of the hotel and as suggested by the characteristics of the communication, it could be an initial attack vector and a potential target.

Although this panel is very useful to start an analysis, you can use tools that have more advanced functionalities—for example, to deobfuscate or decrypt content.

As this is a Windows executable file, we can send these packages to CyberChef to try to get the malicious file for further analysis.

> **Note**
>
> **CyberChef** is a very powerful tool that we can use to create recipes to simplify the removal of these two **HyperText Transfer Protocol** (**HTTP**) headers, giving us a clear visualization of the information that we need to save.

7. Click on the **Send the transcript to CyberChef** button, as shown in the following screenshot. This will open a new CyberChef tab on your web browser with the content of the PCAP:

bKit/537.36 (KHTML, like Gecko) Chrome/97.0.4692.71 Safari/537.36 Edg/97.0.1072.55
, image/webp,image/apng,*/*;q=0.8,application/signed-exchange;v=b3;q=0.9

Figure 14.20 – Sending the PCAP content to CyberChef

In the same way, you can also download the PCAP file to be analyzed in other network packet analysis applications such as **Wireshark** or **NetworkMiner** (you can learn how to use both tools in the *Code in Action* video).

To filter packages, you need to remove the HTTP content to leave only binary content in CyberChef:

1. In the **Operations** textbox, write the word strip to filter the options.
2. Drag the **Strip HTTP headers** field to the **Recipe** section. This will remove the first HTTP header, then do this again to remove the second HTTP header. Now, you should be left with a line starting with MZ.
3. Click on the **Save output to file** button.
4. Change the name of the file to susp_file_01.dat and click the **OK** button to save the file.

The process is illustrated in the following screenshot:

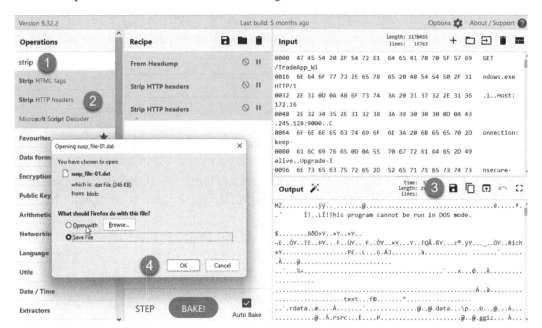

Figure 14.21 – Saving the executable file

We now have the sample of potential malware, and we can review it to identify its functionality.

> **Note**
>
> You may need to disable Windows Defender beforehand because it could catch this malware sample.

5. Move the downloaded file to the following path: `C:\Users\Investigator\Workspace\Labs\Chapter-14`.

6. Open `pestudio.exe` from `C:\Users\Investigator\Workspace\Tools\pestudio`.

7. Drag the `susp_file_01.dat` file to the `pestudio` interface.

You will see the content of the binary file, as shown in the following screenshot:

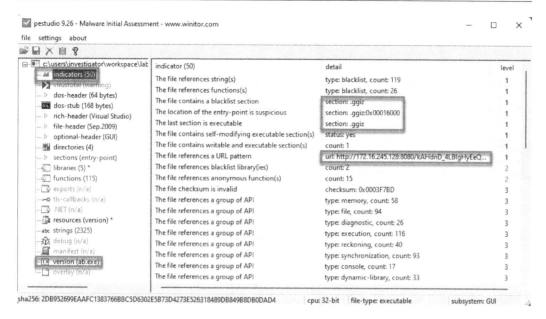

Figure 14.22 – Analyzing the content of the susp_file_01.dat file

Here, you will find interesting things; for instance, on indicators, you will see
section contents tagged as blacklisted or suspicious. You will also see a **Uniform
Resource Locator** (**URL**) where this file could connect once executed.

8.   Now, click on **sections (entry-point)**, as shown in the following screenshot:

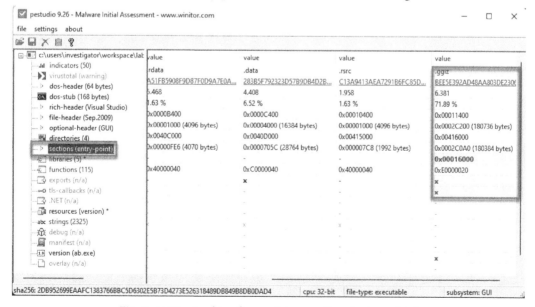

Figure 14.23 – Looking for suspicious sections (entry points)

You will see a suspicious and anomalous section called `.ggiz`. It is not common to find these types of sections in normal executable files.

9. Now, click on **strings**, and you will see a lot of strings within the file that can provide valuable information about the behavior or content of the file, as shown in the following screenshot:

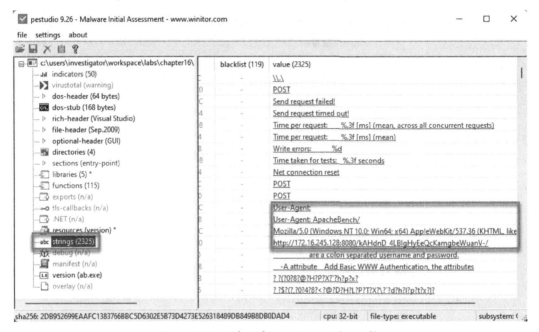

Figure 14.24 – Identifying strings within a file

> **Note**
> Sometimes, malware can be packaged in such a way that the number of strings that can be identified is very small and may not provide much information.

Some strings displayed show indicators related to programs generated in **Metasploit**. Additionally, you can see the URL to which this malicious file would try to connect.

10. Scroll down in the **strings** section to find other relevant information.

At this point, it would be a good idea to create a **YARA** rule from this file to search on other devices on your network to see whether this file is present and ascertain the number of devices compromised with this implant. This is an important step in the first two phases of IR: **identify** and **contain**.

Try to do this yourself with what you've learned. Here's how:

1. Create a YARA rule based on the strings found in the implant.

2. Test the YARA rule on your IR-Laptop VM to validate that it is effective and does not detect false positives.

Now that we have verified malicious activity on at least one of the systems, we will open a new case on the IR platform built into Security Onion to formally initiate the investigation process.

Opening a new IR case

Once we validate that this malicious file is related to the incident, we will open a new case from the alert, using the new **Cases** tool integrated into Security Onion. Here's how to do this:

1. In Security Onion's **Alerts** console, on the **ET MALWARE Possible Metasploit Payload Common Construct Bind_API (from server)** event, click on the **Escalate** button, then select **Escalate to new case** (remember to filter based on date, as you did in the *Starting the investigation* section of this chapter), as illustrated in the following screenshot:

Figure 14.25 – Escalating an alert to create a new case

2. Go to the **Cases** panel on Security Onion, and you will see listed the recent case created, as shown in the following screenshot:

Figure 14.26 – Looking for cases in the Cases panel

3. To edit and manage the case, click on the **View** button, as illustrated in the following screenshot:

Figure 14.27 – Opening a case

You will see the case management interface where you can start assigning tasks—including evidence and observables—and documenting the investigation, as shown in the following screenshot:

ET MALWARE Possible Metasploit Payload Common Construct Bind_API (from server)

Review escalated event details in the Events tab below. Click here to update this description.

COMMENTS   ATTACHMENTS   OBSERVABLES   EVENTS   HISTORY

+   ↻

Ⓐ **Add Comment**

M↓

Provide follow-up information to this case

CANCEL   ADD

Summary   ︿

Assignee:
unassigned

Status:
new

Details   ︿

Severity:
high

Priority:
0

TLP:
unknown

PAP:
unknown

Figure 14.28 – Case management interface

As this incident is about an information leak, not just malware, you need to modify the default incident's name.

4. Click on the incident name to enter into **Edit** mode.

5. Change the name to `202201-IR-Data_Leak_Incident`, and click on the **SAVE** label.

You can also add a description of the incident by just clicking on the **Click here to update this description** section.

You can see an illustration of the process in the following screenshot:

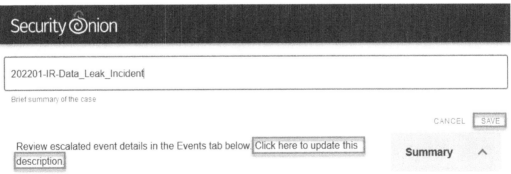

Figure 14.29 – Changing the name and description of a case

We are going to add the first observable of the case. This will be the **Message Digest 5 (MD5)** and **Secure Hash Algorithm 256 (SHA256)** hashes of the malicious file.

6. Click on the **OBSERVABLES** label.

7. Click on the blue plus (+) button.

8. Expand the classification list.

9. Finally, select the **hash** option.

10. Add the MD5 and SHA256 hashes of the file. (You can copy these hashes from `pestudio` by clicking on the filename, including the path at the very top of `pestudio`. Next, right-click on either `md5` or `sha256` and then copy the value(s).)

11. Add a description of the observable.

12. Check the box above **Enable this field if this is an Indicator of Compromise**.

13. Define the **Traffic Light Protocol (TLP)** as **red**.

14. Add **confirmed** and **malware** tags.

15. Click on the **ADD** button to save the changes.

You can see an overview of the process in the following screenshot:

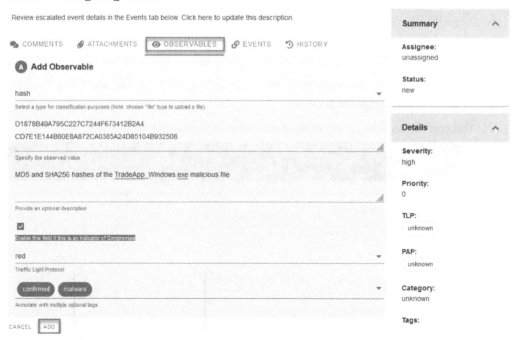

Figure 14.30 – Adding a new hash observable

Now, try for yourself by adding a new file-type observable and uploading the malicious file; this is important because you may need to share it with other teams for further analysis.

I recommend that you compress the malicious file in 7-Zip (.7z) format with a password of `infected` (without quotes) to prevent it from being accidentally executed or deleted by antivirus software.

Investigating the security incident

Now that we have the vector of compromise, we can continue our investigation by looking for evidence about what happened after the initial compromise. Proceed as follows:

1. Go to the **Alerts** panel on Security Onion.

2. On the **Options** menu, click to open the list and select **Acknowledged** and **Escalated** to see an alert regarding the malware, as shown in the following screenshot:

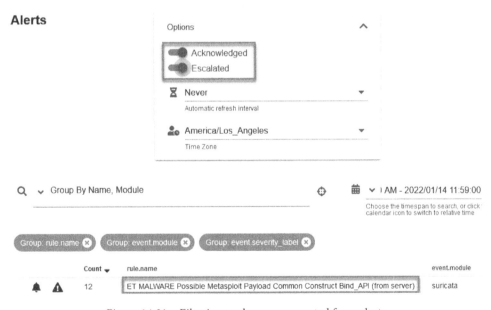

Figure 14.31 – Filtering to show cases created from alerts

3. To see details about this alert, click on the `rule.name` column and select **Actions** then **Hunt** (*remember to filter by date, as you did before*).

    You will see a list of events associated with this alert again; because we already analyzed traffic related to port `9000` communication, we can now try to investigate traffic related to port `445`.

4. Click on the second event that connects from port `445`, then **Actions**, and then click on **PCAP**, as shown in the following screenshot:

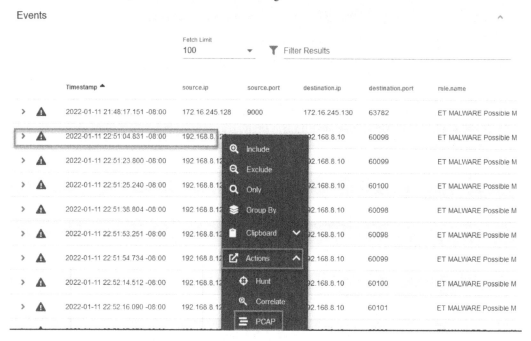

Figure 14.32 – Opening a new PCAP from an event

You will see unwrapped network packages, identifying some interesting strings. As in the previous section, we will use CyberChef to have a better visualization.

5. Click on the **CyberChef** button at the top of the dashboard, as shown in the following screenshot:

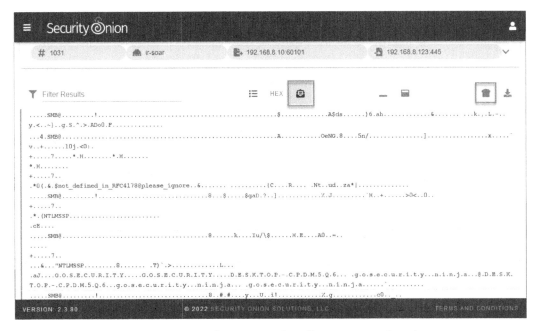

Figure 14.33 – Analyzing network traffic in unwrapped mode

This will open CyberChef in a new tab of your browser with the information obtained from Security Onion.

6. In the **Operations** section, type the word `strings` in the text field, drag this operation to the **Recipe** section, and select **All** on the **Encoding** list, as shown in the following screenshot:

Figure 14.34 – Analyzing PCAP content on CyberChef

At first glance, we can identify some interesting strings.

7. Scroll down, and you will see what seems to be a **New Technology LAN Manager (NTLM)** authentication process of the `admin01` user from the `Desktop-CPDMSQ6` computer of the `gosecurity.ninja` domain to the `WIN-AIR09F7CBLS7` server, as illustrated in the following screenshot:

```
"NTLMSSP.
G.O.S.E.C.U.R.I.T.Y.
.G.O.S.E.C.U.R.I.T.Y.
.D.E.S.K.T.O.P.-.C.P.D.M.5.Q.6.
. .g.o.s.e.c.u.r.i.t.y...n.i.n.j.a.
.@.D.E.S.K.T.O.P.-.C.P.D.M.5.Q.6...g.o.s.e.c.u.r.i.t.y...n.i.n.j.a.
. .g.o.s.e.c.u.r.i.t.y...n.i.n.j.a.
SMB@.
>NTLMSSP.
G.O.S.E.C.U.R.I.T.Y.a.d.m.i.n.0.1.W.I.N.-.A.I.R.0.9.F.7.C.B.L.S.
.G.O.S.E.C.U.R.I.T.Y.
.D.E.S.K.T.O.P.-.C.P.D.M.5.Q.6.
. .g.o.s.e.c.u.r.i.t.y...n.i.n.j.a.
.@.D.E.S.K.T.O.P.-.C.P.D.M.5.Q.6...g.o.s.e.c.u.r.i.t.y...n.i.n.j.a.
. .g.o.s.e.c.u.r.i.t.y...n.i.n.j.a.
Df}f
.$.c.i.f.s./.1.9.2...1.6.8...8...1.2.3.
```

Figure 14.35 – Analyzing the strings of a network package on CyberChef

8. Continue scrolling down and identify additional information that could be valuable for your investigation, such as other programs or files and what you think this means, according to the context of the case.

To get more context about the incident, you request information from the **Information Technology** (**IT**) department about the domain the admin01 user found previously in the network traffic strings. They mentioned that this is not a known user of the system.

It is possible that this account was created by threat actors to maintain persistence, and it could also mean that there is a possible previous compromise of some accounts with administrator privileges, so it is a good idea to look for information related to this account and all activities that were performed with it.

Using Sigma rules to find a user creation event

We will start our hunting by using a Sigma rule from the **Playbook** platform on Security Onion. On the left menu of Security Onion, under **Tools**, select the **Playbook** option, as shown in the following screenshot:

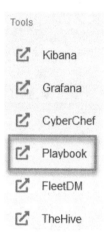

Figure 14.36 – Opening the Playbook tool from Security Onion

We can create a new Sigma rule from scratch, as you learned in the previous chapter, you can use a Sigma rule from the **Detection Playbooks** platform in Security Onion, or you can search for Sigma rules externally.

In this case, we can assume that a user may not have been created using **Active Directory Users and Computers (ADUC) Microsoft Management Console**, so we will use a Sigma rule that detects the creation of local user accounts on this system that are not in **Active Directory (AD)**, published in the following blog: https://www.patrick-bareiss.com/detecting-local-user-creation-in-ad-with-sigma/.

In this blog, you will find a Sigma rule that detects Event 4720 on a non-domain controller computer, so it is perfect to use in this case.

On the **Detection Playbooks** platform, proceed as follows:

1. Click on the **Create New Play** option.
2. Copy the Sigma rule from the blog post and paste it into the **Sigma** rule section.
3. Click on the **Convert** button.

    On the right side of the dashboard, you will now see the converted rule.

4. Click on the **Copy** button.

    The preceding interface is shown in the following screenshot:

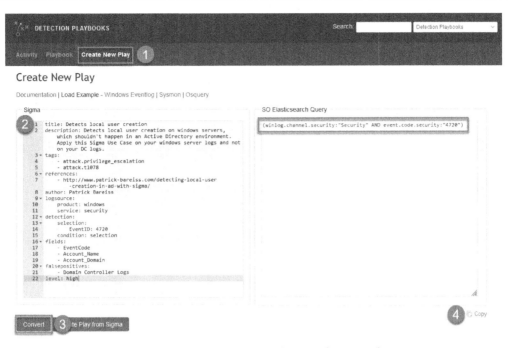

Figure 14.37 – Converting a Sigma rule to an Elasticsearch query

5. You can use this query to search directly in the **Hunt** section of Security Onion, or you could also search on the **Kibana** dashboard. In this case, we are going to do it in the **Hunt** dashboard of Security Onion.

    From the menu on the left side of Security Onion, select the **Hunt** option, as shown in the following screenshot:

Figure 14.38 – Opening the Hunt dashboard

6. Paste the query created from the Sigma rule into the **Search** section, making sure that the date range filter is defined appropriately, as shown in the following screenshot:

Figure 14.39 – Looking for security events with code "4720"

7. You will see an event generated by the user creation.

8. Click on the **Timestamp** dropdown to sort events so that the oldest ones appear first, and then display the content of the first event by clicking on the arrow that appears on the left side of the event, as shown in the following screenshot:

Figure 14.40 – Analyzing the details of a log event

As you will notice, the event code corresponds to the creation of a new user, and this account was created by the MINWINPC$ user, so we are verifying that that account was compromised.

9. Scroll down to collect more information; you will identify the name of the WDAGUtilityAccount created account and some other details that make it look suspicious, as shown in the following screenshot:

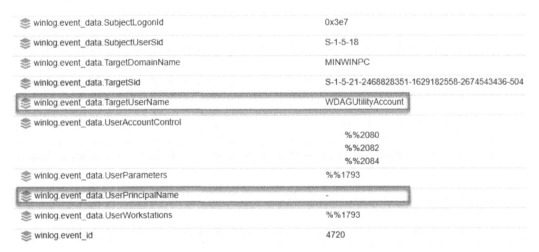

Figure 14.41 – Identifying additional details regarding this log event

If you check the UserPrincipalName field, it is blank, which indicates that this account was created without following the company's user creation standards. You can use this information to search more deeply for activities carried out with this account.

Searching by the activity of devices involved

At this point, we can focus on search information from the device's activity in the period when we believe that the incident occurred, as follows:

1. To limit the amount of information and focus on what may be useful, we will apply an `event.dataset:conn | groupby source.ip destination.ip network.protocol destination.port` filter that is predefined by default in the **Hunt** queries section, as shown in the following screenshot (ensure that the search is carried out in the period mentioned before):

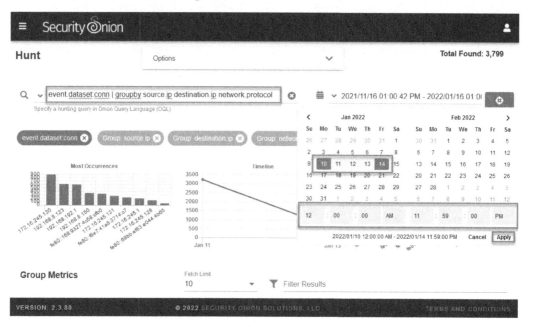

Figure 14.42 – Filtering events using a predefined query

We are particularly going to focus on devices that had some activity out of the ordinary—in this case, those that connected to HTTP ports `9000` and `4444`, as shown in the following screenshot:

	Count ▲	source.ip	destination.ip	network.protocol	destination.port
⚠	1	172.16.245.131	44.238.3.246	ssl	443
⚠	1	172.16.245.130	172.16.245.128	http	9000
⚠	2	172.16.245.128	142.251.32.234	ssl	443
⚠	2	192.168.8.150	192.168.8.255	dns	137
⚠	2	192.168.192.1	255.255.255.255	dhcp	67
⚠	2	192.168.8.123	192.168.8.10	ssl	3389
⚠	2	172.16.245.130	172.16.245.128	http	80
⚠	3	172.16.245.128	172.16.245.255	dns	137
⚠	3	192.168.8.123	192.168.8.10	dce_rpc,smb,krb,gssapi	445
⚠	3	172.16.245.130	172.16.245.128	http	4444

Figure 14.43 – Filtered communications in a range of time

As you can see, this communication was made between the `172.16.245.130` and `172.16.245.128` IP addresses. Investigating a little more, you will verify that the first IP address (`172.16.245.130`) was assigned to the `Corp-Laptop` VM by the **Dynamic Host Configuration Protocol** (**DHCP**) of Michael Scott's hotel.

2. To filter and analyze traffic from these devices, change the order of the **Count** field to see the lower occurrence of communications and click on the `destination. ip` value to select the **Include** option, as shown in the following screenshot:

Figure 14.44 – Filtering for a specific communication

You will see all communication established by these computers in the defined period. In this case, all the communications were under the `http` protocol and the following destination ports:

- `9000`

- `80`

- `4444`

- `8080`

You can see confirmation of this in the following screenshot:

	Count ▲	source.ip	destination.ip	network.protocol	destination.port
⚠	1	172.16.245.130	172.16.245.128	http	9000
⚠	2	172.16.245.130	172.16.245.128	http	80
⚠	3	172.16.245.130	172.16.245.128	http	4444
⚠	6	172.16.245.130	172.16.245.128	http	8080

Figure 14.45 – Communications filtered by ports

3. First, let's filter the communication made to port `9000`. Click on the port number and select the **Only** option, as shown in the following screenshot:

Figure 14.46 – Grouping and analyzing a specific port

4. To analyze this traffic, below the **Events** section, click on the first row where there is communication between these two IPs, and under **Actions**, select **PCAP**, as shown in the following screenshot:

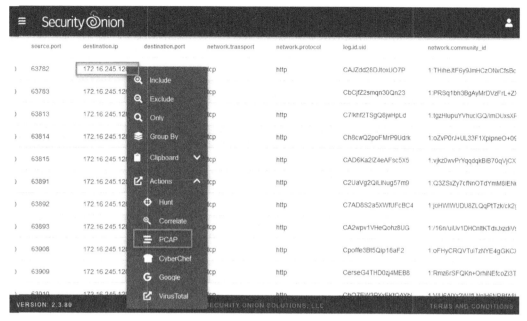

Figure 14.47 – Selecting the PCAP option to analyze traffic

You will be redirected to the PCAP analysis console; apply only the **Raw Packages** option and you will see the content of the package. Now, let's analyze the content of communications between these two computers using port `80`.

In the **Hunt** console, apply the following filter in the **Queries** section: `"172.16.245.128" AND destination.ip:"172.16.245.128" |groupby source.ip destination.ip network.protocol destination.port`. You will again see communications filtered by the destination port, as in the previous search, as illustrated in the following screenshot:

	Count ▲	source.ip	destination.ip	network.protocol	destination.port
⚠	1	172.16.245.130	172.16.245.128	http	9000
⚠	2	172.16.245.130	172.16.245.128	http	80
⚠	3	172.16.245.130	172.16.245.128	http	4444
⚠	6	172.16.245.130	172.16.245.128	http	8080

Figure 14.48 – Communications filtered by ports

5. As you did before, click port 80 of the destination.port column and select the **Include** option to filter the traffic of that port, as illustrated in the following screenshot:

Figure 14.49 – Grouping and analyzing a specific port

Now that you've filtered the traffic of port 80, let's analyze the PCAP packets.

6. Click on the destination.ip first package and then select **PCAP** under **Actions**, as shown in the following screenshot:

Figure 14.50 – Selecting the PCAP option to analyze port 80 traffic

You can now analyze the content of the packages. In this case, you can see the download of the `procdump.zip` file using the GET command from the same URL previously identified.

Again, a binary file appears in the content of the package, so we will perform the same procedure we did earlier, as follows:

Figure 14.51 – Analyzing the content of the PCAP

7. Click on the **Send the transcript to CyberChef** button. This will open a new **CyberChef** tab in your web browser with the content of the PCAP. Remove the HTTP content and leave only the binary content.

8. In the **Operations** textbox, write `strip` to filter the options.

9. Drag the **Strip HTTP headers** option to the **Recipe** section. Repeat this one more time.

10. Click on the **Save** button.

11. Change the name of the `procdump.dat` file, as shown in the following screenshot:

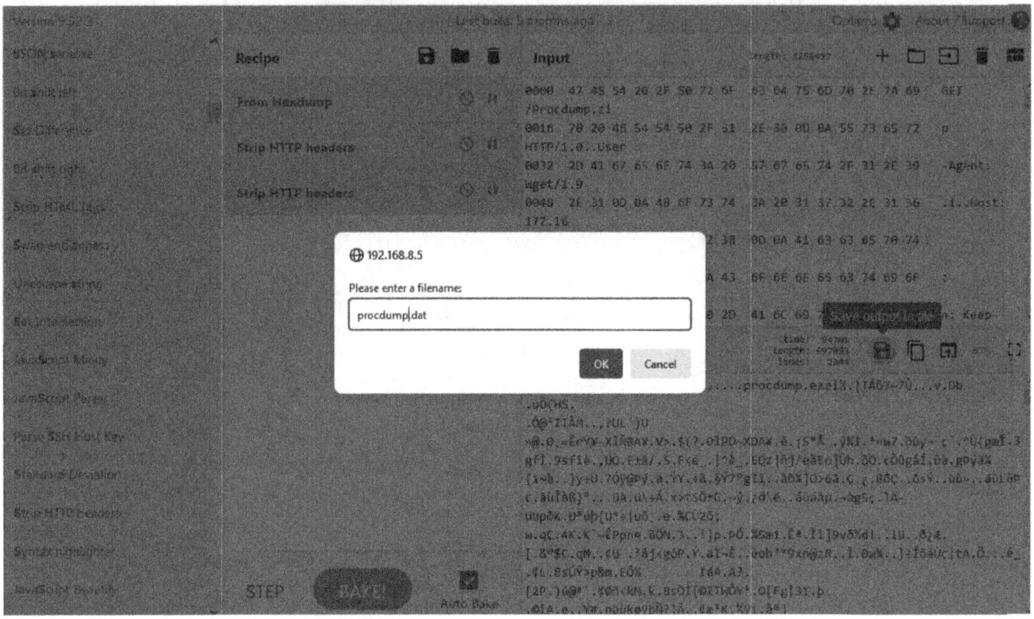

Figure 14.52 – Saving the binary content

12. Save the file to `C:\Users\Investigator\Workspace\Labs\Chapter-14`.

Open a new instance of `pestudio` and drag the `procdump.dat` file to the center of the program.

In this case, you can see that the **virustotal** section appears in green, and no antivirus apparently detects it as malicious. This is because this is a legitimate program abused by threat actors:

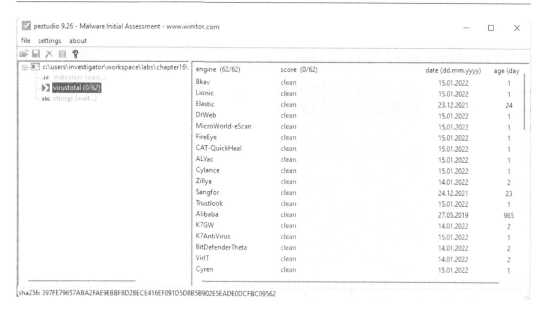

Figure 14.53 – Analyzing the procdump.dat file in pestudio

Now, let's go back to the **Hunt** console to analyze the second packet filtered by port 80, as shown in the following screenshot:

Figure 14.54 – Selecting the PCAP option to analyze port 80 traffic

In this case, you will find what seems to be the download of the Mimikatz program, which is used to dump passwords and can be used in conjunction with the ProcDump tool:

Figure 14.55 – Analyzing the content of the PCAP

To review the file, as on previous occasions, we will send it to CyberChef, save it on our VM, and analyze it with pestudio.

13. Click on the **Send the transcript to CyberChef** button.

14. In the **Operations** textbox, write `strip` to filter the options.

15. Drag the **Strip HTTP headers** option to the **Recipe** section. Repeat this one more time.

16. Click on the **Save** button.

17. Change the name of the `mimikatz.dat` file and press the **OK** button, as shown in the following screenshot:

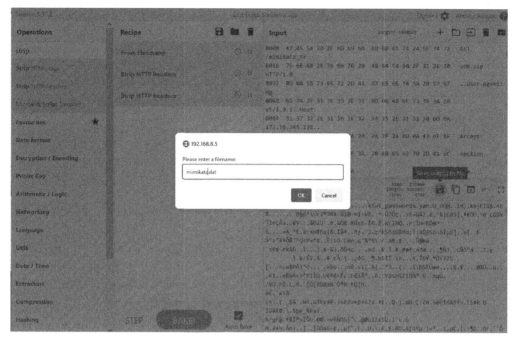

Figure 14.56 – Saving the binary content

18. Open a new instance of `pestudio` and drag the `mimikatz.dat` file to the center of the program.

Unlike the previous file, you can see in the **virustotal** section that this file is detected and identified by almost all antiviruses, as you can see in the following screenshot:

Figure 14.57 – Analyzing the mimikatz.dat file on pestudio

With this, we confirm that one of the intentions of the threat actor was to obtain the user's credentials.

Both files, `procdump.dat` and `mimikatz.dat`, are `.zip` files, so if you want to analyze the binaries in their content, you just need to change the extension and decompress them. Just remember that this must be done in a controlled environment to avoid accidents.

Up to this point, you have obtained very valuable information to help you understand some of the techniques used by threat actors, some **indicators of compromise (IoCs)**, as well as some samples of implants and programs used by attackers.

It is very important that you begin to document all these findings on TheHive and include **indicators of attack (IoAs)** and IoCs.

Now, you will begin to use your instinct, apply the knowledge acquired with this book, and research different sources to find as much evidence as possible, using this information to identify the dimension of attacks and develop the best strategy to contain them.

Try to find evidence that will help you answer the following questions:

- Which other programs and tools did the threat actor use?
- Which **tactics, techniques, and procedures (TTPs)** were used?
- Which credentials could be compromised?
- What information was exfiltrated during the process?
- What was the attacker's main motivation?
- Are there other network devices compromised?

I am sure that you will do an excellent job if you take the time to work on this security incident investigation. Feel free to analyze the evidence further to discover additional artifacts to figure out what could happen, the attacker's possible objective and motivation, and how far they went in this attack.

Summary

In this last chapter, you had the opportunity to apply some of the IR concepts learned in this book.

From a security breach incident, you opened and managed a case and started an investigation by analyzing events and behaviors detected from network traffic monitoring and the centralization of logs from different systems in the corporate network.

Additionally, you learned to perform network traffic and file analysis to get valuable artifacts for your investigation.

I sincerely hope that this book will be helpful for you, whether it is for your professional development as reference material or simply for you to learn something new.

Knowledge evolves quickly, and environments and tools change frequently, so I invite you to visit the repository of this book (`https://github.com/PacktPublishing/Incident-Response-with-Threat-Intelligence`), where you will find updated versions of the tools mentioned in the book and additional tools that will help complement your knowledge.

You will also find guides, short videos, and complementary support material.

Thank you for joining me on this journey; it has been an honor to share some knowledge with you.

I wish you success in your career as a professional incident responder, and I hope we can meet at some place or event in the industry.

Index

`Packt.com`

Subscribe to our online digital library for full access to over 7,000 books and videos, as well as industry leading tools to help you plan your personal development and advance your career. For more information, please visit our website.

Why subscribe?

- Spend less time learning and more time coding with practical eBooks and Videos from over 4,000 industry professionals

- Improve your learning with Skill Plans built especially for you

- Get a free eBook or video every month

- Fully searchable for easy access to vital information

- Copy and paste, print, and bookmark content

Did you know that Packt offers eBook versions of every book published, with PDF and ePub files available? You can upgrade to the eBook version at `packt.com` and as a print book customer, you are entitled to a discount on the eBook copy. Get in touch with us at `customercare@packtpub.com` for more details.

At `www.packt.com`, you can also read a collection of free technical articles, sign up for a range of free newsletters, and receive exclusive discounts and offers on Packt books and eBooks.

Other Books You May Enjoy

If you enjoyed this book, you may be interested in these other books by Packt:

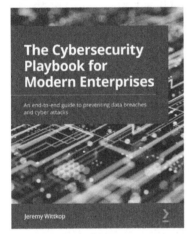

The Cybersecurity Playbook for Modern Enterprises

Jeremy Wittkop

ISBN: 9781803248639

- Understand the macro-implications of cyber attacks
- Identify malicious users and prevent harm to your organization
- Find out how ransomware attacks take place
- Work with emerging techniques for improving security profiles
- Explore identity and access management and endpoint security
- Get to grips with building advanced automation models
- Build effective training programs to protect against hacking techniques
- Discover best practices to help you and your family stay safe online

Mastering Cyber Intelligence

Jean Nestor M. Dahj

ISBN: 9781800209404

- Understand the CTI lifecycle which makes the foundation of the study
- Form a CTI team and position it in the security stack
- Explore CTI frameworks, platforms, and their use in the program
- Integrate CTI in small, medium, and large enterprises
- Discover intelligence data sources and feeds
- Perform threat modelling and adversary and threat analysis
- Find out what Indicators of Compromise (IoCs) are and apply the pyramid of pain in threat detection
- Get to grips with writing intelligence reports and sharing intelligence

Packt is searching for authors like you

If you're interested in becoming an author for Packt, please visit `authors.packtpub.com` and apply today. We have worked with thousands of developers and tech professionals, just like you, to help them share their insight with the global tech community. You can make a general application, apply for a specific hot topic that we are recruiting an author for, or submit your own idea.

Share Your Thoughts

Now you've finished *Incident Response with Threat Intelligence*, we'd love to hear your thoughts! Scan the QR code below to go straight to the Amazon review page for this book and share your feedback or leave a review on the site that you purchased it from.

https://packt.link/r/1801072957

Your review is important to us and the tech community and will help us make sure we're delivering excellent quality content.

46664205R00263